Scottish Elites

Scottish Elites

Proceedings of the
Scottish Historical Studies Seminar
University of Strathclyde
1991–1992

Edited by

T. M. DEVINE

JOHN DONALD PUBLISHERS LTD
EDINBURGH

ISBN 0 85976 402 8

A catalogue record for this book
is available from the British Library

Phototypeset by ROM-Data Corporation, Falmouth, Cornwall
Printed and bound in Great Britain by Hartnolls Limited, Bodmin, Cornwall

Preface

The papers published in this book were first presented at the Scottish Historical Studies Seminar in the University of Strathclyde in 1991–2 are now made available to a wider audience. All are based on original research and present some fresh and intriguing perspectives on the dominant groups who have governed and influenced Scotland over the last three hundred years. The collected studies do not attempt to provide a coherent and systematic examination of the nation's urban and rural elites. That possibility is still a long way off. Research in this field, and especially the history of the dominant classes in Scottish cities and towns, is still in its very early stages and no convincing overview is yet feasible. The contributors do however attempt to provide an analysis of some key aspects of elite experience and in the process question much received historical wisdom. Allan Macinnes, as a result of a detailed investigation of estate papers and legal records for Argyllshire, presents a picture of landownership in that county which is far removed from the stereotyped image of the Highland aristocracy of the eighteenth and nineteenth centuries. The impression that comes through is of a more active and dynamic class than that often suggested in the textbooks. Like their counterparts elsewhere in Gaeldom, the Argyll elites abandoned the responsibilities of clan leadership in favour of entrepreneurship. But they seem to have been much more committed, at least for a period, to effective estate management and diversified investment than landowners in other west Highland counties. The depth of factual detail and the new perspectives in Macinnes's chapter question several conventional beliefs about the Highland landed class in the age of the Clearances and suggest that they had more similarities with the Lowland Improvers than is often assumed.

The papers by Graham Cummings and Tom Devine focus on landowners and tenant farmers in the age of agricultural transformation. Grant of Monymusk, the subject of Cummings' chapter, is best known in Scottish history as a famous and enlightened 'improver' of the eighteenth century. Here he is seen from a more critical point of view. He is revealed as a man deeply involved in one of the shadier business schemes of the early eighteenth century who resorted to agricultural improvement to escape financial ruin. However, Grant's career also demonstrates the intimate connections which existed between the land, industry, commerce and the world of finance in the era of the Union and the Scottish Enlightenment. A neat division of elite families into 'landed', 'mercantile' and 'professional' in this period is not always possible. Threads of different interests ran through most kin groupings. It was this kind of economic diversification which partly helped to preserve the power of the landowners in the age of industrialisation and urbanisation and gave a considerable social resilience to the class as a whole. For most of the eighteenth and nineteenth centuries the new economic system was as much an opportunity as a threat to the old elite because of the landowners' close familial ties with commerce, finance and industry. In his paper, Devine questions another orthodoxy of Scottish historiography in the age of improvement, namely that small farmers were largely removed on a large-scale in the Lowlands and replaced by a new elite of 'capitalist' farmers. This process, known as the 'Lowland Clearances' is often seen to have had significant effects on migration from the land and the proletarianisation of the rural population. Devine argues on the basis of estate records and government data that the scale of these changes after c.1750 has been exaggerated and that the 'Agricultural Revolution' was accomplished not only by a new elite of 'big' husbandmen but by a whole range of rural occupiers. In very many lowland districts the small family farm survived and in some counties remained the norm. The notion of wholesale consolidation of land into larger units and the squeezing out of the smaller tenantry is rejected as too simplistic.

The final two papers on rural society by Iain Hutchison, David McCrone and Angela Morris return to the subject of the greater Scottish landowners. In different ways they examine why and to what extent this class managed to maintain their political and social influence in Scotland even when their economic power was apparently disintegrating. Both pieces bring an interesting and illuminating Scottish perspective to the debate on 'the Decline of the British Aristocracy' initiated by David Cannadine and independently demonstrate that specifically Scottish factors influenced the experience of the landed elite from the later nineteenth century.

The papers by Allan MacLaren, Irene Maver and Anthony Slaven provide pioneering discussions of urban professional and business elites. Focusing specifically on Aberdeen, MacLaren examines clergy, doctors and lawyers in comparative perspective. Both clerics and lawyers enjoyed high status and lawyers had proceeded furthest down the road to professionalism, but doctors were in a much less secure position with, on the whole, weak regulatory structures and inadequate training.

Mavor provides a detailed and richly documented analysis of Glasgow's governing class from a somewhat different perspective. Hers is a case-study of how the social elite in a major industrial city managed to maintain and enhance its position in a period of rapid economic change. Slaven concentrates on 'Scottish business leaders' over the century from 1860 to 1960. This is the first aggregative study to be published on the basis of the Glasgow University Scottish Business Biography Project. The results of the analysis of several hundred individual biographies are important not simply for the discussion of business elites but for an understanding of modern Scottish society and economy in more general terms. Slaven notes the growing dominance of family control and interconnected directorships in Scottish industry and tentatively concludes that the erosion of independent Scottish businesses may be partly linked to this concentration which could have made Scottish business less flexible and responsive than it had been during its halcyon era of expansion in the nineteenth century.

It is difficult to isolate general conclusions from this varied selection of studies. However, one theme is prominent throughout much of the volume. Despite the speed and scale of Scottish urbanisation and industrialisation, the ancient elite of aristocrats and lairds maintained their grip on power at both national and local level for much longer than might have been anticipated. Even in the twentieth century, as Hutchison, McCrone and Morris suggest, their influence had not disappeared. At one level this is puzzling since by the middle decades of the nineteenth century, industry and commerce had come to dominate the Scottish economy, employment on the land was in rapid decline and the first Reform Act of 1832 had enfranchised the urban middle classes. The continuing power of the landed elite coexisted with a society in the throes of an economic and social revolution.

This, of course, was not a peculiarly Scottish phenomenon. In England, too, the landed class proved adept at perpetuating their authority despite the challenge of a new economic order and the menace of an incipient democracy. The British aristocracy as a whole were not swept aside by industrialisation because they had an enormous stake in it. It swelled their rent rolls through urban demand for foods, drink, raw materials and minerals. Land, therefore, remained a major source of wealth and wealth conveyed power. In addition, both Scottish and English landed elites exploited their traditional authority to great effect by carrying out a tactical retreat which helped to preserve much of their position in a changing world. 1832 can be interpreted in this light. It was not so much a surrender of political authority as a measured concession designed to defuse more extreme radical demands. Not until the later nineteenth and early twentieth centuries, therefore, did specifically 'anti-landlord' legislation reach the statute book in the form of enactments for crofting reform and the imposition of death duties.

But there were also peculiarly Scottish factors at work in the perpetuation of landlord authority. Landownership in Scotland was more concentrated than in England. Particularly in the Highlands, Borders and along much of the eastern Lowlands a few great landed families dominated the structure of control. These powerful landowners and the smaller lairds had also inherited formidable powers of local patronage, which did not disappear overnight, in the two key Scottish institutions of church and education. The nature of Scottish industrialisation also worked to their advantage. Its main distinctive feature was territorial concentration. Large-scale urbanisation, with the exception of Dundee and Aberdeen, was confined to the Forth Clyde valley. Elsewhere, the pattern to a large extent was one of small towns, rural villages and farming landscape. Scotland had indeed become an industrial society, as measured by employment statistics and the composition of gross national product, by the 1850s. But much of the land mass of the country remained rural in character and in these districts the social influence of 'the big house' and the local laird families remained considerable.

T. M. Devine

Contributors

A. J. G. Cummings
Lecturer in History, University of Strathclyde

T. M. Devine
Professor of Scottish History and Director of the Research Centre in Scottish History, University of Strathclyde.

I. G. C. Hutchison
Lecturer in History, University of Stirling.

David McCrone
Reader in Sociology, University of Edinburgh.

Allan J. Macinnes
Burnett-Fletcher Professor of History, University of Aberdeen.

A. Allan MacLaren
Senior Lecturer in Historical Sociology, University of Strathclyde.

Irene Maver
Lecturer in Scottish History, University of Glasgow.

Angela Morris
Lecturer in Rural Resource Management, Scottish Agricultural College, Edinburgh.

Anthony Slaven
Professor of Business History, University of Glasgow.

Contents

1. Landownership, Land Use and Elite Enterprise in Scottish Gaeldom: From Clanship to Clearance in Argyllshire, 1688–1858
    Allan I. Macinnes   1

2. The Business Affairs of an Eighteenth Century Lowland Laird: Sir Archibald Grant of Monymusk, 1696–1778
    A. J. G. Cummings   43

3. The Making of a Farming Elite? Lowland Scotland 1750–1850
    T. M. Devine   62

4. The Liberal Professions within the Scottish Class Structure 1760–1860: A Comparative Study of Aberdeen Clergymen, Doctors and Lawyers.
    A. Allan MacLaren   77

5. Politics and Power in the Scottish City: Glasgow Town Council in the Nineteenth Century.
    Irene Maver   98

6. The Nobility and Politics in Scotland, c.1880–1939.
    I. G. C. Hutchison   131

7. The Origins and Economic and Social Roles of Scottish Business Leaders, 1860–1960
    Anthony Slaven with the assistance of Dong-Woon Kim   152

8. Lords and Heritages: the Transformation of the Great Lairds of Scotland
    David McCrone and Angela Morris   170

Index   187

1

Landownership, Land Use and Elite Enterprise in Scottish Gaeldom: from Clanship to Clearance in Argyllshire, 1688–1858.

Allan I. Macinnes

Following the demise of clanship, historical perceptions of Scottish Gaeldom in the eighteenth and nineteenth centuries have tended to be dominated by the creation and clearance of crofting communities.[1] Albeit the removal and relocation of people was an issue affecting the whole of Scottish Gaeldom, crofting, as a recent magisterial study has demonstrated, was primarily an issue affecting the north and western Highlands.[2] Arguably, the most significant impact of the first phase of Clearance between the 1730s and the 1820s—when traditional townships were broken up to make way for cattle-ranches and sheep-walks as well as crofting communities—was the shift from proactive to reactive landlordism throughout Scottish Gaeldom.[3] The switch from resource management under clanship to demand management under commercial landlordism, a switch rationalized by the Whiggish belief in progress and fortified by the political economy emanating from the Scottish Enlightenment,[4] occasioned the central paradox of Highland history: despite the common espousal of improvement on the part of landlords, the principal features of estate management in the Highlands would appear to be the persistent underdevelopment of landed resources and a marked failure to industrialize beyond the level of extractive industries. Whereas the Scottish Lowlands were embarking on a second phase of industrialization associated with the heavy industries from the 1830s, the Highlands were undergoing a second phase of Clearance characterized by the wholesale switch to sheep-farming or deer-forestry at the expense of the crofting community. In the process, landlords moved from the aggressive apostatizing of commercial over customary relationships prior to the Forty-Five rebellion to the defensive maintenance of economic individualism in the wake of the Great Highland Famine of 1845–50.[5]

Differing patterns of development give superficial credence to an

analysis which sees the Lowlands as a beneficiary of the British Empire
and the Highlands as another internal colony on the Celtic fringe.[6]
Yet, this contrast between regions is more subtle than stark in terms of
entrepreneurial endeavour, as can be suggested by a case study of
landownership and land use in Argyllshire, where a manifest drive for
commercial growth led by the clan elite between the 1690s and the
1750s was neither sustained nor sufficiently diversified by their landed
successors between the 1760s and the 1800s. The result was that estate
management was marked by an increasing, but by no means a pervasive,
recourse to commercial pastoralism and recreational capitalism between the 1810s and the 1850s.

In Argyll, where systematic tenurial change to terminate clanship was
instituted in the first half of the eighteenth century and where crofting
was subsequently popularised if not pioneered,[7] land use remained
notably diversified in the middle of the nineteenth century. Indeed by
the 1850s, Argyll was marginally ahead of Sutherland, but significantly
behind the other three Highland counties of Caithness, Inverness and
Ross & Cromarty in terms of crofting as defined by occupants renting
below £20, by their amount of arable acreage and by their livestock.
Conversely, Argyll was the foremost Highland county in terms of mixed
farming, with the highest rates of farming occupancy renting at not
less than £20 and of arable acreage characterised by the balanced
production of white crops, green crops and pasture. Moreover, the
county's highest livestock figures cannot be attributed wholly to sheep-
farming as Argyll ranked only third in the Highlands in proportion to
pastoral acreage given over to sheep-walks. Argyll was the only Highland
county which retained a vigorous cattle trade and where dairy farming
featured prominently. Moreover, Argyll had extensive quarrying, particularly for slate; small scale chemicals and an iron works indigenously
supplied with charcoal; commercial forestry and fishing; significant
distilling, marketing and even tourist demands to sustain planned
villages; and a burgeoning construction industry.[8]

Given such diversity which was largely promoted, if not always
maintained, by the landed interest, Argyll does not necessarily fit
deterministic interpretations of Highland history: notably, that the role
of landowners as the principal instruments of social and economic
change was so constricted by geographic, financial and demographic
factors that native entrepreneurship failed to flourish.[9] Such interpretations require substantial modification with respect not only to cultural
considerations and feudal technicalities affecting estate management
but also to regional diversity within the Highlands and, above all, to
the imperial context in which Highland history must be examined in

the eighteenth and nineteenth centuries. Undoubtedly in Argyll, as
elsewhere in Scottish Gaeldom, the clan elite abandoned the traditional
concept of heritable trusteeship, their *duthchas*, in favour of the legal-
istic concept of heritable title, their *oighreachd*, to enhance their
assimilation into the Anglo-Scottish landed classes. Yet, this traditionalist concept was never abandoned by the victims and critics of
commercial landlordism.[10] At the same time, Highland landlords were
not only aspiring members of the Anglo-Scottish ruling elite but, as was
particularly evident in Argyllshire, members of the imperial exploiting
classes as planters, slave traders, colonial officials, military commanders
and merchant adventurers. Ultimately, the issue linking landownership, land use and enterprise was that of mentality. That the clan elite
operated within a prevailing Anglo-Scottish cultural climate was confirmed by the failure of the Forty-Five. Notwithstanding their imperial
aspirations, indigenous Highland landlords were never entirely di-
vested of the cultural baggage of clanship and even incomers felt
obliged to exercise paternalism to offset periodic economic distress
among their tenantry.[11]

I

A significant starting point for the current analysis is to disregard
traditionalist notions that Highland society was monolithic and static
prior to the Forty-Five. Argyll, moreover, is the best served of the
Scottish, not just Highland, shires with respect to extant records which
list, describe and evaluate the estates of heritors—that is, landowners
with a direct managerial or financial interest in land rather than the
indirect interest exercised heritably by superiors—according to each
parish and territorial division within the shire. Albeit valuation rolls
provide no more than cadastral snapshots, they not only indicate
continuity and change but also afford an inquisitorial picture on the
incidence, extent and enterprising nature of landownership.[12] In Argyll, for example, the land-market was notably buoyant and
landownership was expanding progressively, to the order of 25% in the
course of the seventeenth century. A comparison of extant valuation
rolls for 1629 and 1688, together with an examination of 1615 land
transfers in the registers of sasines between 1617 and 1675 reveal a
considerable expansion in landownership brought about by the indebtedness of chiefs and leading clan gentry which enabled lesser clan
gentry to acquire heritable titles to lands formerly held in tack (lease),
initially by way of wadset (mortgage), subsequently by sale. In effect,

the land market was fuelled by two forces—the negative impact of debt occasioned by the irrevocable social commitment of the clan elite to Scottish politics from the 1640s coupled to the positive impact of the London-led expansion of the cattle trade whose dominance by Highland drovers from the later seventeenth century provided the capital for the more frugal, lesser gentry to acquire wadsets in return for advances of credit to the clan elite. Because the lesser gentry were content to hold their newly acquired property within the feudal superiority of the clan elite rather than directly as freeholders from the Crown, the land-market conveyed the deceptive appearance of stability.[13]

Whereas the dual impact of debt and enterprise led to the expansion of the land-market in the seventeenth century, this situation was subsequently to fluctuate markedly, as evident from the number of landowners cited as heritors in the extant valuation rolls for the shire in 1688, 1751, 1802 and 1858. Albeit heritors were cited by their parochial rather than their total shire holdings, the number of heritors cited and the actual number of landowners both decline, suggesting a measure of estate consolidation throughout the eighteenth century.[14] This contraction of landownership was not uniform. Ownership of lands in more than one parish increased marginally, while the number of landowners declined by 1751. The holding of land in more than one parish was cut back and the number of landowners continued to decline in the second half of the century. In like manner the increase in both categories in the first half of the nineteenth century, suggests the opening up of the land-market and the fragmentation of estates, although landowners continued to purchase estates in more than one parish.

While the contraction of landownership in the eighteenth century and its expansion in the first half of the nineteenth is apparently in keeping with national trends,[15] fluctuations in landownership in Argyllshire can be measured more precisely than in other Highland or Scottish shires, partly because of the relatively shorter intervals between

Table 1. *Incidence of Landownership*

Year	Parochial Heritors	% change	Actual Landowners	% change
1688	392		337	
1751	358	(8.7)	256	(24.0)
1802	294	(17.9)	193	(24.6)
1858	360	22.4	285	47.7

extant valuation rolls and primarily because Argyll was unique among Scottish shires in attaining parliamentary sanction for a comprehensive revaluation in 1749, after two years of judicious lobbying by the shire's commissioners of supply in association with their member of parliament, Sir Duncan Campbell of Lochnell. The valuation roll of 1688 had conformed to existing Scottish practice in so far as the basis of valuation had sustained the ancient fiscal rating of pound (£), merk (m) and penny (d) lands rather than actual rents, a basis which came to be regarded not only an anachronistic, but inequitable. In effect, up to two-thirds of actual rents were apportioned as the valued rent from which the heritors met their fiscal liabilities. In the wake of the Forty-Five, the landed classes in Argyll, trading on their predominantly Whig sympathies in a region noted for its Jacobite affinities, successfully petitioned the British parliament for a more authentic assessment of rents.[16] The valued rents duly recorded in the roll of 1751, reputedly half of the real rents after deduction of public burdens, were on average one-sixth higher than in the roll of 1688. But the fiscal liabilities of heritors from 1751 fell notably. Valued rents now ranged from around two-fifths to as low as a twelfth of actual rents, a range which continued to expand in real terms by 1802 when a valuation roll was compiled merely to update changes in landownership without altering the basis of evaluation. Indeed, by the 1790s, valuations for landowners in Argyllshire were on average rated nine times below their actual rents; comparative figures for the 1840s suggest that valuations on average had fallen to around 18 times the actual rents.[17] The valuation rolls, therefore, do not serve as a useful indicator to changing rental as against fiscal expectations prior to the comprehensive overhaul of the rating system on an annual basis from 1854. Until this date, moreover, no standardization or comparison of landownership on the basis of estate acreage is possible.

Nonetheless, by taking the revaluation of and the parochial boundaries for 1751 as the standard for cadastral comparison, landownership can be categorized according to estate valuations in £ sterling.[18] The broad spectrum of landownership within the parishes of Argyll demonstrates a remarkable consistency despite fluctuating numbers of parochial heritors. Three clear categories emerge to define landownership by the value of individual holdings within every parish. The perceptible swing from small to large landholdings between 1688 and 1802 is partially checked by the decline and resurgence in the middle range. When further adjustment is made for the massive revaluation from 1854, the expansion of landownership in the first half of the nineteenth century suggests a resurgence in small landholding through

Table 2. Spectrum of Landownership

Year	Range (# Sterling)		Number	Percentage
1688	Large	(85+)	25	6.4
	Middle	(84–17)	129	32.9
	Small	(16–)	238	60.5
1751	Large	(100+)	30	8.4
	Middle	(99–20)	113	31.6
	Small	(19–)	215	60.
1802	Large	(100+)	30	10.2
	Middle	(99–20)	108	36.7
	Small	(19–)	156	53.1
1858	Large	(3300+)	15	4.2
	Middle	(3299–700)	90	25.
	Small	(00–)	255	70.8

piecemeal sales of large and, to a lesser extent, middle range estates.[19]

For administrative and fiscal purposes, Argyll was divided into six maritime districts. Two, Mull and Islay, were predominantly island, the other four, Lorne, Mid-Argyll, Cowal and Kintyre, were mainland. Divisional variations in landownership within Argyllshire can serve as a useful construct for Highland diversity. The lack of uniformity in the spectrum of landownership is underscored divisionally both with respect to incidence (see appendix 1) and extent (see appendix 2). The high incidence of medium sized estates throughout the eighteenth century is supportive of estate consolidation, primarily at the expense of smaller estates. The turn-around in the nineteenth century is most marked by the significant fall in the number of large estates and the steady decline in medium-size estates. Fragmentation of estates was not a consistent feature in every division, however. Changes in the extent of landownership, though generally supportive of eighteenth century consolidation and nineteenth century fragmentation, also cannot be presented as a consistent feature. The uniform expansion in the incidence of small estates which was not matched by changes in extent, does not rule out consolidation as well as fragmentation through the operation of the land market during the nineteenth century.

Despite the general tendency towards fragmentation in the early nineteenth century, any attempt to correlate changes in incidence and extent of landownership with the changing orientation of estate management during the first phase of Clearance can only be tentative. Mixed farming with a considerable arable emphasis was practised in Kintyre and Islay, the two divisions dominated by large estates in the eighteenth century; yet their divisional spectrum of landownership diverged markedly in the nineteenth century. Islay, and more especially

Mull, were the two divisions in which crofting was a significant feature of estate management. But again patterns of landownership diverged with Mull having more in common with the other predominantly hill-farming divisions where medium-sized estates tended to prevail. Albeit the recreational use of land in terms of creating country retreats does help explain the growth in small estates in Cowal, the recreational use of land for deer-forests and salmon fishings in Lorne and to a lesser extent, Mid-Argyll, occurred in divisions where small landownership was in decline and cannot be convincingly tied to the break-up of large estates.[20]

Divisional divergence in landownership is further evident in the parochial distribution of heritors (see appendix 3). In no division did the number of parochial heritors decline or rise uniformly. A net increase in the number of parochial heritors was recorded in the divisions of Mull and Kintyre, while in Islay a marked upsurge of ownership by 1751 had receded by 1802 only to resurge by 1858. For this division as a whole, as for individual parishes in other divisions, the unsustained upsurge in landownership during the eighteenth century can partially be attributed to grants of land under wadset, grants that were subsequently redeemed following the passage of the Montgomery or Entail Act of 1770, which allowed landowners to apportion up to two-thirds of costs incurred by estate improvements on to succeeding generations. The apparent national trend of a slower decline in parochial heritors in lowland as against upland or highland districts cannot be linked neatly to the pace of agricultural improvements or to proximity to urban markets in Argyllshire.[21] In the three larger divisions, the relative decline in landownership in Cowal and Mid-Argyll—the divisions which contained the majority of planned villages or towns in Argyllshire—was less pronounced than in Lorne. Yet, Mid-Argyll continued to decline while the other two divisions experienced a resurgence in landownership in the nineteenth century. Despite their ongoing creation from the 1750s to the 1840s, the principal cadastral significance of planned villages and towns would appear to be their conspicuous failure to check the decline in land-ownership. Unlike Lowland Scotland, the creation of planned villages and towns cannot convincingly be correlated with the expansion of petty proprietorship in Argyllshire.

Major fluctuations in the number of parochial heritors can readily be associated with a lack of continuity in landownership, a trend accelerated not instigated in all divisions after 1751. While the valuation rolls do not indicate the number of times estates changed hands, the following tables certainly underestimate the actual continuity of landed

Table 3. Eighteenth Century, 1688–1802

Division	Heritors in 1688	Continuity		Percentage	
		1751	1802	1751	1802
Mull	22	10	6	45.5	31.8
Lorne	95	72	37	75.8	38.9
Mid-Argyll	134	69	42	51.5	31.3
Cowal	95	42	15	44.2	15.8
Kintyre	37	7	4	18.9	10.8
Islay	9	2	1	22.2	11.1

interests as the datasets from which these figures have been extracted relate to individual families not to family groups and their cadets.[22]

Lack of continuity, which was certainly a feature of clanship in the seventeenth century, notably increased in the aftermath of the last Jacobite rising and the onset of Clearance. The land market, as reflected in the redemption of mortgages as well as the sale of estates, would appear to have been most active in Kintyre and Islay. Notwithstanding the establishment of Whig political hegemony at the Revolution, Jacobitism had no significant impact on the land market. Indeed, the division with the highest continuity in the early 18th century, Lorn, was arguably the most militantly Jacobite. Albeit 19 gentry from Argyllshire were identified as Jacobite activists after the Forty-Five, no more than 6 landowners were affected by attainder and annexation which was eventually reversed in 1784. In turn, interventionist agencies supported by the government to civilize the Highlands made little impact in Argyllshire, save for the promotion of Tobermory in Mull as a planned village by the British Fisheries Society.[23]

The second phase of Clearance, though compounding lack of continuity, did indicate a recovering stability in the land-market by mid-nineteenth century in relation to the eighteenth century as a whole, but also a more active land-market in all divisions except Lorne in relation to the later eighteenth century. The land market in Argyll, while apparently less active than elsewhere in the Highlands and Islands

Table 4. Later Eighteenth Century, 1751–1802

Division	Heritors in 1751	Continuity 1801	Percentage 1751
Mull	31	17	54.8
Lorne	8	36	52.9
Mid-Argyll	125	53	42.4
Cowal	73	30	41.1
Kintyre	40	22	55.0
Islay	20	7	35.0

Table 5. *Early Nineteenth Century, 1802–1858*

Division	Heritors in 1802	Continuity 1858	Percentage 1858
Mull	32	11	34.3
Lorne	49	25	51.0
Mid-Argyll	105	33	31.4
Cowal	56	20	35.7
Kintyre	43	15	34.9
Islay	9	3	33.3

from the 1820s, was not as stagnant as that purportedly prevailing in Britain in the decades ensuing through to the 1850s.[24]

II

Despite the manifest shifts in landownership and contemporaneous lamentations for the passing of the ancient families of Argyll, incomers established no significant presence in the county until the nineteenth century.[25] Increasing numbers notwithstanding, few incomers appeared to pass on their estates to a second generation prior to the nineteenth century, a feature particularly evident among landowners owning estates elsewhere in Scotland. Few if any of the incomers conformed to the stereotyped recreational capitalists who were buying up the Highlands. By the outset of the nineteenth century, the pattern of incoming entrepreneurs acquiring lands in Argyllshire had been augmented to include gentlemen farmers from other Highland as well as Lowland shires. The opening up of the land market to incomers is particularly evident in Cowal and Kintyre, the two divisions closest to the Lowlands. As these divisions had been importing Lowland farmers since the mid-seventeenth century, the most noteworthy aspect is not so much the location of incomers within these divisions as their limited presence during the first phase of Clearance.

Clannish associations continued to dominate the parochial distribution of heritors in Argyllshire.[26] The acquisitiveness of the Campbells at the expense of other Argyllshire clans remained the most pronounced feature of landownership in the eighteenth century (see appendix 4). Special political factors do much to explain the upsurge in Campbell dominance from 1688 to 1751. The Revolution of 1689–90 terminated the forfeiture of the house of Argyll effected in 1681 and underscored by the rebellion of Archibald Campbell, the ninth earl, in 1685. Lands vested in the Crown as an institution and incomers, primarily Lowland nobles favoured by James VII, were restored wholesale to Archibald, the tenth earl (later the first duke), by William of Orange. Also restored were 13 Campbell gentry and five landed associates involved in the rebellion of 1685. Conversely, the restoration of the tenth earl cemented the expropriation of the Macleans of Duart in the Mull division. At the same time, the replacement of episcopacy by presbyterianism in the Kirk primarily worked to the landed advantage of the house of Argyll at the expense of the dissolved bishoprics of Argyll and the Isles. John Campbell, first earl of Breadalbane, however, demonstrated that individual enterprise could take precedence over clan cohesion when he secured the extensive but indebted estates of Lord Neil Campbell of Ardmaddy for £20,000 Scots (£1666-13/4) in 1693, thereby pre-empting their return to the house of Argyll, Lord Neill being uncle to the tenth earl.[27]

Although the house of Argyll remained the principal Whig interest in the shire, political factors were not of primary significance in determining the density of family settlement in the later eighteenth century (see appendix 5). The density of Campbell heritors both in terms of extent and incidence of landownership, which diminished marginally despite a doubling of incomers into the Argyllshire landed classes in the later eighteenth century, was not seriously challenged until the first half of the nineteenth century and then principally by entrepreneurial, indigenous, non-Campbell families. Notwithstanding their pervasive presence, the Campbells never entirely or consistently

Table 6. Density of Family Settlement—Campbells

Year	Spectrum	Value	% of total value
1688	Total	£5030-0/5	43.5
	Large	£2350-9/2	51.4
	Medium	£1949-19/2	39.5
	Small	£729-12/2	35.6
1751	Total	£8332-8/10	67.0
	Large	£4708-17/4	83.5
	Medium	£2685-8/2	55.6
	Small	£938-2/3	47.6
1802	Total	£8237-2/7	66.3
	Large	£5036-8/8	86.4
	Medium	£2644-14/-	50.8
	Small	£555-19/11	39.8
1858	Total	£99235-13/4	39.0
	Large	£44618-6/10	54.1
	Medium	£45075-8/10	36.6
	Small	£9541-4/7	19.6

dominated the groupings for large, medium and small estates in each or every division between 1688 and 1858. Campbell dominance in Argyll, though threatened temporarily in the aftermath of the abortive rebellion of 1685, had only declined permanently by 1858 as a result of market-forces affecting, most noticeably, the acquisition of medium and small estates in the early nineteenth century.

Given endemic lack of continuity of landownership, the persistent dominance of the Campbells can be attributed less to hereditary conveyancing than to assiduous playing of the land market. In addition to their commercial acumen, the Campbells did have the inbuilt advantage of the massive feudal superiority exercised by the house of Argyle to supervise and, if necessary, pre-empt or force through sales. This feudal privilege was generally used constructively to place checks on indebtedness for the benefit of creditors and sureties for loans. John Campbell, the second duke, used his powers of superiority in 1720 to enforce the sale rather than permit the collateral inheritance of the estate of Phantilans in Mid-Argyll. Not only was the designated heir Hew MacCorquodale resident in England, but the debt burden on Phantilans was equivalent to 60 years rents. Superiority could also be exercised destructively, however. Even although feudal services of a military nature were abolished in the aftermath of the Forty-Five, John Campbell, the fourth duke, enforced a bankruptcy order against Archibald MacAllister of Tarbet in 1762 for his failure to maintain a boat and uphold a mansion house for the reception of his feudal superior.[28]

Campbell dominance of landownership is further manifest by their continuing prominence among the elite groups of large landowners (see appendix 6). The 18 heritors recorded as having lands valued over £85 sterling in 1688 composed an elite 5% of landowners who held 36% of the valued rent of Argyllshire. In 1751, the 21 heritors holding lands over £100 composed an elite of 7% who held 45% of valued rent. The comparative figures for 1802 were 20 heritors, an elite of 8% who held 47% of valued rents. The nine heritors owning land worth over £3000 in 1858 composed a reduced elite of 3% who held around 33% of the valued rent. Of no less significance than these elite proportions, was the growing tendency of the Argyllshire elite to concentrate their landed influence in single parishes. Also marked was the relative lack of continuity among the elite despite the continuing Campbell preponderance among great landowners. Only four families (three Campbells) featured in the initial three elite lists. No more than seven families (five Campbells) in the elite of 1688 figured in the elite of 1751, a figure that did rise to 12 (nine Campbells) between 1751 and 1802. The three landowners out of the nine in 1858 whose predecessors had featured in earlier elite lists were all Campbells. The relative resilience of the Campbells is further attested by the continued, if diminished, landed presence in the county of representatives of all ten leading cadet families of the house of Argyll at the end of the seventeenth century—albeit the heads of four of these cadet families had lost their estates.[29]

The Campbells, nonetheless, were becoming increasingly vulnerable as family solidarity among indigenous landowners in all divisions began to break down in the more open land market that seemingly prevailed by the outset of the nineteenth century. The pervasive feudal influence of the house of Argyll was gradually eroded by the willingness of other indigenous landowners as well as incomers to advertise sales by public auction in the burgeoning national press.[30] Advertising, a well established practice in Argyllshire by the 1770s, not only opened out the land market, but even made the Campbells vulnerable to market forces. A pertinent, but by no means comprehensive indicator of change, has been provided by the comments on changed ownership appended by the shire's commissioners of supply, first to the valuation roll of 1751 before its updating in 1802 and secondly to that of 1802 before its overhaul in 1854. Comments specified both new buyers and sellers in the later eighteenth century, but only the sellers are indicated after 1802.

The land-market for new buyers, which was most active in Mid-Argyll but dominated throughout the shire by indigenous sales, was concerned principally with the purchase of medium and small estates, a situation which changed dramatically after 1802, when large estates were sold in every division, either in whole (w) or in part (p). Mid-Argyll again dominated the land-market with Campbells as the principal victims among indigenous families.

Table 7. Buyers (B) and Sellers (S), 1751–1802

Division		Totals	Campbell	Mac	Clan	Incomer
Mull	(B)	4	1	2	0	1
	(S)	3	1	0	1	1
Lorne	(B)	3	0	1	1	1
	(S)	3	2	1	0	0
Mid-Argyll	(B)	12	2	4	1	5
	(S)	15	8	6	1	0
Cowal	(B)	4	1	1	0	2
	(S)	4	2	0	2	0
Kintyre	(B)	11	3	4	1	3
	(S)	7	0	5	0	2
Islay	(B)	1	0	1	0	0
	(S)	1	0	1	0	0

Table 8. Sellers Post-1802

Division		Totals	Campbells	Mac	Clan	Incomer
Mull	(w)	7	1	5	0	1
	(p)	4	2	2	0	0
Lorne	(w)	14	7	5	0	2
	(p)	2	1	1	0	0
Mid-Argyll	(w)	61	38	16	3	4
	(p)	6	4	5	4	3
Cowal	(w)	16	4	5	4	3
	(p)	5	4	0	0	1
Kintyre	(w)	14	10	2	0	2
	(p)	0	0	0	0	0
Islay	(w)	3	3	0	0	0
	(p)	1	1	0	0	0

The opening up of the land-market in the nineteenth century, though undoubtedly accelerated by the economic depression in the aftermath of the Napoleonic Wars,[31] was giving such cause for concern to the commissioners of supply by 1813, that an inquiry was instituted into changes in landownership which were already threatening to make the updated valuation roll of 1802 outdated. In just over a decade, 34 heritors had sold estates in every division of the shire to 39 buyers, an indication that the trend towards consolidation was not inevitably bound to continue as Argyllshire headed towards the second phase of Clearance.[32]

No more than three landowners appear to have figured as both buyers and sellers (most prominently, the house of Argyll). Sales, which occurred in every division, mostly dealt primarily with small and secondarily with medium but no large estates. The substantive significance of the commissioners' findings was that in just over a decade, 13.3% of parochial heritors listed in 1802 as holding 5% of the valued rent of Argyllshire were actively involved in the land-market. More than a fifth (22.4%) of estates recorded as sold in the first half of the nineteenth century had already changed hands within eleven years. It can be contended, therefore, that Argyllshire evidence suggests a manifest opening up of the land market in advance of the economic depression which undoubtedly accelerated the process of sale in the

Table 9. Land Market, 1802–13

Designation	Campbell	Mac	Clan	Incomer
Seller	13	13	4	4
Buyer	10	19	2	8

Western Highland and Islands. The question remains, however, as to whether changes in landownership and, in particular, the shake-out during the Napoleonic Wars was a reflection of inadequate land use, conspicuous consumption and general indebtedness or an aspect of the enterprise culture which viewed the acquisition of land as productive and progressive and not just a recreational activity.

III

Questions of land use and enterprise notwithstanding, consideration must also be given to political connections affecting the land market. The incursion of noted improvers like the maverick Sir Alexander Murray of Stanhope in the Mull division in 1724 and the affluent George Hay, seventh marquis of Tweeddale in Lorne by 1788 owed much to the political influence of the house of Argyll. In the interim, Lord Chief Justice, James Montgomery, the author of the Entail Act and noted colonial adventurer in Prince Edward Island, was a prominent backer of James Riddell in his successful endeavours during 1768 to secure the overextended estates of Murray of Stanhope in Ardnamurchan and Sunart and across the Sound of Mull in Kilfinichen.[33] Conversely, Argyllshire landowners, such as Neill Malcolm of Poltalloch intent on promoting experimental farms, herring fishing and planned villages in Mid-Argyll, took advantage of the broader political and social horizons opened up by their involvement from the 1780s in the Highland and Agricultural Society and the British Fisheries Society; particularly as both these improving agencies were directed initially by John Campbell, fifth duke of Argyll. Political connections accruing partly from imperial service and partly from a judicious marriage into the upper echelons of the resurgent Tory party not only facilitated the acquisition of Lowland estates and the office of receiver-general of the revenues of Scotland, but no less significantly for Colonel Alexander Maclean of Ardgour, led him to oversee the neighbouring estates in East Lothian of his former colonial associate George Ramsay, ninth earl of Dalhousie, during the 1820s.[34]

Ideological considerations were no less apparent in endeavours to improve and diversify land use. The tenurial reforms instigated piecemeal in Kintyre from the outset of the eighteenth century, but promoted systematically by John, second duke of Argyll in the Mull division from 1737, were motivated by the Whig belief that material and cultural progress necessitated the replacement of customary by commercial relationships. This death-blow to clanship marked by the introduction of competitive bidding between tacksmen and tenants for the right to farm townships became the model for estate reorientation not only in Argyll but in the rest of the Highlands in the course of the eighteenth and early nineteenth century.[35] More immediately, the prospect of tenurial reform had stimulated the formation of the Argyll Company of Farmers as a co-partnery in October 1735, with a capital stock of £3000. The Company, which was articled to operate as exemplary improvers for 23 years, was intent on leasing one farm in each of the shire divisions. The subscribing partners were all landowners in their own right;28 were Campbells and the remainder longstanding associates of the clan. As all 38 were either signatories or direct descendants of the 63 heritors who subscribed the loyal address to George I in 1715, the Company can be deemed the Whig vanguard in Argyll. In the event, the Company was more significant for espousing than accomplishing improvement.[36]

Undaunted, the Whig interest in the county, complementing the political aspirations behind the British Linen Company headed by Archibald, third duke of Argyll, sought to promote a linen manufactory at Inveraray as a patriotic endeavour in the aftermath of the Forty-Five. Spinning schools were to be established throughout the county and premiums paid for the growing of flax and the spinning of yarn except in the divisions of Kintyre and Islay, where the business of spinning is already arrived at a considerable degree of perfection. Looms were to be supplied and further premiums paid to designated gentry who were currently promoting the manufacture of coarse cloth in Cowal, Lorne and Mull. Although the commissioners of supply apparently baulked at the consequent fiscal commitment during 1753, this initiative did serve to occasion an eleven-fold increase in linen production in the county, an increase which temporarily elevated Argyllshire to the forefront of Highland counties producing linen stamped for sale between the 1750s and the 1760s.[37] The endeavour of John Campbell, the fifth duke of Argyll, to promote the manufacture as well as the export of wool from the county, did lead to the establishment of a carpet factory in 1776 at Clunary near Inverary which lasted almost a working generation being sustained fitfully until 1806 by favourable advances of loans from supportive shire gentry at interest rates of 2.5%—half the current rates.[38] As Whig grandees, the house of Argyll from John the second to John George the eighth dukes—with the exception of George the spendthrift sixth duke—were commended and sought public approval for their patriotic and benevolent endeavours as innovative estate managers in eradicating tacksmen, founding planned villages, instituting textile works, sponsoring fishing communities, developing quarries and encouraging plantations; activities which they regarded as integral not colonial aspects of British economic and social development between the 1730s and the 1850s.[39]

Nonetheless, despite the manifest but not uncritical desire for improvement among the landed and professional classes in the county, the latter half of the eighteenth century witnessed a shift from proactive to reactive estate management. Proactive management, signposted by the introduction of competitive bidding, by diversified land-use and proto-industrialization, and by commercial expansion within an imperial framework was, arguably, by the 1790s and certainly by the end of the Napoleonic Wars, giving way to reactive management characterized by over-reliance on hill-farming, by largely unsustained planning, and by growing dependence on external sources of income accumulated from marriages, imperial service and stocks and shares. By the 1790s, limited improvements had actually been effected in Argyllshire outwith the properties directly managed by committed improvers. Tenurial reform through competitive bidding, rent raising, the engrossing of farms for cattle-ranches and sheep-walks, the haphazard extraction of timber and minerals and the piecemeal creation of crofting communities to exploit kelp, fishing and quarrying had taken precedence over livestock breeding, enclosures and plantations, land reclamation, the break-up of runrig, proper attention to manuring and the introduction of green crops, the termination of work-services, the planned creation of villages and the establishment of a cohesive infrastructure geared to exports.[40]

The upsurge in commodity prices, which sustained high rent rolls during the Napoleonic Wars and certainly agitated the land-market in Argyllshire, hastened estate policies of removal and relocation rather than perceptible improvements in land-use.[41] Nonetheless, the attractiveness of acquiring Argyllshire estates was certainly enhanced by official encouragement from the Board of Trade as from the Highland and Agricultural Society to promote hill-farming in particular in Mull, Lorne and Cowal. Among the most significant group of new landowners were indigenous working farmers like Angus Gregorson who so successfully exploited large tacks on the Argyll estates in Mull and Morvern that he was able to acquire the medium sized estate of Durran in Kilchrenan parish, Mid-Argyll, in 1795 and another at Acharn in Morvern by 1808, the former for an undisclosed sum, the latter for £14,500. Even incomers to the landed class in Argyllshire, such as John Ramsay of Kildalton, who initially made his money as a distiller in Islay also made such a profitable living as a tenant-farmer on the island that he was able to acquire around a third of the Campbell of Shawfield estates on Islay for £82,265 following their enforced sale in 1853. Moreover, across the broad spectrum of landowners in Argyll, sellers and purchasers were well aware of the economic potential of estates when linked to productive and diversified land-use.[42] Undoubtedly, gradual but significant progress was made in all divisions in this capital absorbing direction by the 1840s. Although run-rig was not entirely eradicated and deer forestry was intruding most notably in Lorne, the burgeoning of local agricultural societies in the previous decade had institutionalized the concerted endeavours of landowners and farmers to further livestock breeding, the reclamation of land for pastoral farming, scientific crop rotation, the drilled cultivation of root crops and the draining and dyking of fields. In like manner, the nurturing of plantations was being pursued more systematically partly in the aesthetical interest of landscaping and partly by the persistent and ubiquitous commercial demand for charcoal from Bonawe on Lochetive, the one surviving offshoot of the English iron-industry from the later eighteenth century.[43]

The virtual tripling of towns and villages in the first half of the nineteenth century from the 14 featured in the 1790s certainly indicates less limited diversification and greater variety of planning than hitherto identified in Argyllshire.[44] The curtailing of illicit distilling from the 1820s was counterpoised by the establishment of small rural industrial villages most notably in Islay and the diversification of commercial activity especially in Campbeltown for the licensed production of malt whisky. At the same time, the advent of steamships, which enhanced the development of existing villages such as Tobermory and Oban as divisional market centres, created coastal trading and recreational centres particularly in and around Dunoon on the Clyde Coast. Indeed, as early as 1819, Mrs Elizabeth Campbell of Glendaruel, having scaled down the slate quarries on her estate of Orchard Park, was intent on establishing a village for sea-bathing which was to be called Little Dalling. On a less lavish but more commercial scale, landowners instigating villages for quarrying and, more generally for fishing, too often condoned reliance on crofting and unplanned growth rather than sustained investment in marketing.[45] Yet, the quarries in the Lorne division were becoming the foremost providers of roofing slates in Scotland and realising at least £14,000 annually for quarrying proprietors, principally, John Stewart of Ballachulish and John, first marquis of Breadalbane, by the end of the Napoleonic Wars. This was a remuneration that increased substantially with the lifting of fiscal restrictions on coastal trade from the 1820s. Albeit the iniquities of salt laws prior to 1790s had subsequently been replaced by inconsistencies of bounties and compounded by the contrariness of herring shoals, whole communities around Loch Fyne and in the Inner Hebrides depended on pelagic and to a lesser extent on white fishing for their livelihood with as many as 1500 boats with three or four man crews catching fish worth reputedly between £40,–50,000 in the opening decades of the nineteenth century.[46]

Moreover, despite a corresponding growth in seasonal hiring fairs and local livestock markets in the early nineteenth century, particular landlords as well as the county interest embodied by the commissioners of supply signally failed to establish a cohesive communications network. Arguably, too great an emphasis was placed on roads rather than quays. While difficulties of tides and currents on the western seaboard cannot be understated, significant progress was made in the development of market-towns such as Tobermory, Oban and Bowmore in Islay once adequate piers had been established by the 1790s; a lesson belatedly learned by Dunoon with the advent of steam navigation on the Clyde. By the 1840s, the provision of piers and slips on Jura and Colonsay placed these islands at a distinct advantage for the export of livestock and other marketable commodities in comparison to Gigha and remote maritime districts like Ardnamurchan.[47] It can also be contended that the county tied up too much capital in expensive but soon to be outmoded canal projects, not only that accomplished at Crinan facilitating access to and from Lochfyne cutting out the Mull of Kintyre, but also those projected to avoid the stormy point of Ardnamurchan and link Loch Eil and Loch Moidart via Loch Shiel and the cross-country linking of the Crinan Canal to Loch Awe with a possible extension through Glen Orchy and Glen Dochart to Perth.[48]

The Crinan Canal, which opened for trade seven years after work commenced in 1794, virtually followed a land route originally suggested by the Company at Lochgilphead trading with the Isles, a co-partnery promoted by frustrated merchants at Inveraray seeking to open up trading outlets to the Baltic as well as the Western Isles from 1727. Initially projected for the coastal and fishing trade and expanded with a view to accommodating Baltic and West Indies trade, the Crinan Canal had insufficient breadth to cope with large steam vessels. Nonetheless, its accomplishment helped secure the dominance of Argyllshire quarries as the leading slate producers in Scotland, enhanced tourism by steam packet and, through the initiative of John MacNeill of Oakfield, occasioned the establishment of two planned villages at Ardrishaig at its outlet to Lochfyne and contiguously at Lochgilphead. But, the canal with its leaky embankments was a burdensome and embarrassing expense to its original subscribers headed by John, fifth duke of Argyll, and including other prominent county landowners who were obliged to commit almost £100,000 in stocks and secured loans without any meaningful returns before the Treasury assumed financial oversight and vested management in the Commissioners for the Caledonian Canal by 1814.[49]

The shift from proactive to reactive landlordism in the wake of the wholesale switch from resource to demand management during the first phase of Clearance was compounded by rising social expectations. Investment in estate management remained a secondary pursuit to investment in social standing. Reactive landlordism among both indigenous and incoming heritors was particularly symbolized by the building mania of the 1830s and 1840s, when Argyll, despite its relatively backward agrarian development within a British context, was to the fore in the building of mansion houses which synthesized re-emergent gothic and the picturesque. This trend, probably begun by Kirkman Finlay after his acquisition of the Castle Toward estate in 1818 and continued, notably at Ballimore around 1832, by his Cowal neighbour Mungo Nutter Campbell, reached its apogee with the mansion building of the Malcolms of Poltalloch. Having commenced a mansion house at the family seat in Kilmartin parish around 1793, Neill Malcolm and his son Neill proceeded with substantial refurbishments to Duntroon Castle and Kilmartin House in the same parish in Mid-Argyll, after their respective acquisitions from indebted Campbell lairds in 1796 and 1829. By 1844, his grandson Neill was preparing to abandon the family seat having decided on a more favourable location for a more splendid edifice which was completed at the staggering cost of £100,000 in 1848.[50]

Given such investment priorities, debt continued to fuel the land-market despite a quadrupling of rents in the late eighteenth century and a further doubling in the early nineteenth century. Hard pressed landlords, who could expect to receive a purchase price equivalent to six years rents until the 1780s, thereafter sought and frequently received a purchase price equivalent to 25–30 years rents. Albeit purchase rates did not consistently or uniformly rise from the 1820s, Argyllshire would appear to be coming into line with prevailing British trends during the Napoleonic Wars.[51]

At the same time, too involved and accusatory explanations for changes in the land-market can underplay the impact of failure of heirs male and overstate the negative features of the unenlightened entail laws. The Entail Act of 1770 should not be accepted unquestionably as either a spur to improvement or a supportive measure to promote continuity of landownership. The land-market in Argyll was arguably at its most volatile by 1812, when around one-third of all estates in the county were estimated to be under entail. Entail, particularly after the liberalising amendments of 1848, was more an excuse than a reason for belated agricultural improvement—albeit enabling legislation to change the entail of particular estates was often protracted and expensive.[52] In like manner, absenteeism, which was estimated to afflict two-thirds of Argyllshire estates by 1812, was not necessarily an impediment to improvement as evident from the general approbation of the estate management of Walter Campbell of Shawfield who reputedly never lived more than three months of the year in Islay during the 1790s. While the personal supervision of a landlord was certainly preferable to studious neglect, the varied experience of the house of Argyll would seem to suggest that the calibre of bailies and factors selected by landlords was a more significant determinant of viable estate management. Absenteeism, however, was certainly significant in the removal of rental income from an estate, income which was diverted away from reinvestment in land use to support assimilation in Anglo-Scottish landed society.[53]

Social assimilation did yield windfall dividends in the shape of marriage dowries, a source of income subsequently expanded through alliances with industrial as well as landed and commercial families in the nineteenth century. However, the short-term gains from dowries were often offset by the longer-term need to make provision for dowagers, daughters and younger sons.[54] The accumulation of debts was a recurrent, but by no means inexorable, feature of social assimilation among Argyllshire landowners. Recourse to trusteeship or placing estates in commission, though an accelerating aspect of estate management by the outset of the nineteenth century, was not necessarily occasioned by excessive debts. Trusteeship, which was primarily a measure for the avoidance of bankruptcy and the enforced sale of estates, was often occasioned by absenteeism on political and imperial service. This latter tradition, established by the dukes of Argyll as Whig grandees at the outset of the eighteenth century, was continued notably by Sir Alexander Campbell of Inverneil while governor of Madras in the 1780s. Landlords, such as Colonel Alexander MacLean of Ardgour in the 1810s, were named as trustees of their own estates when political or imperial business necessitated long periods of absenteeism. Moreover, although recourse to trusteeship could force down the purchase price for indebted estates whenever they came on the market, landlords in Argyll were not frequent victims of sequestrations. While they do feature in judicial processes for financial delinquency, in common with other members of their class they were able to take advantage of legal deference and protection not afforded to tradesmen or even commercial companies.[55]

Superficially, a case can be made that the active land market in Argyll by the end of the eighteenth century represented a failure to adapt and diversify land use in certain key districts, notably Knapdale in Mid-Argyll. However, the shake out in landownership which occurred in this district can primarily be attributed to the enforced bankruptcy of the major heritor, Sir James Campbell of Auchinbreck in 1760. Auchinbreck not only carried an inherited burden of debt from the seventeenth century, but was also financially compromised because of his association with Jacobitism. No less significantly, his debts were underwritten by a plethora of local landowners, some of whom had also borrowed from him. While their financial acumen can undoubtedly be questioned, they did not lack enterprise. Most were involved in the ill-fated Crinan Trading Company, whose endeavours to promote direct trading links with the West Indies had collapsed by 1738. While they variously sought to recover their fortunes by exploiting the droving of black cattle, the herring fishing, the extractive industries and the demand for timber from English ironmasters, the collapse of the Ayr Bank in 1772 paved the way for enforced sales throughout the district. The two principal beneficiaries of these sales, Sir Alexander Campbell of Inverneil and Neill Malcolm of Poltalloch were from indigenous landed families who had successfully exploited the imperial dimension; the former as governor of Jamaica and Madras, the latter as a colonial planter in Jamaica. Their particular acquisition and consolidation of large estates serves to confirm the general trend that Argyllshire landowners were required to demonstrate entrepreneurship to sustain their status and enhance their social aspirations.[56]

IV

Indeed, from the outset of the eighteenth century, younger sons of cadet families as of lesser gentry who had no immediate prospect of acquiring land were actively encouraged to accumulate capital through trade as well as the law and military service, the latter avenue being opened up imperially in the wake of the Treaty of Union. Even small landowners from the outset of the eighteenth century, such as Malcolm MacNeill of Carskey in Kintyre, sought to diversify their economic activities in association with the mercantile community in Campbeltown.[57] Commercial contact with the Clyde ports and to a lesser extent Ireland stimulated commercial enterprise throughout Argyllshire. The furtherance of such entrepreneurship is particularly manifest in the career of Daniel Campbell of Shawfield, a younger son of the laird of Skipness, who not only acquired his own estate near Glasgow and built a mansion house in the city, but was able to purchase Islay in 1726. In addition to the £6000 he had already advanced under wadset to his indebted kinsman John Campbell of Cawdor, the acquisition of the island was greatly facilitated by the £6080 compensation he received from the city after riotous citizens razed his mansion for his purported failure as M.P. for the Clyde Burghs to oppose the imposition of the malt tax on Scotland in 1725.[58]

The Glasgow connection with Argyll was formalized by the establishment of a Highland Society in the city in 1727; 13 Argyllshire landowners being among its 78 founder members. Operating formally as a charitable body intent on promoting apprenticeships and educational services, the Society brought together aspiring and assured entrepreneurs among the landed, commercial and professional classes. Argyllshire landowners were consistently well represented among the Society's membership throughout the eighteenth into the early nineteenth century. A socially elite offshoot of the Highland Society was the Gaelic Club of Gentlemen established in 1780 for landowners, industrialists, West Indian traders and city financers; the club deemed the most enterprising in the city by the 1800s. Among the leading lights of this Club, whose membership from 1798 was neither exclusively Highland nor primarily Gaelic speaking, were such textile entrepreneurs as David Dale and Kirkman Findlay. While the former was content to sponsor ill-fated linen and cotton mills in Argyll, at Oban and near Corpach in Kilmallie parish, the latter furthered his tenuous Highland ties by acquiring Castle Toward estate in Cowal, a move which set exemplary standards for the establishment of landscaped coastal retreats from 1818.[59]

That commercial enterprise was as much indigenous as imported seems evident from interlocking network of companies that made up the marketing portfolio of the Campbells of Ardchattan, their cadet family of Inveresregan and their Loch Etive kinsmen of Achnaba. This Campbell family cannot be regarded among the leading landowners in Argyllshire, their landed influence being largely concentrated on the parish of Ardchattan and Muckairn throughout the eighteenth and early nineteenth century. Commencing in 1688 as agents for recovering debts owed to Clyde merchants, the Inveresregan Trading Company was launched in 1706. This company, which traded until 1774 and even dabbled in coal mining in Perthshire, was complemented by a series of lesser merchandising operations, notably the Loch Etive Trading

Company of 1741–42 and the Oban Company specializing in tobacco imports between 1736 and 1743, which catered for the growth in consumerism stimulated but not creditably secured by the droving trade. Their own marketing of black cattle was furthered by a Droving Company operative between 1741 and 1775. Having acquired an agency from a Dublin consortium to export tree barks for the tanning industry, their timber dealings were entrusted to the Letterewe Wood Company from 1733 to 1737. Their Lorne Meal Company, 1730–1774, and their associated Loch Etive Meal Company, 1729–1843, were particularly active in shipping grain from Caithness. Although they promoted direct trade links with the West Indies and the American South and although they encouraged tobacco spinning as a cottage industry in Argyllshire, their company portfolio was more impressive on paper than in practice. Three of their companies did not last a decade and only two lasted beyond two generations. Their entrepreneurship merely enabled them to stand still in the middle range of landowners in Lorne.[60]

Highly profitable diversification into the extractive industries did facilitate a measure of landed expansion for indigenous heritors, notably the Stewarts of Ballachulish in Lismore and Appin parish. The commencement of slate quarrying on their estate in Lorne during the 1690s led directly to their movement from small to medium sized landowners by the mid-eighteenth century. The enterprising importation of skilled workers from Cumberland and the standardisation of slate to Welsh sizes to offset the punitive tariffs on coastal trade imposed during the Napoleonic Wars, and, above all significant capital investment in wagonways, haulage machinery and pumping equipment ensured that the slate quarries of Ballachullish by the 1830s were outperforming the larger, but more dispersed operations in the Slate Islands which, since 1745, were under the commercial direction of the Easdale Slate Company established by John Campbell, second earl of Breadalbane. Nonetheless, commercial expansion to meet increasing demand from Glasgow and other urban areas in Lowland Scotland and north-east England for roofing-slates, was not necessarily the key to landed expansion as evident from the financial difficulties encountered by the Stewarts of Ballachulish from the 1820s, albeit these difficulties were compounded less by conspicuous social expenditure than by the ripple effect of bankruptcies among financially interdependent Argyllshire entrepreneurs which forced the estate into trusteeship by the late 1850s.[61]

Despite the perennial risks of inadequate working capital and over-extended credit, commercial entrepreneurship remained not only the prime but an expanding avenue into landed society, the ranks of indigenous landowners being augmented by distillers, general merchants and bankers in the early nineteenth century. Thus, John Sinclair, descended from a line of tacksmen on Loch Etive, first made his mark commercially as a general merchant and coastal trader then as a distiller at Tobermory on Mull before building up the substantial estate of Lochaline through a series of land purchases and exchanges in the Morvern parish between 1813 and 1841 at a net outlay of £20,000.[62]

Entrepreneurial connections were of paramount significance in promoting the financial viability of estates in Argyllshire. While proximity to the industrial centres of Lowland Scotland was certainly a key determinant in this achievement from the later eighteenth century,[63] arguably a no less significant factor from the 1730s was access to the colonies and imperial service. Differentiation must be made in terms of the scale and location of imperial entrepreneurship. In North Carolina, the Argyll Colony originally projected in 1739 was based on small scale plantations around the Cape Fear River which exploited tar, turpentine and tobacco as well as the more familiar cattle, flax and timber. Although supported and sustained by tacksmen and tenants who lost out in tenurial reforms as competitive bidding was implemented throughout the county, this Colony was principally an undertaking of entrepreneurial landlords predominantly from the small and middle spectrum that offered an outlet for the commercial frustrations occasioned by the restrictive feudal superiority of the house of Argyll, especially in the Mid-Argyll and Kintyre divisions. Of the original projectors, only the MacNeills of Lossit and of Ardelay accorded priority to sustaining the necessary colonial presence to develop profitable plantations from the 1740s. Families such as the MacAllisters of Balinakill, the MacTavishes of Dunardry and the Campbells of Kilduskland opted, with varied degrees of frustration, to direct their operations from Argyllshire principally as colonial promoters rather than planters; their endeavours to profit from mercantile links with the Carolinas, West Indies and the Canadian Maritimes, enjoyed mixed fortunes that ultimately resulted in the loss of their landed estates in both North Carolina and Argyll by the outset of the nineteenth century.[64]

On the other hand, in Jamaica, where the original 'Argyll Colony' was established at least a decade before that in North Carolina, large-scale plantations in the western parishes of Hanover, Westmoreland and St. Elizabeth concentrated on sugar and rum production. Some Argyllshire landowners adventured in both colonies while other maintained a connection through the slave-trade. Whereas the Clarks of

Braleckan in Mid-Argyll had settled permanently on the island by the 1750s, most Argyllshire landed families endured tropical conditions to build up their capital reserves before returning to Scotland—albeit some like the Campbells of Orangebay renamed their estate in Glassary parish in honour of their Jamaican plantation. Undoubtedly, the pre-eminent benificiaries of this imperial connection were the Malcolms of Poltalloch who accrued immense profits not only as planters but as store-keepers. From their base in Lucca in Hanover parish, they expanded their activities to supply primarily Scottish planters throughout the island and extended their trading ventures in the Caribbean, including the selling and leasing of slaves, from Tobago to Honduras. By the outset of the 1770s, the Malcolms of Poltalloch were repatriating profits in excess of £40,000 from a yearly turnover of around £110,000, principally to build up their commercial interests and social position in London from where their West Indian trade continued to be serviced into the 1850s. At the same time, they enhanced their landed position in both Jamaica, where their ownership of five plantations in 1771 had increased to eight by 1821 and in Argyll, where they progressed from small landowners in Mid-Argyll at the outset of the eighteenth century to among the largest in the shire by the mid-nineteenth.[65]

However, the Caribbean connection was high risk and not invariably profitable. The efforts of Archibald Maclaine of Lochbuie to establish himself as a colonial adventurer were terminated by his fatal encounter with pirates on the high seas near Cuba in 1784. The credit constrictions imposed on planters, particularly those involved directly in the slave trade from Africa, were aggravated by discriminatory colonial rates of interest. The one leading Argyllshire family involved both as colonists and slave traders in North Carolina and the Caribbean—in St. Christophers—were the MacNeills of Taynish whose trading ventures in the West Indies and North Atlantic more than recouped the heavy indebtedness afflicting them in the 1730s. Unfortunately, overextended lines of credit climaxed by Neil MacNeil's absconding with the funds of his trading partnerships to the Danish island of St. Croix, enforced the sale of his estates in Mid-Argyll and Kintyre by the 1780s. Despite increasing industrial demand for cotton at the close of the eighteenth century, the West Indies trade was materially disrupted during the Napoleonic Wars, a situation compounded by the anti-slavery legislation in the early nineteenth century which pushed up overheads for labour supply and provisioning.[66]

Nonetheless, ownership of large plantations coupled to the availability of cheap native labour in Batavia enabled the Maclaines of Lochbuie, who had first moved into this former Dutch colony around 1811, to stave off bankruptcy. Sequestration proceedings were dropped by creditors and their estates in Mull rescued from trusteeship following the accession in 1852 of Donald Maclaine, whose activities as a coffee planter trading in London and Rotterdam were run concurrently with his diplomatic commission as British consular agent at Samarang, Java. But, imperial service proved a variable source of profitability. An army, naval or diplomatic commission was often a means of compensating landowners such as Lachlan MacQuarrie of Ulva who lost his family patrimony in the Mull division by 1780, but rose to the rank of major-general in the British army seeing active service in North America, Jamaica, India and Egypt before becoming colonial governor of New South Wales between 1809 and 1821. Imperial service did not sustain sundry army and naval officers on the rolls of Argyllshire landowners. While Lieutenant-Colonel Charles MacQuarrie had regained Ulva and acquired the estate of Glenforsa in Torosay parish by 1830, both estates were sold prior to 1843.[67]

Undoubtedly, service in India was the most lucrative and secure imperial prospect as evident from the rapid rise of Sir Alexander Campbell of Inverneil in the 1780s—as later, Colonel Alexander Maclean of Ardgour in the 1820s—into the elite group of large estate owners. The income Inverneil accrued from his Argyllshire estates during the 1780s, on average around £1550 yearly, was but a fraction (just over a tenth after adjustments for arrears) of the monies he accumulated annually from his stocks and shares in the East India Company, the Scottish Banks and Consolidated Government Funds and as financier to his regimental and diplomatic associates. Conversely, the sums initially expended (£7977) in acquiring the estates of Inverneil and Danna in Mid-Argyll, were but a tenth of his total expenditure in 1776, over £9785 being laid out in stock and £55,560 in interest bearing loans.[68]

Colonial plantations and imperial service can be connected with a notable expansion in individual landholding. The Malcolms of Poltalloch and the Macleans of Ardgour do serve to demonstrate that not all landowners with a hereditary connection to the Highlands were on the defensive from the 1820s. Yet, the evidence that imperial service made a significant contribution to improved and diversified land-use is at best patchy, certainly more sustainable with respect to the Malcolms of Poltalloch than to Inverneil, Ardgour or Lochbuie. Incoming landowners were arguably more aggressive in publicizing competitive bidding for leases and competitive tendering for sales of timber and other landed resources which, in turn, made indigenous landowners more aware of the power of the press to mobilize interest in sales by public auction. Imperial entrepreneurs had sufficient resources not only to compete with incomers, but to sit out and exploit long delays in affecting sales on account of disputed ownership, entail or feudal technicalities. However, the extent to which land prices were pushed up through the imperial connection is an aspect awaiting further analysis along with detailed scrutiny of the sums invested from the Empire in Argyllshire. Nonetheless, the most significant feature about landownership in Argyll, among both indigenous and incoming heritors from the outset of the nineteenth century, was the growing dependence on external funding which underwrote reactive estate management tied as much to the fluctuations in the financial as in the agricultural markets.

V

That changes in landownership was largely a self-contained affair during the eighteenth century was testimony to the commercial acumen of Argyllshire landed families. Albeit this acumen was increasingly under threat by the outset of the nineteenth century, entrepreneurial horizons had undoubtedly been broadened by imperial as much as by urban connections. While the Argyllshire land market was never closed between 1688 and 1858, more research is required in to the role of lawyers not only as estate agents but in directing investments and in forming companies. The Malcolms of Poltalloch and Campbells of Inverneil had established sophisticated legal and commercial agencies to handle their financial affairs by the 1770s with the result that they obtained far greater returns from commercial ventures and from stocks and shares than from their Argyllshire estates. While the clannish character of Argyllshire landowners was only gradually being undermined at the outset of the nineteenth century, it can be postulated that the large shake out in the land-market between 1802 and 1813, when the landed economy was actually on the upturn, was less the product of inadequate estate management than of unsound or unremunerative investments by landlords of small and medium sized estates who, with the noted exception of the duke of Argyll, lacked the external resources to ride out banking constrictions during the liquidity crisis of 1797, 1802–03 and 1810, a time when the Crinan Canal was also making its largest claims on its Argyllshire investors.[69] Conversely, external sources of income no less than buoyant rentals maintained by commercial pastoralism do much to explain the lack of a corresponding shake out in the wake of the great famine of 1845–50, an agrarian crisis which aggravated rather than caused the financial difficulties which forced insolvency upon two substantial landowners in Argyll, Walter Frederick Campbell of Shawfield and Sir James Riddell of Ardrnamurchan.[70]

The increasing dependence of estates on external funding does not absolve landlords from the responsibilities of estate management, notably for the diaspora of the dispossessed and the distressed that scarred the second phase of Clearances in Argyllshire as elsewhere in the Highlands from the 1820s.[71] The piecemeal, but systematic, removal of tacksmen which characterised the first phase of Clearance from the 1730s had undoubtedly hampered the capacity of indigenous no less than incoming landlords to sustain community support for their changes in land use. Nonetheless, purported resistance to tenurial and commercial change in all divisions of Argyll during the Clearances cannot be equated with endemic resistance to enterprise on the part of the commonality within the county.[72] The conservatism manifest in the acceptance of rampant sub-division within traditional townships and thereafter in crofting communities must be counterpoised by the commercial experience accrued from regular hiring and livestock fairs, from the opening up of marketing and travel by steamers, and from the different labour rhythms accrued in the course of seasonal migration. Even emigration which on one level can be viewed as a community protest against estate re-orientation, on another level involved entrepreneurial flair—at least during the first phase of Clearance. As is evident from the Glenaladale settlement on Prince Edward Island at the outset of the 1770s, potential emigrants, who included families from the Mull division, were required to negotiate both their acquisition of single-tenant farms and conditions for indentured labour.[73] Arguably, the innate conservatism of the commonality in Argyll had more to do with cultural diffidence than opposition to enterprise. The celebrated Gaelic poet, Duncan Ban Macintyre took solace in the predatory inclination of foxes after his removal from Glenorchy with the advent of sheep-farming in the 1760s. While William Livingstone in Islay was an outspoken critic of Clearance and the anglicization of the landed classes in the 1830s, the only contemporaneous work specifically attacking a landlord was an anonymous tirade against the unfortunate Sir James Riddell of Ardnamurchan.[74]

The cultural issue, nonetheless, raises a final question about whether landed families with imperial aspirations could realistically be expected to retain the cultural baggage of Gaelic and, in particular, traditional expectations of trusteeship. It is not altogether surprising that a family such as the Malcolms of Poltalloch who ruthlessly exploited the slave trade in the West Indies, where they regarded the naming of their slaves of a piece with the naming of their livestock, should show limited sympathy in effecting Clearance. Neill Malcolm had to be restrained by his factor, John Campbell, an Inveraray lawyer, from effecting wholesale clearances in his recently acquired estate of Oib in 1801. His grandson Neill, deprived of this restraining influence, instigated the riotous clearance of the crofting community of Arichonan in Knapdale, at the height of the great famine in the 1848, a clearance that prejudiced folk memories against his own and his family's sustained endeavours to improve and diversify land use in Mid-Argyll since the later eighteenth century.[75]

REFERENCES

1. J. Hunter, *The Making of the Crofting Community*, (Edinburgh, 1976); M. Gray, *The Highland Economy, 1750–1850*, (Edinburgh, 1957, reprinted 1976); E. Richards, *A History of the Highland Clearances*, vol. 1, (London, 1982).
2. T.M. Devine, *The Great Highland Famine*, (Edinburgh, 1988).
3. A.I. Macinnes, 'Scottish Gaeldom: The First Phase of Clearance' in *People and Society in Scotland, vol. 1, 1760–1830*, T.M. Devine & R. Mitchison eds, (Edinburgh, 1988), pp.70–90.
4. A.J. Youngson, *After the Forty-Five*, (Edinburgh, 1973); R. Mitchison, 'The Highland Clearances', *Scottish Economic & Social History*, 1, (1981), pp.137–49.
5. Sir Alexander Murray of Stanhope, *Letter and Remonstrance*, (London, 1740); John George Campbell, eighth duke of Argyll, 'On the Economic Condition of the Highlands of Scotland', *Journal of the Statistical Society of London*, (December, 1866), pp.503–34.
6. M. Hechter, *Internal Colonialism: the Celtic Fringe in British National Development*, (London, 1975).
7. E.R. Cregeen, 'The Tacksmen and their successors', *Scottish Studies*, 13, (1969), pp.93–144; John George Campbell, eighth duke of Argyll, *Crofts and Farms in the Hebrides*, (Edinburgh, 1883), pp.4–17; M.M. Leigh, *The Crofting Problem, 1780–1883*, (Edinburgh, 1929); J.B. Caird, 'The creation of crofts and new settlement patterns in the Highlands and Islands of Scotland', *Scottish Geographic Magazine*, 103, (1987), pp.67–75.
8. 'Agricultural Statistics', *T[ransactions of the] H[ighland and] A[gricultural] S[ociety of] S[cotland]*, second series, (1853–55), pp.491–3, 498; (1855–57), pp.68, 207–11, 216, 465–69, 476–77; D. Clerk, 'On the Agriculture of the County of Argyll', *THASS*, fourth series, X, (1878), pp.11–105; A[rgyll &] B[ute] D[istrict] A[rchives], Argyllshire Valuation Roll, 1858–59.
9. D. Turnock, *Patterns of Highland Development*, (London, 1970); E. Richards, *A History of the Highland Clearances*, vol. 2, (London, 1985).
10. A Highlander, *The Present Conduct of the Chieftains and Proprietors of Lands in the Highlands of Scotland towards their clans and people, considered impartially*, (London, 1773); *Report of Her Majesty's Commissioners of Inquiry into the condition of the Crofters and Cottars in the Highlands and Islands of Scotland*, (P[arliamentary] P[apers], 1884), p.8.
11. Throughout this period, the proportion of landlords to the general population

in Argyllshire seemingly fluctuated from a high of around 1.6% in the late seventeenth century to a low of around 0.3% following the institution of the national census in 1801, marginally increasing to around 0.4% by the mid-nineteenth century. Although the landed elite cannot be deemed a numerically significant grouping, they did, of course, exercise a disproportionate and dominant political, economic, social, religious and cultural influence (A.I. Macinnes, Who Owned Argyll in the Eighteenth Century? Continuity and Change from Clanship to Clearance', *Power, Property and Privilege: The Landed Elite in Scotland from 1440 to 1914*, (Association of Scottish Historical Studies, 1989), pp.95–113).

12. The valuation rolls of 1688, 1751 and 1802, the three which have survived for the years prior to the parliamentary enactment of 1854 requiring the annual compilation of rolls, have been dataprocessed, together with a fourth roll for 1858, to provide a broad perspective for continuity and change in landownership from the late seventeenth to the mid-nineteenth century (ABDA, Valuation Rolls of Argyllshire, 1688, 1751, 1802, 1858–59). The data from the valuation rolls has been processed comprehensively using DISHDATA, a data entry program devised by the DISH laboratory at Glasgow University. This task was funded by the Economic and Social Science Research Council (ESRC award number R 000 23 1710), by the John Robertson Bequest and by John Burroughs Ltd. Technical aspects of the datasets and preliminary findings are discussed in A.I. Macinnes, 'From Clanship to Commercial Landlordism: Landownership in Argyll from the Seventeenth to the Nineteenth Century', *History & Computing*, 2, (1990), pp.176–86.

13. ABDA, Valuation Roll of the Presbytery of Argyll, 1629; A.I. Macinnes, 'The impact of the Civil Wars and Interregnum: Political Disruption and Social Change within Scottish Gaeldom' in R. Mitchison & P. Roebuck eds, *Economy and Society in Scotland and Ireland, 1500–1939*, (Edinburgh, 1988), pp.170–90.

14. An index to the valuation roll for 1751 in the Scottish Record Office (SRO, E 106/3/2) has allowed greater accuracy in identifying landowners who held lands in more than one parish and to provide a corrective to the misleading figures of 200 heritors in 1751 and 156 in 1802 provided in J. Smith, *General View of the Agriculture of the County of Argyle*, (London, 1813), pp.13–14.

15. R.F. Callander, *A Pattern of Landownership in Scotland*, (Finzean, 1987), pp.45–79.

16. ABDA, Minute Book of the Commissioners of Supply of Argyllshire, 1744–95, pp.52–53, 62–64; Act for making an Authentick Roll of Valuation for the Shire of Argyll, (London, 1749).

17. ABDA, Minute Book of the Commissioners of Supply of Argyllshire, 1744–95, pp.117; Smith, *General View of Argyle*, pp.324–25; D.J. Withrington & I.R. Grant eds. *The Statistical Account of Scotland, 1791–99 edited by Sir John Sinclair: Argyll*, vol. VIII, Wakefield (1983), pp.4, 18, 76, 102, 143, 168, 192, 249, 260, 271, 291, 353, 370, 407–08; & *Western Isles*, vol. XX, (Wakefield, 1983), pp.330, 381, 439; (hereafter, *OSA*); *New Statistical Account of Scotland: Argyle*, (Edinburgh, 1845), pp.44, 57, 115, 181, 391, 431, 435, 460–61, 528, 609, 639–40, 763, 699, 717; (hereafter, *NSA*).

18. Though a useful starting point for comparative analysis, the classification by £-Scots of landowners into the great, those with estates whose valued rent exceeded £2000 Scots, the small, those with estates under £100 Scots valued rent, and the middle range in between (L.R. Timperley, 'The Pattern of Landholding in Eighteenth-Century Scotland', *The Making of the Scottish Countryside*, M.L. Parry and T.R. Slater (eds), (London, 1980), pp.137–54), has serious technical deficiencies for gauging the range and changing nature of landownership. Even although the total valued rent for a shire remained constant from the later seventeenth century, the distribution and division of landowners perpetuates inbuilt discrepancies if no allowance is made for the piecemeal revaluation and

redistribution of landlords' estates within shires since the Restoration. Lands could be exchanged between heritors without any significant alteration in their respective valued rents. Conversely, lands could be mortgaged but wadsetters not entered on the valuation roll by private agreement with the proprietors who continued to bear fiscal liabilities in return for favourable advances of credit. The parcelling out of lands to cadets diminished an individual heritor's valued rent but not necessarily his territorial influence.

19. With regard to comparative analysis, neither L.R. Timperley's *Directory of Landownership in Scotland c1770*, (Scottish Record Society, Edinburgh, 1976), nor Sir Kenneth MacKenzie of Gairloch's 'Changes in the Ownership of Land in Rossshire, 1756–1853', *T[ransactions of the] G[aelic] S[ociety of] I[nverness]*, XII, (1885–86), pp.293–324, give a clear indication of the range or changing nature of landownership. Differentiation must be observed between heritors directly managing estates solely as proprietors or conjointly as portioners, between those profiting from mortgages and annuities as wadsetters and liferenters, between those controlling teinds as titulars and tacksmen or between those stripped temporarily of their managerial role through sequestration or permanently by attainter.

20. 'Agricultural Statistics', *THASS*, second series, (1853–55), pp.493, 498; (1855–57), pp.211, 216, 469, 476–77.

21. Callendar, *A Pattern of Landownership in Scotland*, pp.57, 60–61.

22. As well as not taking account of estates created for younger sons, a process which could serve to consolidate the density of family settlement within a parish or shire, the rates of continuity have been tabulated without full knowledge of exchanges of estates among indigenous landowners or changes of landed designation that occasionally followed the acquisition of larger, more prestigious estates.

23. N[ational] L[ibrary of] S[cotland], Saltoun Papers, vol. XII, MS 175222, fo. 65; *OSA*, Western Isles, pp.328, 330–31. By way of comparison, only 22.4 per cent of estates remained in the same families in Ross-shire between the mid-eighteenth and mid-nineteenth century; at the same time, the drop in the number of heritors from 188 to 133, left no more than 56 families (29.8%) with a continuous landed presence (MacKenzie, *TGSI*, XII, pp.302–05).

24. T.M. Devine, 'The Emergence of the New Elite in the Western Highlands and Islands, 1800–60' in T.M. Devine ed. *Improvement and Enlightenment*, (Edinburgh, 1989), pp.108–42; F.M.L. Thompson, "The Land Market in the Nineteenth Century", *Oxford Economic Papers*, second series, 9, (1957), pp.268–308.

25. *OSA*, Argyll, pp.310–12; *NSA*, Argyle, pp.18, 180–81, 259, 261–62, 472, 555, 630, 684; S. MacMillan, *Families of Knapdale: Their History and Their Place-Names*, (Paisley, 1960).

26. Albeit Gaelic patronymics had generally given way to clan names by the close of the seventeenth century, the anglicization of clan names from the eighteenth century presents particular problems in detecting continuity and change of landownership. Names such a McIlmichell anglicized as Carmichael, MacCallum or McCallum as Malcolm, Mcinturner or Mcinturneour as Turner, Mcilvernoch or Macilvernock as Graham and Macinlea or McLea as Livingstone can only be matched if the division and preferably the parish and estate correspond in succeeding valuation rolls.

27. *The Acts of the Parliament of Scotland*, vol. VIII, (1670–86), T. Thomson ed., (Edinburgh, 1820), p.493, c.55; pp.592–93, c.17; p.630, c.61; p.648, c.78; Sir J.B. Paul ed., *The Scots Peerage*, vol. I, (Edinburgh, 1904), p.360.

28. I[nveraray] C[astle] A[rchives], bundle 45/9; bundle 47/6; bundle 64/1; bundle 92/220, /225; bundle 94/282; bundle 105/398; *Decisions of the Court of Session*, vol. I, 1760–64, (Edinburgh, 1772), pp.172–74. Material extracted from the Inveraray Castle Archives has been sponsored by major research grants from the British Academy.

29. Genealogical listings of the leading Campbell cadet families of the house of Argyll were kindly supplied by Alasdair Campbell of Airds, Chief Executive of Clan Campbell and Inveraray Castle Archivist.

30. *Caledonian Mercury*, 25 May 1774, p.4; ABDA, Minute Book of the Commissioners of Supply of Argyllshire, 1744–95, p.9. 372–73; NLS, Yester Papers, MS 14744, fos 16–17, 19, 21–22, 55.

31. Devine, 'The Emergence of the New Elite in the Western Highlands and Islands, 1800–60', pp.109–14.

32. ABDA, Minute Book of the Commissioners of Supply of Argyllshire, 1808–21, pp.119–21.

33. SRO, Sir James W. Montgomery Papers, RH 4/56/4; Strathclyde Regional Archives, Glasgow Burgh Court Register of Deeds, B 10/15/5784; Sir C.E. Adam ed, *View of the Political State of Scotland in the Last Century*, (Edinburgh, 1887), pp.43–49; P. Gaskell, *Morvern Transformed: A Highland Parish in the Nineteenth Century*, (Cambridge, 1980), pp.136–37.

34. ABDA, Malcolm of Poltalloch Papers, DR 2/19–20; E.R. Cregeen ed, *Argyll Estate Instructions, 1771–1805*, (Edinburgh, 1964), xxx–xxxi; Argyll, *Crofts and Farms in the Hebrides*, p.4; SRO, Dalhousie Muniments, GD 45/14/552; J. Mitchell, *Reminiscences of My Life in the Highlands (1883)*, vol. I, (Newton Abbot, 1971), pp.180–81.

35. ICA, bundle 79/8–9; *Argyll Estate Instructions*, pp.xiv–xvii; Macinnes, 'Scottish Gaeldom: The First Phase of Clearance', pp.82–85.

36. Glasgow University Archives, Angus McKechnie Papers, DC/23/2, /102–03, /105, /107; ICA bundle 45/11. The capital stock was divided into 300 shres of £10 each. No dividends were to be paid for five years. The 12 directors of the company (10 of whom were Campbells) were not appointed until June 1736, seven months after the initial share subscription had commenced.

37. ABDA, Minute Book of the Commissioners of Supply of Argyllshire, 1744–95, pp.39, 47, 90; A.J. Warden, *The Linen Trade, Ancient and Modern*, (London, 1864), pp.477–79.

38. *OSA*, Argyll, p.147; Smith, *General View of Argyle*, pp.302–03; J. Watson, 'Account of that district of Argyle and Inverness-shire, having the Atlantic Ocean on the west; the Sound of Mull on the south; Linnhe Loch, Locheil, and the Caledonian Canal to Loch Lochy, on the east; and on the north, Loch Archaig and Loch Nevish', *Prize Essays and Transactions of the Highland Society of Scotland*, IV, (1816), p.528.

39. *Argyll Estate Instructions*, pp.xxix–xxxvi, xxxviii; E.M. MacArthur, *Iona: the living memory of a crofting community, 1750–1914*, (Edinburgh, 1990), pp.18–21, 29–40, 76–83; Argyll, *Crofts and Farms in the Hebrides*, pp.16–33.

40. *OSA, Argyll, passim; Western Isles*, pp.255–446; J. Robson, *General View of the Agriculture in the County of Argyll and Western Part of Inverness-shire*, (London, 1794).

41. Smith, *General View of Argyle*, pp.314–20; Watson, 'Account of Argyle', pp.501–29; SRO, Robert Robertson's Report of Netherlorn, 1796, RHP 972/5; SRO, Riddell Papers, AF 49/6.

42. Gaskell, *Morvern Transformed*, pp.28, 133, 145; F. Ramsay, *John Ramsay of Kildalton*, (Toronto, 1969), pp.14–15, 27–29; ADBA, Malcolm of Poltalloch Papers, DR 2/15; Letter Book of Duncan Campbell, Sheriff-Substitute at Inveraray, 1805–09, DR 1/86/2; NLS, Yester Papers, MS 14777, fos 102–08.

43. *NSA, Argyle, passim;* Clerk, 'On the Agriculture of the County of Argyll', pp.11–105; *Argyllshire Monthly Magazine*, vols 1–4, (1833); M.C. Storrie, 'Landholdings and Settlement Evolution in West Highland Scotland', *Geografiska Annaler*, 47, (1965), pp.138–61; M.C. Storrie, 'Land use and settlement history of the southern Inner Hebrides', *Proceedings of the Royal Society of Edinburgh*, 83B, (1983), pp.549–66.

44. D.G. Lockhart, 'Planned Village Development in Scotland and Ireland, 1700–1850' T.M. Devine and D. Dickson eds., *Ireland and Scotland, 1600–1850*,

(Edinburgh, 1983), pp.132–45; C.W.J. Withers, *Gaelic Scotland: The Transformation of a Culture Region*, (London, 1988), pp.91–96.

45. SRO, Skene, Edwards & Garson Papers, RHP 315; *Report from the Select Committee on Emigration from the United Kingdom*, (P.P., 1826), qq.637–39; *Evidence to Her Majesty's Commission of Inquiry into the Condition of the Crofters and Cottars in the Highlands of Scotland*, (P.P., 1884), IV, q.44731.

46. J. Anderson, *An Account of the Present State of the Hebrides and Western coasts of Scotland*, (Edinburgh, 1785), pp.34–41; *Sketch of a Tour in the Highlands of Scotland*, (London, 1819), pp.222–23; ABDA, Malcolm of Poltalloch Papers, DR 2/19; Smith, *General View of Argyle*, pp.306–08; Watson, 'Account of Argyle', pp.516–22; *British Sessional Papers*, (P.P., 1830–31), X, Slate, Tiles & Brick, p.448.

47. ICA, bundle 94/291; *OSA: Argyll*, p.283; *Western Isles*, pp.328, 330–31, 409; *NSA, Argyle*, pp.156, 403, 543, 546, 618; M.M. McKay ed., *The Rev. Dr John Walker's Report on the Hebrides of 1764 & 1771*, (Edinburgh, 1980), pp.112, 138, 154, 180; J. Knox, *A Tour through the Highlands of Scotland and the Hebride Isles in 1786*, (Edinburgh, 1975), pp.42, 66–67, 69, 72, 80; ABDA, Minute Book of the Commissioners of Supply of Argyllshire, 1744–95, pp.27, 34–35, 37, 49, 128, 157, 164, 167.

48. Anderson, *An Account of the Present State of the Hebrides*, pp.55, 394–402; *NSA, Argyle*, pp.122–23; ABDA, Malcolm of Poltalloch Papers, DR 2/2; Watson, 'Account of Argyle', p.528.

49. ABDA, Burgh of Inveraray Minute Book, 1721–75, BI/1/2; NLS, Crinan Canal MSS, fos 3–4, 35–38; *NSA, Argyle*, pp.265–71; *Report from the Select Committee on the Caledonian & Crinan Canals*, (P.P., 1839), IV, appendix 15, p.200; E.F. Bradford, *MacTavish of Dunardry*, (Whitby, 1991), pp.93–97.

50. M.C. Davis, *The Lost Mansions of Argyll*, (Ardrishaig, n.d.), pp.24–25, 31–35; *NSA: Argyle*, pp.365–66; 610; H.A. Clemenson, *English Country Houses and Landed Estates*, (London, 1982), pp.46–47, 96.

51. *OSA, Argyll*, p.247; SRO, Court of Session Productions, CS 96/3346; G[lasgow] U[niversity] L[ibrary], Campbell of Inverneil Papers, vol. 6, fos 20, 100–06, 113, 159–60; ABDA, Malcolm of Poltalloch Papers, DR 2/15, /22–25; NLS, Yester Papers, MS 14777, fos 102–08; H. McKechnie, *The Lamont Clan, 1235–1935*, (Morgantown, West Virginia, 1984), pp.336, 350–51; Thompson, 'The Land Market in the Nineteenth Century', pp.289–90. Landlords were prepared to ask for purchase prices as high as 40 years rents from the outset of the 1780s (F. Ramsay (ed.), *The Day Book of Daniel Campbell of Shawfield, 1767*, (Aberdeen, 1991), pp.192, 202–04). Although estates did fetch exceptionally high prices, equivalent to 65 years rents during the wartime boom, prices subsequently fell during the recession, albeit the Napoleonic Wars served to place purchase prices in Argyll on a higher plateau (Gaskell, *Morvern Transformed*, pp.130–66).

52. R.H. Campbell, 'The Landed Classes' in *People and Society in Scotland, vol. I, 1760–1830*, pp.91–108; Smith, *General View of Argyle*, p.15; R. Somers, *Letters from the Highlands on the Famine of 1846*, (Inverness, 1977), pp.178–79; *NSA*, Argyle, p.509; McKechnie, *The Lamont Clan*, pp.362, 364; *The Day Book of Daniel Campbell of Shawfield*, pp.180–204.

53. Smith, *General View of Argyle*, pp.14–15, 319–20; *OSA*, pp.391–92, 394, 397, 409–10; *Argyll Estate Instructions*, pp.xxxvi–xxxviii, 15–16, 32–34, 63–73, 186–91, 196–206.

54. SRO, Court of Session Productions, CS 96/1626, /3336; ICA bundle 47/10; McKechnie, *The Lamont Clan*, pp.313–46; Clemenson, *English Country Houses and Landed Estates*, pp.16–17.

55. ICA, bundle 62/6; bundle 76/2; bundle 82/5; GUL, Campbell of Inverneil Papers, vol. 6, fos 101–03, 106, 116, 162–63, 161; SRO, Melville Castle Muniments, GD 51/1949/1–2; SRO, Court of Session Productions, CS 96/241, /282,/1330,/3135, /3230.

56. A. Fraser, *North Knapdale in the XVII and XVIIIth Centuries*, (Oban, 1964), pp.54–55,

71–72, 81–87, 94–95; SRO, Court of Session Productions CS 96/1626; SRO, Inveraray Sheriff Court Processes, SC 54/2/49/1, -/50/4, -/52/1; Bradford, *MacTavish of Dunardry*, pp.6–8, 97–105.

57.　D. Graham-Campbell, 'The Younger Generation in Argyll at the beginning of the Eighteenth Century', *Scottish Studies*, 18, (1974), pp.83–94; Fraser, *North Knapdale*, pp.67–68; F.F. Mackay (ed.), *MacNeil of Carskey: His Estate Journal, 1703–1743*, (Edinburgh, 1955), pp.32, 45.

58.　*The Day Book of Daniel Campbell of Shawfield*, pp.1–2.

58.　*Glasgow Highland Society, Regulations Thereof and Lists of Members*, (Glasgow, 1861), pp.3–8, 21–101; J. Strang, *Glasgow and its Clubs*, (London, 1856), pp.128–51; Robson, *General View of Argyll*, p.23; Watson, 'Account of Argyle', p.528; *NSA: Argyle*, pp.607–08.

60.　Macinnes, 'Who Owned Argyll in the Eighteenth Century?', p.98; SRO, Loch Etive Trading Company Records, RH4/93/1–4; SRO, Inveraray Sheriff Court Processes, SC 54/2/49/1, -/50/4, -/51/7, -/52/4–5, -/54/1.

61.　*OSA, Argyll*, pp.173–74; *Western Isles*, pp.362–63; *NSA, Argyle*, pp.77–78, 247–51; J. Leyden, *Journal of a Tour in the Highlands and Western Islands of Scotland in 1800*, J. Sinton ed., (Edinburgh, 1903), p.128; SRO, Court of Session Productions, CS 96/162/1–4, -/3381; D.G. Tucker, 'The History of the Scottish Slate Industry', *Business History*, 19, (1977), pp.18–36.

62.　Gaskell, *Morvern Transformed*, pp.29–32; SRO, Court of Session Productions, CS 96/3368–69; Clerk, 'On the Agriculture of the County of Argyll', pp.49, 63.

63.　Campbell, 'The Landed Classes', pp.100–01.

64.　N[orth] C[arolina] S[tate] A[rchives], McAllister Family Papers Cumberland County, 1747–1935, PC.1738.1/4, /11–12, /14–15, /19–37, /40, /43, /53–60; ICA bundle 9/10; bundle 10/152, /191; SRO, Inveraray Sheriff Court Processes, SC 54/2/50/5, -/53/2–3, -/54/4; SRO, Minutes of the Presbytery of Inveraray, 1715–45, pp.346, 350386–87; SRO, Campbell of Stonefield Papers, GD 14/10/1; A. Murdoch (ed.), 'A Scottish document concerning Emigration to North Carolina in 1772', *The North Carolina Historical Review*, LXVII, (1990), pp.438–49. A less successful contemporaneous effort was also made to establish a colonial settlement in New York State, principally by wadsetters and tacksmen from Islay discomfited by the estate management of the island's new landowner (*The Day Book of Daniel Campbell of Shawfield*, pp.21–36).

65.　NCSA, General Accessions Register, box 1, Petition of Alexander Campell, December 9, 1777; ABDA, Malcolm of Poltalloch Papers, DR 2/52, /64, /80/7; *The Oban Times*, Letter from Dugald Clerk, April 14, 1930; *Monumental Inscriptions of Jamaica*, (Society of Genealogists, London, 1966), p.177; Bradford, *MacTavish of Dunardry*, pp.144–61.

66.　SRO, Maclaine of Lochbuie Papers, GD 174/174–76; SRO, Court of Session Productions, CS 96/4370; SRO, Inveraray Sheriff Court Processes, SC 54/2/49/5, -/50/5, -/53/3; J.M. Price, 'Credit in the slave trade and plantation economies' in B.L. Solow ed. *Slavery and the Rise of the Atlantic System*, (Cambridge, 1991), pp.293–339.

67.　SRO, Maclaine of Lochbuie Papers, GD 1741/10, /14, /18, /20, /31, /32–33, /36–37, /287–92, /2343, /2346–53; *NSA*, Argyle, pp.286, 349–50. Investment outwith the empire was also problematic. The Stevensons of Belnahua, who had progressed from managers to owners of quarries on the Slate Islands in the mid-eighteenth century and then turned their hand to the development of Oban as a market centre noted for shipping, tanning and distilling, invested surplus profits in Buenos Aires; the returns from which enabled the family to maintained solvency during the recession that followed the ending of the Napoleonic Wars in 1815 but did not prevent their insolvency by 1829. In the interim, Thomas Stevenson had imported llamas which he farmed with limited success at Oban

(SRO, CS 96/423–25; Robson, *General View of Argyll,* p.22; *OSA: Argyll,* p.283; *NSA: Argyle,* p.681).

68. GUL, Campbell of Inverneil Papers, vol. 6, fos 20–24, 100–20, 159–76; NSA: Argyle, pp.634–35. Having died in 1791, Sir Archibald Campbell passed his vast estates to his elder brother James who features among the landed elite in 1802 as Campbell of Ross (see appendix 6).

69. S.G. Checkland, *Scottish Banking: A History, 1695–1973,* (Glasgow, 1975), pp.223–25; SRO, Court of Session Productions, CS 96/241,/713, /1530, /2646, /3135, /3336, /3346; McKechnie, *The Lamont Clan,* pp.321, 336.

70. Devine, *The Great Highland Famine,* pp.83–105.

71. *Report from the select committee on Emigration from the United Kingdom,* (P.P., 1826), appendix 14, pp.356–57; *Third Report from the Select Committee on Emigration,* (P.P., 1827), appendix 1, pp.500–08.

72. R.A.A. McGeachy, 'Aspects commerce, community and culture: Argyll, 1730–1850', (University of Glasgow, M. Litt., 1988).

73. Prince Edward Island Provincial Archives, MacDonald Papers, MS 2664/70–72, /75, /138–55.

74. A. MacLeod ed., *The Songs of Duncan Ban Macintyre,* (Scottish Gaelic Text Society, Edinburgh, 1978), pp.178–83, 346–49; Uilleam MacDhunleibhe, *Duain agus Orain,* (Glasgow, 1882), pp.151–55; A. & A. MacDonald eds., *The MacDonald Collection of Gaelic Poetry,* (Inverness, 1911), p.355.

75. ABDA, Malcolm of Poltalloch Papers, DR 2/15, /18; SRO, Inveraray Sheriff Court Minute Book, JC 13/92; SRO Lord Advocate's Papers, AD 14/48/319; *The Oban Times,* Speech of Rev. Donald MacCallum to Crofter Delegates in London, January 3, 1885.

Appendix 1. Spectrum of Landownership—Incidence

Year	Size	Mull	Lorne	Mid-Argyll	Cowal	Kintyre	Islay
1688	Large	6	6	6	1	5	1
	Medium	11	24	39	35	16	4
	Small	4	66	89	59	16	4
1751	Large	6	6	7	4	5	2
	Medium	11	17	38	21	17	8
	Small	14	45	80	48	18	10
1802	Large	6	7	7	4	4	2
	Medium	13	18	36	21	17	4
	Small	14	24	62	31	22	3
1858	Large	3	2	3	2	2	3
	Medium	18	21	23	13	11	4
	Small	47	37	60	55	39	17

Appendix 2. Spectrum of Landownership—Extent

Division	Size	1688	1751	1802	1858
Mull					
	Large	1243-19/3	990-15/11	951-4/7	10878-8/11
	Medium	518-14/6	59-15/7	701-10/7	22190-5/1
	Small	42-12/9	128-13/11	167-7/2	9588-7/-
Lorne					
	Large	1038-6/8	965-6/9	1122-10/1	14973
	Medium	697-0/6	688-15/-	773-19/9	27417-3/11
Mid-Argyll					
	Large	652-8/2	1009-19/7	980-18/9	16207-10/9
	Medium	1412-10/3	1590-10/11	1739-2/2	29376-1/9
	Small	772-13/9	686-3/-	516-1/-	10566-6/-
Cowal					
	Large	199-12/3	788-8/2	806-7/6	7797-3/-
	Medium	1280-12/8	888-3/4	1031-12/8	18770-16/4
	Small	495-16/4	409-1/4	235-7/2	12935-13/-
Kintyre					
	Large	1001-2/6	1223-9/-	1094-16/8	16013-16/4
	Medium	788-10/11	729-2/8	828-15/3	19582-3/8
	Small	137-14/4	206-11/9	230-2/5	8921-0/8
Islay					
	Large	439-5/7	661-7/11	873-7/9	19760-3/7
	Medium	243-18/9	271-18/3	153-19/8	6928-1/-
	Small	N45-16/8	93-10/5	11-1/1	1847

Appendix 3. Parochial Distribution of Heritors

Division/ Parish	1688	1751	1802	1858
Mull				
Small Isles	1	(3	2	3
Coll	1	(	2	2
Tiree	1	1	1	4
Kilninian	3	8	7	17
Torosay	4	4	2	9
Kilfinichan	3	4	8	11
Morvern	4	6	6	13
Ardnamurchan	(3	1	1	(5
Sunart	(	1	1	(
Kilmalie	2	3	3	4
	22	31	32	68
Lorne				
Lismore	33	26	21	21
Ardchattan	22	14	7	14
Kilmore	21	15	10	13
Kilninver	10	8	6	6
Kilbrandon	8	6	5	6
	95	69	49	60
Mid-Argyll				
Inishael	15	11	7	9
Kilchrenan	22	18	16	10
Kilmelford	7	4	4	5
Craignish	8	7	7	8
Kilmartin	19	18	14	9
Glassary	34	22	23	15
N. Knapdale	(14	18	13	6
S. Knapdale	(	16	12	12
Kilberry	15	11	9	11
	134	125	105	86
Cowal				
Glenaray	7	7	1	2
Lochgoilhead	14	2	4	6
Strachur	12	11	10	11
Kilmodan	11	8	5	8
Kilfinan	19	11	10	11
Inverchaolan	12	10	5	9
Kilmun	20	24	21	23
	95	73	56	70
Kintyre				
Killean	14	9	16	14
Campbeltown	9	10	11	23
Kilcolumkill	10	13	13	11
Gigha	4	8	3	4
	37	40	43	52
Islay				
Islay	2	12	2	16
Kilchattan	3	1	1	(8
Jura	4	7	6	(
	9	20	9	24

Appendix 4: Parochial Distribution of Clans

Division	Total	Campbell	Year Mac	Clan*	Institution	Incomer
		1688				
Mull	22	2	13	1	5	1
Lorne	95	48	26	13	7	1
Mid-Argyll	135	53	49	11	13	4
Cowal	98	26	35	11	13	8
Kintyre	37	13	13	1	5	5
Islay	9	3	2	0	4	0
	392	145	138	37	47	19

(6 unidentified, 4 in Mid-Argyll and 2 in Cowal)

		1751				
Mull	31	6	17	5	0	3
Lorne	70	40	19	10	0	0
Mid-Argyll	125	81	39	3	0	2
Cowal	73	34	16	14	0	9
Kintyre	40	11	23	1	0	5
Islay	20	14	4	0	0	2
	358	186	118	33	0	21

(1 unidentified, in Lorne)

		1802				
Mull	32	8	16	3	1	4
Lorne	49	26	13	6	0	4
Mid-Argyll	105	64	28	6	0	6
Cowal	56	24	9	11	0	12
Kintyre	43	18	17	2	0	6
Islay	9	5	3	0	0	1
	294	145	87	28	1	33

		1858				
Mull	68	9	21	5	1	24
Lorne	60	19	15	9	1	11
Mid-Argyll	86	37	23	2	2	11
Cowal	70	17	10	9	0	27
Kintyre	52	7	21	2	0	18
Islay	24	2	9	3	0	6
	360	91	99	30	4	97

(39 unidentified, 8 in Mull, 5 in Lorne, 11 in Mid-Argyll, 7 in Cowal, 4 in Kintyre & 4 in Islay).

* All clan names other than Campbells or Macs.

Appendix 5. Parochial Estates—Family Composition

Year	Size					
1688	Large (£85+)					
Division		Total	Campbell	Mac	Clan	Institution Incomer
Mull		6	—	3	—	2	1
Lorne		6	5	—	1	—	—
Mid-Argyll		6	3	—	1	2	—
Cowal		1	1	—	—	—	—
Kintyre		5	3	—	—	—	2
Islay		1	1	—	—	—	—
	Medium (£17–84)					
Mull		11	1	8	1	1	—
Lorne		24	17	3	3	1	—
Mid-Argyll		39	14	15	6	3	1
Cowal		35	13	9	5	4	3
Kintyre		16	7	5	—	3	1
Islay		4	1	1	—	2	—
	Small (£16–)					
Mull		4	1	2	—	1	—
Lorne		65	26	26	6	6	1
Mid-Argyll		89	35	34	5	7	3
Cowal		59	11	24	6	9	5
Kintyre		16	3	8	1	2	2
Islay		4	1	1	—	2	—
1751	Large (£100+)					
Division		Total	Campbell	Mac	Clan	Institution Incomer
Mull		6	4	1	—	—	1
Lorne		6	5	—	1	—	—
Mid-Argyll		7	6	1	—	—	—
Cowal		4	3	—	1	—	—
Kintyre		5	3	2	—	—	—
Islay		2	2	—	—	—	—
	Medium (£20–99)					
Mull		11	1	7	3	—	—
Lorne		17	10	4	3	—	—
Mid-Argyll		38	27	9	2	—	—
Cowal		21	14	2	2	—	3
Kintyre		17	6	9	—	—	2
Islay		8	6	2	—	—	—
	Small (£19–)					
Mull		14	1	9	2	—	2
Lorne		45	24	16	4	—	—
Mid-Argyll		80	48	29	2	—	1
Cowal		48	17	14	11	—	6
Kintyre		18	2	12	1	—	3
Islay		10	6	2	—	—	2

Appendix 5. Continued.

Year	Size					
1802	Large (£100+)					
Division		Total	Campbell	Mac	Clan	Institution Incomer
Mull		6	4	1	—	— 1
Lorne		7	5	1	—	— 1
Mid-Argyll		7	7	—	—	— —
Cowal		4	3	—	1	— —
Kintyre		4	3	1	—	— —
Islay		2	2	—	—	— —
	Medium (£20–99)					
Mull		13	1	9	2	— 1
Lorne		18	12	1	3	— 2
Mid-Argyll		36	20	13	2	— 1
Cowal		21	14	1	3	— 3
Kintyre		17	7	7	1	— 2
Islay		4	2	2	—	— —
	Small (£19–)					
Mull		14	3	7	1	1 2
Lorne		24	9	11	3	— 1
Mid-Argyll		62	37	15	4	— 6
Cowal		31	7	10	7	— 7
Kintyre		22	8	9	1	— 4
Islay		3	1	1	—	— 1
1858	Large (£3300+)					
Division		Total	Campbell	Mac	Clan	Institution Incomer
Mull		3	1	1	—	— 1
Lorne		2	2	—	—	— —
Mid-Argyll		3	1	2	—	— —
Cowal		2	1	—	—	— 1
Kintyre		2	2	—	—	— —
Islay		3	—	—	—	— 3
	Medium (£700–3299)					
Mull		18	4	2	4	— 8
Lorne		21	8	2	3	1 7
Mid-Argyll		23	13	5	2	1 2
Cowal		13	7	1	2	— 3
Kintyre		11	1	5	1	— 4
Islay		4	1	2	—	— 1
	Small (£699–)					
Mull		47	4	17	5	— 13
Lorne		37	10	9	5	— 7
Mid-Argyll		60	23	14	4	1 7
Cowal		55	9	7	11	— 21
Kintyre		35	4	17	1	— 13
Islay		17	1	5	3	— 4

Appendix 6. Landed Elites

Past Position	Present Position	Total Parish Landowner	Valued Rent	Presence
		1688		
	1	Campbell of Cawdor	537–13/9	2
	2	Maclean of Duart	500	3
	3	Lord Lorne	445–17/2	3
	4	Crown	406–1/2	3
	5	Earls of (Erroll (Strathmore	277–12/8	1
	7	Lord Neil Campbell	240–14/10	3
	8	Campbell of Ardkinglas	199–12/3	1
	9	Maclean of Coll	178–7/10	1
	10	Maclaine of Lochbuie	151–7/1	1
	11	Earl of Breadalbane	140–8/11	1
	12	Marquis of Atholl	134–0/9	1
	13	Campbell of Lochnell	118–4/10	1
	14	Stewart of Ballequhan	104–7/-	1
	15	Stewart of Appin	99–9/3	1
	16	Bishop of the Isles	95	4
	17	Campbell of Skipness	93–12/3	1
	18	Campbell of Barrichbeyan	92–15/7	1
		1751		
(3)	1	Duke of Argyll	1882–0/5	8
	2	Campbell of Shawfield	538–0/5	1
(11)	3	Earl of Breadalbane	507–17/1	3
(8)	4	Campbell of Ardkinglas	328–16/3	1
(13)	5	Campbell of Lochnell	273–10/7	1
	6	Campbell of Auchinbreck	222–3/3	1
	7	Murray of Stanhope	182–8/11	1
	8	Campbell of Craignish	144–18/3	1
	9	MacMillan of Dunmore	138–4/11	1
	10	Lamont of Lamont	136–6/10	1
(15)	11	Stewart of Appin	128–13/10	1
	12	Campbell of Ederline	126–18/8	1
(10)	13	Maclaine of Lochbuie	124–11/1	1
	14	Campbell of Airds	123–4/-	1
	15	Campbell of Jura	122–18/7	1
	16	Campbell of Barcaldine	117–16/-	1
	17	MacNeill of Taynish	117–5/10	1
(17)	18	Campbell of Skipness	110–16/2	1
	19	Campbell of Otter	107–6/1	1
	20	MacDonald of Largie	102–18/7	1
	21	Campbell of Inverawe	102–2/8	1

Appendix 6. Landed Elites

Past Position	Present Position	Total Parish Landowner	Valued Rent	Presence
		1802		
(3/1)	1	Duke of Argyll	1899–18/2	8
(—/2)	2	Campbell of Shawfield	832–19/1	2
(11/3)	3	Marquis of Breadalbane	566–19/11	3
(13/5)	4	Campbell of Lochnell	294–5/7	1
(—/4)	5	Campbell of Ardkinglas	260–18/11	1
	6	Campbell of Ross	186–3/9	1
	7	Riddell of Ardnamurchan	182–8/11	1
(—/15)	8	Campbell of Jura	164–10/-	1
(—/10)	9	Lamont of Lamont	162–5/1	1
(—/16)	10	Campbell of Barcaldine	132–18/2	1
	11	Campbell of Stonefield	131–16/5	1
(10/13)	12	Maclaine of Lochbuie	130–9/11	1
(—/14)	13	Campbell of Airds	125–5/10	1
	14	Campbell of Kilberry	123–1/-	1
	15	Campbell of Southall	108–11/7	1
	16	MacNeill of Gigha	108–7/9	1
	17	Campbell of Silvercraigs	107–10/3	1
	18	MacDougall of Dunnolly	107–3/1	1
(—/21)	19	Campbell of Inverawe	102–2/8	1
	20	Marquis of Tweeddale	102–0/10	1
		1858		
(3/1/1)	1	Duke of Argyll	23,405–8/6	4
(—/—/—)	2	Morrison of Islay	16,312–3/7	2
(11/3/3)	3	Marquis of Breadalbane	11,087–10/6	2
(13/5/4)	4	Campbell of Lochnell	10,126–9/9	1
(—/—/—)	5	Malcolm of Poltalloch	9,966–13/3	2
(—/—/—)	6	Dalgleish of West Grange	4,114–4/8	1
(—/—/—)	7	Callender of Ardkinglas	3,708–10/-	1
(—/—/—)	8	Ramsay of Kildalton	3,447–19/-	1
(—/—/—)	9	Maclean of Ardgour	3,444–4/3	1

2

The Business Affairs of an Eighteenth Century Lowland Laird: Sir Archibald Grant of Monymusk, 1696–1778

A.J.G. Cummings

The years following the Union of the Parliaments of Scotland and England in 1707 witnessed some profound changes in Scottish society, although development was neither immediate or rapid.[1] The removal of the major elements of government to London completed the change begun in 1603 when James VI of Scotland also became King of England and ruled both kingdoms from London. Thus London became increasingly attractive to many Scotsmen and led Dr. Johnson to exclaim, 'The noblest prospect which a Scotchman ever sees, is the highroad which leads him to England.' In consequence the nobility now looked ever more clearly to the court in London for patronage and left something of a social and political vacuum in Scotland itself.[2] Part of this gap was to be filled by the middling rank of lairds, merchants and professional groups of whom the lawyers were among the more important. Edinburgh remained an important administrative and legal centre and it was the lawyers who gained considerably from employment within the major courts of Session, Justiciary and Exchequer as well as the less important ones of Commissary and Admiralty. In addition the General Assembly of the Church of Scotland and the Convention of Royal Burghs met annually in the city, which also played host to several administrative bodies such as the Scottish Board of Customs and the Board of Excise.[3] Thus Edinburgh became an important centre of patronage, much of which, between 1725 and 1761, was centred around Andrew Fletcher of Saltoun, Lord Milton, a Court of Session judge who acted as the Duke of Argyll's political manager in Scotland.[4] Thus both the upper classes and the middling sort were drawn into this network of patronage.[5]

Who precisely constituted the upper and middle classes in eighteenth century Britain is less easy to define. In England Peter Earle has defined the gentry as 'men with a private income who did not need to work

43

for a living.'[6] In Scotland the situation was not so clear cut. The reason
for this, as John Shaw has shown, was that the comparatively low
incomes yielded by their estates, meant that many members of both
the upper class and lesser landowners needed to supplement their
incomes by gainful employment. The law became a favourite outlet
and the social base of the legal profession was widened as a result.[7] A
further consequence of this was that this gainful employment would
not necessarily rule a man out of the elite. In the Lowlands of Scotland,
therefore, Lenman has stated that a fairly complex rural society had
emerged.[8] Among the leading legal families of the early eighteenth
century was that of Grant of Monymusk in Aberdeenshire. The object
of this case study is to examine the affairs of one of this family, Sir
Archibald Grant (1696–1778), the second baronet of Monymusk in
order to ascertain the nature of his financial and business activities and
to set them within the context of the elite society in which he operated.
The traditional view of him has been as a noted improver.[9] On the
other hand his notoriety as a principal player in the Charitable Corporation has also been examined.[10] Emphasis on the latter has tempted
Bruce Lenman to decry the former school of thought as embalming
him in 'an oudour of sanctity' whereas 'contemporaries knew him to
the end of his days as the notably unpleasant and greedy trickster he
was.'[11] Existing examinations have, therefore, tended to concentrate
on one side or another of Grant's character. The aim of this examination, however, is not to rehabilitate or to condemn Grant, but to assess
his career in the context of the conditions in which he operated.
Particular attention will be paid to the 1720s and 1730s, as these years
proved to be a critical stage in his life.

By any definition of the word, Sir Archibald Grant of Monymusk
must be counted among the elite of Scotland of his day. He was born
on 25 September 1696, the eldest son of the lawyer Francis Grant who
became Lord Cullen, a Senator of the College of Justice, and the first
baronet of Monymusk. His younger brother, William Grant, was to
become Lord Advocate under Lord Ilay's patronage, and in 1754, a
senator of the College of Justice under the title Lord Prestongrange.[12]
Archibald was thus born into, and lived, within the higher echelons of
the legal profession. Like all advancing lawyers, Cullen tried to raise
his status among the landed classes. In 1713 he sold his paternal estate
at Gamrie in Banffshire and purchased the estate of Monymusk in
Aberdeenshire from Sir William Forbes who had gone bankrupt.[13] The
comparative poverty of the Scottish economy as reflected in the relatively backward state of agriculture, and the lack of success in
promoting new trading schemes as witnessed by the catastrophe of the

Darien project had contributed to landed insolvencies. Anything up to a quarter of Scottish estates had changed hands because of bankruptcy between 1660 and 1710.[14] Such a trend provided much work for the legal profession whose numbers began to grow, and, as in Cullen's case, provided the wealth to enhance their status among the landed gentry by the acquisition of real estate.

Grant's education was typical of those of his class and social standing. He was educated to the law, not only as befitted the son of a noted lawyer, but also as dictated by the Scottish practice of educating the eldest son in this way. He qualified as an advocate,[15] and would appear to have practised in Edinburgh from c. 1717 until he entered Parliament in 1722, when he became a member of Lincoln's Inn in London. Grant was part of a changing trend within the Scottish legal profession whereby the Faculty of Advocates, which before 1670 had been mainly recruited from the ranks of the lesser gentry and those of lower social orders, now came to include the sons of peers and baronets.[16] The reason for this as we have already seen was financial necessity. How far these pressures applied to Sir Archibald Grant is difficult to say, but the fact that the estate of Monymusk yielded only £617 Sterling per annum,[17] is indicative of his need to supplement this from a further source. However as he was able to become a member of parliament there is no doubt that his standing as one of the elite was recognised by his contemporaries and, moreover, was acceptable to the political managers of Scotland.

In retrospect Cullen was none too enamoured of his purchase of the estate of Monymusk and felt he had been badly advised in doing so. His legal duties meant that he spent most of his time in Edinburgh, and so, in 1716, he handed over the running of his northern property to Archibald.[18] In essence it is not hard to see why Cullen had second thoughts about Monymusk. Of its 10,743 acres, some 4,735 were moor and moss and 1,933 consisted of woodland. The more useful land consisted of 844 acres of pasture and 3,231 acres of arable land.[19] In 1712, the money rent of the estate was £1,591 Scots, the equivalent of £133 Sterling, to which was added the victual rent or rent in kind. By 1733 the money rent had increased to £3586 Scots (£299 Sterling) while, Hamilton has estimated, the victual rent remained much the same.[20] As Grant claimed in 1732 that the rental value of the estate was £617 Sterling (£7404 Scots), the victual rent must have been worth approximately £320 Sterling per year. Ironically, even as late as 1770, this would have placed Grant among the top one hundred Scottish landowners.[21] However even in 1712, the cash element of the rent seemed smaller than was necessary to maintain a family desirous of upward social mobility in a British as opposed to a Scottish context. In order to advance his fortunes it was therefore necessary for Grant to expand his operations. His efforts in this regard were to prove troublesome to say the least. However in the long term, young Archibald was to prove at least equal to the task of consolidating and indeed improving upon his father's work in the limited sphere on his own estate.

Before entering parliament, Grant became more deeply involved in the management of Monymusk. In 1717, on the occasion of his marriage to Ann Hamilton, daughter of James Hamilton of Pencaitland, his father made over the estate to Archibald, reserving only a small annuity to himself. Archibald now proceeded to carry out a range of improvements, including repairs to the house and draining and enclosing the Home Park. Here new farming methods were gradually being introduced, including the planting of leguminous crops by 1719 and turnips by 1726.[22] Grant was also aware of the possibilities of reafforestation and from his earliest days at Monymusk was planting young trees with seeds acquired both locally and further afield in Scotland and abroad. These not only enhanced the appearance of the estate but, by 1730, were also proving to be a profitable business venture in both seed and timber.[23] Thus by the time he left for London sometime after his election as member of parliament for Aberdeenshire in 1722, he had laid the foundations of what was to become the most important work of his life. Ironically, until 1734 he was largely absent from Monymusk, either in Edinburgh or London, but he kept strict control over his factors, gardners and others on the estate by means of weekly reports and voluminous correspondence. It also seems likely that his travels in England greatly influenced his thinking on estate management.[24] What he did prove, therefore, was that absenteeism did not necessarily constitute neglect. On the contrary, Grant was able to use the knowledge gained on his travels to improve both the appearance and the value of his estate. It must be stressed, though, that what Grant was doing was not new to Scotland. As Whyte has shown, particularly in the Lothians, new or converted houses surrounded by enclosed parkland and commercial development of the home farm had been on the increase since the seventeenth century.[25]

In London, Grant quickly became involved in a much wider business and financial world, in the era of the aftermath of the South Sea Bubble, where, despite attempts to control new corporate ventures, speculation continued to flourish. He was a shareholder in the Mines Royal and Mineral and Battery Works, a moribund mining corporation which had been revived during the speculative mania surrounding the South Sea Bubble by the notorious speculator, Case Billingsley.[26] On 2 October

1723, Grant became a director of the York Buildings Company,[27] a London waterworks which be dint of a flaw in its act of incorporation had been expanded by speculators during the boom in company promotions in 1719 and 1720 into a larger concern designed to acquire estates forfeited after the unsuccessful Jacobite Rebellion of 1715 in order to use the revenues to fund a life annuity scheme.[28] Ironically, an outgoing director was Sir John Cockburn of Ormiston, like Grant, one of the most noted agricultural improvers of his age.[29] On 25 October 1725 Grant was also elected to the board of a body with the august title of 'The Charitable Corporation for the relief of the Industrious Poor, by assisting them with small Sums upon Pledges at Legal Interest'.[30] In effect, the Charitable Corporation was a corporate pawn-broker established to keep the poor out of the hands of the more rapacious sector of that profession by charging interest at the legal maximum of 5 per cent.[31] Involvement in both of these organisation was to have immense significance for Grant's future, leading him in to the murky waters of high finance and corporate scandals.

The contacts that he made in London confirmed the widening scope of Grant's interests. One of his fellow directors in both of these operations, and who was also involved in the Mines Royal, was William Squire, a merchant and former mayor of Liverpool and brother-in-law of Edward Norris, one of the town's M.Ps. Squire had come to London during the stock market boom of 1720 to sell shares in river improvement schemes in North-west England and had remained in the capital as a speculator after the crash.[32] Together with Billingsley, Squire had been responsible for the formulation of the highly dubious Harburgh Lottery scheme suppressed by parliament in 1723 before it could get off the ground.[33] In 1724, the York Buildings Company unsuccessfully tried to gain control of the Charitable Corporation's affairs to control its finances and to try to enter banking by the back door. Stockholders in both organisations had strong reservations concerning the scheme and the Solicitor-General was of the opinion that it was illegal.[34] Grant and Squire were probably among the architects of the scheme.[35] Like many Scottish M.P.s in the early years of the union, therefore, Grant was finding London, and indeed England itself, an ideal outlet for the talents which he hoped would advance his fortunes.

Grant also extended his interests through the more conventional paths of matrimony and the development of landed estates. His first wife having died, he married Ann Potts, a Derbyshire woman whose family had interests in lead mining, an activity which was to concern Sir Archibald for many years. In his own right, Grant purchased shares in various Derbyshire mining ventures for a total of £142.13.9

(£142.69). Although these produced a loss before January 1731, in the next eighteen months, the return was £38.15.1 (£38.75) or approximately 18% per annum.[36] With such possibilities for profit it is hardly surprising that Grant was eager to expand these interests. On 15 May 1730 he obtained a lease from the Macleans of Ardgour, allowing him to search for, and develop mines. The cost to him was estimated at £266. In Morvern and Mull, he obtained a sixteenth share in the mines purchased from Sir Alexander Murray of Stanhope at a cost of £635. He advanced a further £395 for the development of the project. In Wales he had a half share in mines in the counties of Cardigan and Brecon at a cost of £267, but by 1730 these seem to have been abandoned, a clear indication of that high return also carried with it a higher risk of loss or failure. In Norway he obtained a fifth share of a lease of mines from the King of Denmark at an initial cost of £275, a further £250 being spent by his brother Francis Grant on travel to Denmark to effect the lease. In both the Morvern and Norwegian ventures, William Squire was also a significant investor.[37]

Among Grant's other business contacts in London were Thomas Watts, founder of an academy providing an education for clerks and accountants as well as courses in natural philosophy. Watts was also the principal force controlling the Sun Fire Office, and also a fellow expatriate Scot. This led Grant into contact with Watts' friend and patron James Brydges, first Duke of Chandos. Together with these luminaries and others, Grant was involved in the setting up of the Scotch Mines Company which obtained a Royal charter in 1729.[38] In association with the Duke of Norfolk and several other partners, he also obtained an interest in the lease of mines owned by Sir Alexander Murray of Stanhope in Strontian on the peninsula of Ardnamurchan across nearby Loch Sunart.[39] In addition, Grant acquired the rights to one-third of the royalties Murray had kept for himself when the lease was enacted, which he reckoned was worth £4,500 over the period of the lease. This clearly illustrates the potential complexity of business relationships in this period as it was assigned to Zachariah Foxall, a London merchant, as security for a £1,000 loan, then further assigned to his brother Francis Grant and finally to his brother William, the three charges to rank in descending order. On 31 July 1730, Grant, and his other partners granted a sub-lease of the Strontian mines to the York Buildings Company, paving the way for one of then greatest financial, scandals of the eighteenth century in which Sir Archibald Grant was to be a leading figure. However Grant's interests in mining were not simply in speculative finance. In 1728, together with the inventor Thomas Tomkyns, Sir Thomas Mackworth, another landowner with extensive business interests, and others, Grant held an interest in a patent for smelting iron using coal. Thus, according to Stewart, 'entrepreneurs, patentees, improving landowners, and natural philosophers found a future in each others' company.[40] Speculators such as Grant, therefore clearly saw developing technology as an essential way of securing the future of high risk investments.

In addition to his mining interests, Grant, like other landowners of his time was concerned with exploitation and development of landed estates. As we have seen, he was gradually developing Monymusk, but other opportunities also began to open up to him. Here again, the York Buildings Company provided an ideal source of potential revenue. Grant was able to do this partly through his own knowledge of the company as a former director, but also because Thomas Fordyce and George Buchan, two of the company's agents were his related to him,[41] and it is fair to assume that these were an additional source of information. Grant was interested in the exploitation of the company's vast estates in Scotland. Among the most important of these was that of the forfeited Earl of Winton at Tranent and Cockenzie in East Lothian. Grant took an interest in the revival of a glassworks at nearby Port Seton, a venture in which the York Buildings Company was also interested and which lost money.[42] When the company withdrew from the venture Grant tried to carry on alone, but cash flow problems and pressure from a London competitor on a supplier to stop providing raw materials contributed to the cessation of production in October 1734.[43]

In order to provide coal for the glassworks, Grant became a silent partner of William Adam, father of the noted architects, who in 1727 was given a lease of the York Buildings Company's coal and saltworks on the Winton estate at Tranent. These had had a turbulent history in the preceding years. In 1722, the York Buildings Company had enlarged the harbour at nearby Cockenzie and invested in a waggonway to link it with the mines at Tranent.[44] In 1724 at the instigation of the Duke of Chandos, one of the most noted aristocratic speculators of the day, the company had embarked on an ambitious scheme to sell coal from the mines on the London market but this had failed, partly because it was difficult to compete with the nearer and less costly operations on Tyneside and partly because it was suspected that the company's employees were not entirely trustworthy[45], hence the decision to salvage what it could by leasing instead of operating the works.

On 11 November 1728, together with his brother-in-law, Alexander Garden of Troup, he became even more deeply involved in the company's affairs when they took a lease of parts of the estates of

Panmure, Southesk and Marischal in the counties of Angus, Kincardine and Aberdeen, together with all of the small estate of Pitcairn in north-east Scotland. The company, finding it difficult to collect and remit rents to London, had settled on leases to local men. Grant was well aware of the potential of these estates as family connections were strong. One of the company's local agents, Thomas Fordyce, was Sir Archibald Grant's uncle.[46] The agreement required Grant and Garden to pay £4,000 per annum. Houses on the estates were to be made habitable by the company before entry after which Grant and Garden would be liable for repairs. Arrears of rent, one of the major factors influencing the company's decision to lease the estates, were also to be sold to Grant and Garden.[47] It is difficult to ascertain just how lucrative the bargain was to Grant and Garden. At the time they took over the estates, the York Buildings Company was engaged in timber works on Speyside and part of the arrangement included an obligation on the leasees to carry some of this timber. It was possibly for this purpose that Grant held a half interest in two ships, which together he felt were worth £150 to him.[48] Certainly when the works ceased, Grant disposed of his interest in the ships. Had the work not ceased, Grant claimed that the costs incurred meant that it would have been necessary to withdraw from the agreement.[49] In 1732, Grant estimated his half share of the lease to be worth £2,500 although part of this was assigned to Garden in respect of money owed to the late Lord Cullen's younger children under his will.[50] If Grant's estimate is accurate, this represented a return of 25% on his outlay, before deducting expenses, a fair return by any standards. Thus later claims that agreement was not altogether profitable must be treated with some caution.[51] The fact that he and Garden held on to the land until their lease expired in 1757, is a clear indication that notwithstanding any problems, the lease had proved reasonably profitable.

Also in London, Grant came into contact with George Robinson, a broker who was to be another factor in Grant's downfall. Robinson, according to Romney Sedgewick, was a stockbroker 'with a reputation for ruining his clients.'[52] It is uncertain how Grant came into contact with Robinson, but certainly it was part of the widening network of his acquaintances and business contacts. Another such contact was John Thompson an Edinburgh merchant and a noted Jacobite with whom Grant is known to have had dealings.[53] Together with these two, Squire and one William Burroughs, Grant was about to embark on what was to prove one of the most gigantic frauds of the eighteenth century.

Since his arrival in London, as we have seen, Grant, with Squire, had been closely involved with both the York Buildings Company and the

Charitable Corporation. Despite the failure of the earlier attempt to merge the companies and develop banking, some of the directors of the Charitable Corporation, including Sir Archibald Grant, were determined to ignore their obligations to meet the needs of the poor and enter the world of high finance. In 1726, the directors had allowed pledges to be made through brokers, thus allowing borrowers to remain anonymous, then in 1727 they empowered Thompson, the corporation's warehousekeeper, to advance up to £2,000 on any one pledge.[54] Both of these actions were totally irrelevant to the needs of the poor. In the meantime, Robinson had become sole banker to the Charitable Corporation in 1726, persuading the company to withdraw funds from the Bank of England and other reputable concerns.[55] On March 1 1729, he obtained permission from the directors to handle notes amounting to £120,000 *per annum* for three years. The directors failed to secure the permission of the shareholders in general meeting and in any case there were no powers in the corporation's charter to sanction such a move.[56] Likewise the directors increased the share capital of the corporation without receiving proper authority from the shareholders. On 21 June 1728, with the consent of the law officers of the crown, the authorised capital was increased from £100,000 to £300,000 and on 31 July 1730 a further increase to £600,000 was allowed. In neither case did the law officers check that such changes had been properly sanctioned by the shareholders.[57] In 1728, though, they had vetoed the original application for an unlimited increase in capital on the grounds that it was unprecedented.[58] Not all of the authorised sum was received by the company as by 30 September 1731, only £353,871 had been paid up.[59] Nevertheless a large pool of funds had been made available for lending and Grant and his associates nominated themselves as the principal 'borrowers'.

Grant together with Robinson, Thompson, Squire and Burroughs had formed a sharedealing partnership in October 1727. Their aim was to deal in the Charitable Corporation's own shares which were now above their par value of £5. To finance their purchases, Thompson raised the necessary finance from the corporation itself by means of fictitious pledges. The money was then given to Robinson as a broker whose task it was to purchase the shares on behalf of the syndicate. Many of the shares in which they dealt had come from the holdings of Sir John Meres, former principal shareholder in the corporation who was liquidating his holding to raise money for other venture. In particular he was involved in the noted speculator William Wood's scheme to smelt iron using coal. Ironically Grant and Robinson were involved in a rival patent.[60]

One must ask why Grant became involved in such a scheme. The most reasonable explanation is that he was indebted to Robinson and was forced to do so out of necessity. John Thompson said later that Robinson had been the bane of Grant's life before he became involved with the Charitable Corporation, and that part of the debt had been settled by the liquidation of a mortgage by Sir William Garden upon a Scottish estate on which Lord Cullen had originally advanced the money. Desperation rather than intent would appear to have motivated Grant. Certainly concealment of their activities was of the essence as when Grant was in Scotland in 1728, fear of an investigation and discovery led to the other four forming a separate partnership to continue dealings without informing Grant.[61]

In order to conceal evidence of the sharedealings still further, Robinson had the shares put into the names of nominees. This also enabled him to indulge in dealings without the knowledge of his partners, sell the holdings and pocket the proceeds.[62] Between 1727 and 1729, the price of the shares rose to over £10.63. Partly, one suspects this increase was due to the activities in the market of the partners themselves as it has been reckoned the two partnerships between them were responsible for the acquisition of almost 31,000 Charitable Corporation shares.[64] Whatever the reason, Grant and the others were keen to offload the shares, take their profit and repay the money 'borrowed' from the Charitable Corporation. It was then, sometime during 1729, that they discovered that Robinson had robbed them.[65] Despite their consternation, there seemed little they could do, as to reveal Robinson's misdoings would only lead to their own downfall.

The only solution which seemed feasible was to trust Robinson yet again. This time the target of the group was the stock of the York Buildings Company. Grant was now able to put his knowledge and contacts with the company to good use. He was well aware of the company's activities in recent years and of the fact that the governor, Col. Samuel Horsey, had obtained an extension to its charter to allow it to embark on trading and industrial ventures. The first such scheme was the development of woods on Speyside owned by Sir Archibald's kinsman, Sir James Grant of Grant. In addition to sawmills to provide timber, iron furnaces were developed to process ore brought over the hills from Tomintoul. More important though, was Horsey's interest in developing lead mines in Scotland. He had already entered into an agreement with Lord Hopetoun to work his mines in West Lothian. He was now persuaded to take a sublease of the lead mines at Strontian in Ardnamurchan in which Grant already had an interest. Squire gained election as a director of the York Buildings Company to promote the conspirators interests, and Grant and Burroughs travelled to the nearby Morvern mines to keep an eye on things.

The aim of the conspirators was to acquire as much stock as possible and then to buy parcels from jobbers who were regarded as 'bears' i.e. those who sold in anticipation of a price fall that would allow them to buy back stock at a profit. By holding on to the stock and by means of rumour and the placement of stories in the press that the success of the lead mines would prove a boost to the company's flagging fortunes, they meant to push the share price up and then sell at the peak of the market. There was even an unsubstantiated rumour that the group was dealing in East India Company stock as well.[66] The plan seemed to go well, as at the turn of the year the price of a £100 stock unit stood at £19.67. On 2 October when a press rumour talked of ships returning from Scotland laden with ore, the price reached a peak of £38.68. However, such was the rate of buying of the partners, not only for the syndicate, but on their own account as well, that they undoubtedly contributed to the rise in prices, a view later confirmed by John Thompson.[69] Despite attempts to control him, Robinson succeeded yet again in defrauding his partners of their already ill-gotten gains, by surreptitiously obtaining the stock and selling it. Thus once again, at the top of the market, the conspirators found themselves the victims of their own crimes. This exacerbated their problems as they were now forced to release their own personal holdings on to a market which had realised the hollow nature of the whole scheme. The price tumbled with the partners as the principal sellers, this time forcing down the price. Grant and the others realised what they were doing to the price and agreed to work as a group instead of against each other. But such was their fear of being the loser in such a deal that they failed to keep to their bargain.[70] Discovery was now certain and Grant and his partners faced potential ruin.

Rumblings of wrongdoings in the Charitable Corporation abounded during the early months of 1731. The directors had an indication of what was afoot in the Spring of that year when on the death of the cashier William Tench it was discovered that large sums were owed by Robinson. Little or nothing had been done to remedy this obvious discrepancy.[71] The other directors, therefore, must take a share of the blame for the fact that it was only with the disappearance of Robinson and Thompson in October 1731 that the Charitable Corporation was forced into action. An internal inquiry revealed that fraud had occurred which led the shareholders to petition parliament for assistance.[72]

In the meantime, Sir Archibald Grant's activities in the market selling

York Buildings stock had been considerable. Between 1 January and 11 November 1731, he disposed of stock in his own name or held by him with a nominal value of £109,000 for which he received £19,764. Among this was £10,000 sold to Robinson on 4 February for £2,600 less £1,695 due to Robinson. Thus even after he knew that Robinson had defrauded him of an incalculable amount, Robinson had such a hold on him that Grant was forced to pay him even more. Due to the falling price, Grant probably lost in excess of £4,000 on these dealings.[73] When Grant's share of the dealings of the partnership are taken into account his losses were even higher. One of Thompson's assistants put the figure in excess of £100,000.[74] It is impossible to determine how much of this was sustained by Grant as much of this stock was held in names other than his own.

During the early months of 1731, Grant had carried on with his public duties as normal. On April 26 he voted in the House of Commons on a matter concerning the Charitable Corporation's charges to its customer.[75] Following the flight of Robinson and Thompson the talk in February 1732 was that Grant would be expelled from the House of Commons.[76] Such was the fear that he might emulate Thompson and Robinson and flee the country that he was ordered into the custody of the Serjeant at Arms on 17 March and only released on bail some three weeks later.[77] The debate concerning the future of Grant and his fellow directors who were Members of Parliament finally came to the floor of the House on 2 May 1732. Grant made a speech in his own defence which Lord Egmont felt did him more harm than good. Significantly, though, Sir Robert Walpole tried to alter some of the motions put before the House to soften their impact on the directors.[78] This was not so much to help Grant as to assist Sir Robert Sutton, one of his fellow directors who had not been one of the fraudsters.[79] It was all to no avail as Grant was expelled from the House on 5 May. He had in fact been caught up in an opposition and Jacobite plot to exploit the situation to embarrass the government. The parliamentary investigation into the corporation's affairs had been instigated by a noted London Jacobite, Col. Samuel Robinson and the opposition Whig, Samuel Sandys had chaired the committee chosen by ballot, which had thrown up an opposition majority.[80]

It is hardly surprising that the revelations had a significant effect on Grant's future. Further information on the partners' dealings came to light when Thompson returned to London in February 1733 and gave evidence to another House of Commons committee examining the affair, ensuring there would be no cover-up.[81] In the short term it appeared that prosecution of the malefactors, including Grant, was a distinct possibility. However, the protection of powerful allies appeared to protect him here.[82] Civil action seemed the only alternative open to the corporation to recover some of its losses. On 28 June 1734 a general court of the Charitable Corporation decided to take action against all of the directors. Friends of Grant tried to oppose this but were unsuccessful.[83] The threat remained for some considerable time as his brother William Grant wrote to him on 1 December 1735 saying that the case was still being actively pursued. However some people now felt that it would be in the corporation's long term interests to try to come to some out-of-court arrangement with Grant as this offered a better chance of a reasonable return for the Charitable Corporation.[84] Sir Archibald was saved from the full consequences of his actions in the longer term when Lord Chancellor Hardwicke was asked to rule in 1742 that John Thompson, the principal witness against the conspirators, was not competent to give evidence as he was himself one of the conspirators and because of an agreement with him, stood to gain a portion of the money he helped to recover for the corporation. Hardwicke referred the matter to the Master of the Rolls, and there the matter appeared to come to an end.[85]

Attempts by Grant to enter public life to any significant extent proved fruitless as the nature of his involvement in the Charitable Corporation was considered unacceptable, even by the lax standards of Walpolian Britain. Sir Robert Sutton who had been held to be guilty of neglect rather than fraud had re-entered parliament in 1734.[86] An attempt by Grant to stand as a parliamentary candidate in 1747 was blocked by the Argyll faction who put up a rival candidate and he had to make do with being appointed Keeper of the Hornings, a minor sinecure awarded to him in 1749.[87]

Grant's discomfiture gives us a detailed insight into his affairs at the time of the Charitable Corporation scandal. As part of parliament's investigation into the affair, he and his fellow directors were required to submit details of their property, in order to ensure it was not put beyond the reach of their creditors.[88] Grant listed his assets and liabilities on 1 January and 30 September 1731 as shown in Table 1.

It can clearly be seen that on 1 January 1731, the largest part of Grant's assets consisted of stocks and shares in the York Buildings company and the Charitable Corporation which were sold at a loss as their market collapsed. It is highly possible that some of his personal debts and liabilities were also for such stock, but the exact nature of these obligations is not spelt out and thus they cannot be accurately determined. What is noticeable is that Grant listed neither debts owed to or sums due from any bank, whether public or private. Thus there

Table 1. *Assets and liabilities of Sir Archibald Grant as at 1 January and 1 September 1731*

Assets		1 Jan		1 Sept
Real estate and leases		£16,741		£17,007
Wadsets and Mortgages		1,889		1,583
Mining Interests		6,395		6,700
Stocks, Shares and Bonds				
Char. Corp.	£22,756			
York Bldgs. Stock	32,335		214	
York Bldgs Annuities	2,700		700	
Bank of Scotland	300		300	
		58,211		1,214
Industrial Ventures		480		
Ships		300		280
Rent Arrears		400		450
Personal Bonds and Debts		2,248		2,336
Household and Personal Possessions		1,626		1,671
		88,290		31,241
Less: Bad and doubtful debts				781
		88,290		30,460
Liabilities				
Family Obligations		£5,443		£5,610
Bonds and Personal Liabilities		14,814		17,107
Lead Royalties and Mining Interests		2,520		220
York Buildings Stock		9,908		
Char. Corp. Shares		8,050		
Wm. Burroughs		2,510		3,810
George Robinson		2,952		
John Thomson		667		1,048
Thomas Watts		2,525		
		52,708		27,795
Net Assets		£35,582		£2,665

Source: Goldsmith's Library, University of London, GL 1732 fol., *Estates of the Directors of the Charitable Corporation: Inventory of Sir Archibald Grant, (1733), pp.5–30.*

is no indication of how he transferred money from Scotland to London. What is clear, though, is that by the end of September 1731 what was essentially paper wealth had disappeared and he was verging on the brink of insolvency.

Grant was fortunate that the Charitable Corporation did not pursue him to the utmost to try to recoup its own losses from him. In fact he was able to pursue some of the ventures previously carried on by the York Buildings Company on his own behalf. By 1737, the York Buildings Company was in serious trouble and Sir Archibald's brother, Francis Grant took on a lease for him to work the mines at Strontian.[89] This was still unsuccessful, and the Grants abandoned their efforts in 1740.[90] Likewise Francis Grant took over the coal and saltworks at Tranent from his brother's erstwhile partner William Adam and continued to operate them until Adam's lease expired in 1739, and the company entered into a new agreement with the Caddell family.[91] Thus despite the seeming failures of the York Buildings Company, Sir Archibald Grant tried to carry on their ideas for his own benefit but with little real success.

Following his expulsion from Parliament, Sir Archibald Grant returned to Monymusk and continued the estate improvement for which he established his historical reputation. As we have already noted, however, such activity had certainly predated his misfortunes in England. Enclosure had been taking place in the 1720s, but this was accelerated in the following decades.[92] This also helped increase the rental value of the estate which rose from £3,586 Scots plus rental in kind in 1733, to £9,709 Scots plus rental in kind in 1767, the latter having diminished somewhat.[93] The scale of the increase can be set in context by the fact that, as we have already seen, Grant himself had valued the total income from Monymusk in 1731 to be worth £617 Sterling. The fact that an element of rent was collected in kind was extremely significant. Like many of his contemporaries, Grant had to make arrangements for the sale of his surplus. In the 1720s, this was usually shipped from Aberdeen and part of it was sold at Leith by his brother Francis, a merchant, who among other things arranged the shipping.[94] Grant himself also held shipping interests in the 1730s.[95] Significantly, the merchant class of Edinburgh drew a fair number of its recruits from the sons of landed families such as the Grant.[96] Thus landowners such as Grant needed a degree of business acumen as well as commercial connections and knowledge of the land in order to ensure that the maximum financial benefit was exacted from their estates.

Like many other improvers, Grant also further attempted to capitalise upon his assets by encouraging industry on his estate. In 1748 he established a lint mill in Kirkton of Monymusk and applied to the Board of Trustees for Manufactures for assistance and premiums to get the industry started. In 1750 he leased out the mill, but the lessees also worked for him in raising lint. In addition he employed both spinners and weavers on a putting-out basis and as Hamilton has said was really acting as an entrepreneur.[97] Grant was nothing if not resourceful in trying to replenish the fortune he had lost in the Charitable Corporation disaster.

Grant, therefore, had a chequered career. As a member of a leading legal family and man of undoubted ability he should have been able to carve out a reasonable career for himself in public life. However his involvement in the Charitable Corporation scandal put paid to that road to success. All later attempts to re-enter public life failed as his reputation was such that, even in Walpolian Britain, a byword for corruption, he was considered beyond the pale. Thus he had to rely much more on his own devices to recover his lost fortune and this helps to explain his attempts to improve his estate and encourage industry. Like many others before and since he had learned the hard way that making a quick fortune on the Stock Market was ringed with perils for the unwary. His misadventures were to the benefit of the agricultural improving movement and his example was to be followed by many of his fellow landowners in the course of the ensuing decades.

Grant's career, however, does tell us much about the role of the Scottish elites in both the Scottish and the wider British economy in the eighteenth century. The broad range of his activities show that he did not depend solely on the income from his own lands to make a living. Like others of his class he spent some time at the bar, but he was not averse to involvement in a broad range of business ventures. He cooperated with those of a similar inclination and standing on both sides of the border and was involved in English as well as Scottish based projects. In the latter, his connection with the York Buildings Company and the Scotch Mines Company both involved English as well as Scottish capital, and led to attempts to bring industry into the Highlands before the '45. Although these ventures were unsuccessful, they clearly indicate that some entrepreneurial minds were aware of the region's potential even if, at this stage, they were unable to turn their ideas into clear profit. By working through London based organisations, men such as Grant were now clearly thinking in terms of a British, as opposed to a purely Scottish or English dimension to industrial finance. As a landowner, Grant was also typical of many of his contemporaries in that he realised that new methods were essential if his estate was to be developed to its fullest potential. He achieved this not only by an interest in up-to-date technology and agricultural sciences, but also by an awareness of the need to ensure proper commercial disposal of surplus produce. In this he was assisted by his brother whose role as a merchant kept the profits within the family and provided a closely knit business network, looking after the entire range of Sir Archibald's many interests. It is therefore fair to say that the career of Sir Archibald Grant of Monymusk pointed the way to the longer term benefits that would accrue to enterprising Scotsmen as a result of the Union of 1707.

REFERENCES

1. T.M. Devine, 'The Union of 1707 and Scottish Development', *Scottish Economic and Social History*, 5 (1985), pp.23–40.
2. John Stuart Shaw, *The Management of Scottish Society 1707–1764: Power, Nobles, Lawyers, Edinburgh Agents and English Influences*, (Edinburgh, 1983), pp.14–15.
3. Alexander Murdoch, *The People Above: Politics and Administration in Mid-Eighteenth Century Scotland*, (Edinburgh, 1980) pp.11–12.
4. *ibid.*, p.12; Shaw, *Management of Scottish Society*, Ch. 7.
5. Many aspects of such patronage are dealt with in Ronald M. Sunter, *Patronage and Politics in Scotland 1707–1832*, (Edinburgh, 1986).
6. Peter Earle, *The Making of the English Middle Class: Business, Society and Family Life in London, 1660–1730*, (1989), p.3.
7. Shaw, *Management of Scottish Society*, p.31.
8. Bruce P. Lenman, 'Scotland between the '15 and the '45,' in Jeremy Black ed., *Britain in the Age of Walpole*, (1984), p.77.
9. This is particularly noted in two selections from the Monymusk Papers viz. Henry Hamilton ed., *Selections from the Monymusk Papers*, (Edinburgh, 1945) and Henry Hamilton, ed.,*Life and Labour on an Aberdeenshire Estate 1735–1750*, (Aberdeen, 1946).
10. See I.J. Simpson, 'Sir Archibald Grant and the Charitable Corporation,' *Scottish Historical Review*, 44, (1965) and A.J.G. Cummings, The York Buildings Company: a Case Study in Eighteenth Century Corporation Mismanagement, (University of Strathclyde unpublished Ph.D. thesis, 1980), Ch. 6.
11. Lenman, 'Scotland between the '15 and the '45,' p.81.
12. Romney Sedgwick ed., *The History of Parliament: The House of Commons, 1715–1754*, (1970), II, pp.78–80.
13. Hamilton, *Life and Labour*, p.ix.
14. N.T. Phillipson, 'Lawyers, Landowners, and the Civic leadership of Post-Union Scotland: an essay on the Social role of the faculty of Advocates 1661–1830 in 18th Century Scottish society', *Juridical Review*, 1976, p.102.
15. Hamilton, *Life and Labour*, p.x.
16. Phillipson, 'Lawyers, Landowners and Civic Leadership', p.101; Sedgewick, *Commons*, II, p.78.
17. Goldsmith's Library, University of London, [Henceforth GL], GL 1732 fol., *Estates of the Directors of the Charitable Corporation: Inventory of Sir Archibald Grant*, (1733), p.5.
18. Hamilton, *Life and Labour*, p.ix.
19. Hamilton, *Monymusk Papers*, p.ix.
20. *ibid.*, lxxiv. £1 Sterling = £12 Scots at this period.
21. Lee Soltow, 'Inequality of Wealth in Land in Scotland in the Eighteenth Century' *Scottish Economic and Social History*, 10, (1990), p.42.
22. Hamilton, *Monymusk Papers*, pp.lviii–lix.
23. *ibid.*, pp.xlviii–xlix.
24. Hamilton, *Life and Labour*, p.x.
25. I. Whyte, 'The Emergence of the New Estate Structure' in M.L. Parry and T.R. Slater eds., *The Making of the Scottish Countryside*, (1980), pp.129–130.
26. *Grant's Estate*, p.10; Hamilton, *Life and Labour*, pp.x–xi; A.J.G. Cummings and L. Stewart, 'The Case of the Eighteenth Century Projector' in B. Moran ed., *Patronage and Institutions: Science, Technology, and Medicine at the European Court 1500–1750*, (1991), pp.243.
27. Cummings, 'York Buildings', p.508.
28. *ibid.*, p.35.

29. *ibid.*, p.514.
30. *ibid.*, p.415.
31. *ibid.*, Ch. 6.
32. T.S. Willan, *River Navigation in England 1600–1750*, (1964), p.70.
33. A.J.G. Cummings, 'The Harburgh Company and its Lottery 1716–23', *Business History*, 28 no.3, (July, 1986), pp.1–18.
34. A.B. Du Bois, *The English Business Company after the Bubble Act, 1720–1800*, (repr. New York, 1971), p.430.
35. Cummings, 'York Buildings', 399–406.
36. *Grant's Estate*, p.6.
37. *ibid.* p.8–9.
38. Larry Stewart, *The Rise of Public Science: Rhetoric, Technology, and Natural Philosophy in Newtonian Britain, 1660–1750*, (Cambridge, 1992), pp.374–377; T.C. Smout, 'Lead Mining in Scotland 1650–1850', in P.L. Payne ed., *Studies in Scottish Business History*, (London, 1967), p.119; P.G.M. Dickson, *The Sun Insurance Office, 1710–1960*, (London, 1960), Appendix 6.
39. Edinburgh University Library, Laing Ms II 693, Defences for Norfolk etc. against John Pringle, 1739.
40. Stewart, *Rise of Public Science*, p. 359
41. David Murray, *The York Buildings Company: a Chapter in Scotch History*, (repr. 1973), p.27
42. SRO, GD345/765/3, Letter P. Grant to Sir A. Grant, 27 May 1732; *Grant's Estate*, p.25.
43. SRO, GD345/765/9, Letter P. Grant to Sir A. Grant, 26 Oct., 1734.
44. George Dott, *Early Scottish Colliery Waggonways*, (1947), p.15; Kenneth Brown, 'The First Railway in Scotland, The Tranent-Cockenzie Waggonway', *Railway Magazine*, January 1938, p.1.
45. *Letter from a Gentleman in Edinburgh to his Friend at London.*
46. Cummings, 'York Buildings', p.350.
47. SRO, GD345/575/1, Grant of Monymusk Ms, Articles of Agreement, 1727.
48. *Grant's Estate*, p.10.
49. SRO, GD345/575/23, Information for Buchan, Grant and Garden, 15 December 1746.
50. *Grant's Estate*, p.9.
51. SRO GD345/575/23, Information for Buchan etc.
52. Sedgewick, *Commons*, II, p.386.
53. *RHC.* 1, p.381; *Grant's Estate*, 15, admits a debt to Thomson of £3,319 on 1 January 1731.
54. *ibid.* p.370.
55. SRO, GD345/712/5, Grant of Monymusk Ms, Answer of Thompson, p.22.
56. *RHC*, I, pp.376–377.
57. *ibid.*, p.365.
58. BL Add. Ms. 36141, 550ff., Hardwicke Papers, Opinion of P. Yorke, 24 February, 1728.
59. *RHC*, I, p.368.
60. J.M. Treadwell, 'William Wood and the Company of Ironmasters', *Business History*, Vol. 16, 1974, p.108; Stewart, *Rise of Public Science*, p.357.
61. *RHC*, I, pp.545–546.
62. *ibid.*, p.545.
63. PRO C11/520/11 Char. Corp. v. Burroughs (1735) Answer of Burroughs.
64. *RHC*, I, p.427.
65. *ibid.*, p.545.
66. SRO, GD345/780/15, Grant of Monymusk MS, Letter W. Grant to Sir A. Grant, 1 December 1735.

67. *Daily Journal,* 1 January, 1730.
68. *Daily Courant,* 2 October, 1730.
69. *RHC,* I, p.545.
70. *ibid.*
71. *ibid.,* p.380.
72. BL 712.k.1(1), *Report of the Gentlemen appointed by the General Court of the Charitable Corporation (1732).*; S. Lambert ed., *Sessional Papers of the House of Commons in the Eighteenth century, Vol.14, The Charitable Corporation,* Reports on the Charitable Corporation, pp.3–4.
73. Cummings, 'York Buildings', pp.442–3.
74. *RHC,* p.383.
75. Historical Manuscripts Commission, *Diary of the First Viscount Percival, subsequently First Earl of Egmont,* Vol.1, p.185.
76. *ibid.,* p.225.
77. *ibid.,* p.242; Simpson, 'Grant', p.57.
78. *Egmont Diary,* Vol 1, pp.264–5.
79. Eveline Cruickshanks, 'The Political Management of Sir Robert Walpole' in Jeremy Black ed., *Britain in the Age of Walpole,* (1984), p.38.
80. Cruickshanks, 'Political Management', p.37.
81. *Daily Journal,* 26 February, 1733.
82. Simpson, 'Grant', p.58.
83. SRO, GD345/573, Grant of Monymusk Ms., Minute of the Charitable Corporation General Court, 28 June, 1734.
84. SRO, GD345/780/15, Letter W. Grant to Sir A. Grant, 1 December, 1735.
85. British Library, Add. Ms. 35786, ff.200–201, Minutes of hearing in Chancery, Char. Corp v. Sutton, 13 August, 1742.
86. Sedgewick, *Commons,* II, pp.456–458.
87. *ibid.,* p.78.
88. *Egmont's Diary,* I, p.271.
89. S[ignet] L[ibrary], Edinburgh, CSP 14;1 Campbell v. Crawfurd, 1753, Answer of Patrick Crawfurd, 1 June, 1751.
90. SRO, CS 228/G2/27, F. Grant v. York Buildings C., 1744.
91. SL CSP2; 23 York Buildings Company v. Adams 1737, Petn of Co. and Francis Grant, 5 January 1737; *ibid.,* p.423; 12, Caddell v. Anderson, 1801, Info. for William and John Caddell, 13 January, 1801.
92. Hamilton, *Monymusk Papers,* p.lxviii.
93. *ibid.,* p.lxxiv.
94. *ibid.,* p.xxvii.
95. *Grant's Estate,* p.10.
96. T.M. Devine, 'The Merchant Class of the Larger Scottish Towns in the later Seventeenth and Early Eighteenth Centuries,' in George Gordon and Brian Dicks eds., *Scottish Urban History,* (Aberdeen, 1983), p.103.
97. Hamilton, *Life and Labour,* pp.xxxvii–xxxix.

3

The Making of a Farming Elite?
Lowland Scotland, 1750–1850

T. M. Devine

I

Over the century between c.1750 and c.1850 the pattern of economy and society in the rural Lowlands of Scotland was transformed. This was the classic period of that process dubbed by some writers as the 'Agricultural Revolution'. Through the adoption of improved rotations, better farm management and higher levels of labour productivity, agriculture was able to dramatically raise levels of food and raw material production to supply an industrialising society where relatively fewer of the working population were themselves engaged in the direct cultivation of the soil or the tending of stock. At the heart of the economic revolution was a fundamental change in rural social structure.[1] Put simply, in the middle decades of the nineteenth century, a much smaller part of the rural population had established rights to land than a hundred years before. The old cottar class, which had provided much seasonal labour in the traditional society, was widely and rapidly displaced in the interests of more efficient land management. Historians have also noted that the tenantry was changing. In general terms, there was a movement from smaller to larger holdings. Consolidation of land into new and more compact holdings meant that many old farmers lost out. In their place, there developed a farming elite, a class with larger units than had been common before the eighteenth century. This new, dynamic group of husbandmen, epitomised most famously by the great East Lothian grain farmers of the nineteenth century, were the agricultural equivalent of the entrepreneurs who transformed industry and commerce. Possessing larger farms, they had the capital and the enterprise to exploit the vast expansion in market opportunities which took place as urbanisation gathered pace. They were the shock troops of the Agricultural Revolution.

This picture of a farming elite who had gained land as their less fortunate neighbours had lost it is deeply embedded in orthodox interpretations of eighteenth century Scottish history. In his influential *A History of the Scottish People, 1560–1830,* Smout observes that the 'new farmers were as deliberate and artificial a creation as the quick-set hedge and the Cheviot sheep'.[2] An integral part of this programme of social engineering was the consolidation of lands. As a result, 'many would . . . fall to the ranks of the landless labourer'.[3] He quotes the contemporary opinion that small holdings were incompatible with the new agriculture. As Thomas Robertson put it in 1796:

> It would be endless to state what is so often repeated in the surveys that the small farm is found to be attended with an insufficient capital, with puny enclosures down to two acres and with wretched husbandry; that the poor farmer is always a bad one, the lower the rent the poorer the tenant, and with husbandry worse; that idleness and laziness, prevail; that a small farm is not worth the attention of any man of ingenuity and property.[4]

Smout's interpretation of the agrarian revolution as a triumph for a farming elite which has replaced this poorer group is then concluded with a detailed examination of the great Lothian tenants, 'in so many ways the quintessence of the new class' who combined large holdings with an opulent style of life.[5] They are seen to represent the improved rural world. In this perspective, big was better.

Gray also notes the same tendencies. The movement towards larger units was inevitable on the grounds of efficiency. He describes how the improving writers regarded about seventy acres as the very minimum for effective working.[6] But even bigger holdings were much preferable because they possessed advantages 'in meeting the expenses of farm buildings and of fencing and could better sustain the overhead costs of the threshing machine'.[7] Thus the consolidation process accelerated with enormous social consequences: 'there was a general movement in every part of Lowland Scotland to lay down larger farms and nearly always larger farms meant fewer tenants: dispossession and eviction became a common experience'.[8] This was the 'Lowland Clearances', a term now in common usage among scholars to convey the radical changes and the scale of tenant displacement which was taking place in the Scottish countryside in this period.[9]

The writers of more general texts concur in accepting the received wisdom. Mitchison asserted that 'larger and more coherent, separate units' were necessary to improved farming.[10] Brown took the view that the dispossession of the small tenants had much wider social consequences as many of those who were evicted found employment in the new urban textile industries.[11] Town growth and the destruction of the small farming class were seen to go together. Slaven, in his study of the

development of the west of Scotland, put forward a similar interpretation while also acknowledging the sheer scale of tenant removal: ' . . .
the majority of the agricultural population probably rented a little land
of their own at the beginning of the period, but only a minority survived
as tenants in 1870'.[12] It can accurately be said, therefore, that the idea
of the creation of a farming elite is a central orthodoxy in current
understanding of Scottish society in the eighteenth and early nineteenth centuries, a notion which impinges not only on discussion of
the rural economy but on the wider analysis of Scotland in its era of
rapid transformation.

Yet, curiously enough, the concept has rarely been subjected to
serious critical examination. On the whole, most authors have simply
accepted the contemporary judgement that small farms were bad and
larger holdings good and assumed a movement from one to the other.
Where quantitative evidence has occasionally been given it is normally
confined to particular counties or districts. For example, to justify his
view that 'the overwhelming tenor of the evidence, in every county, is
of holdings thrown together to make larger farms and of tenants
evicted'; Gray quotes some instances of the fall in the number of farms
in a few East Lothian parishes.[13] But the south east is hardly likely to
yield representative data on the Lowland experience because it was
precisely in that region that the big farm was dominant and, as the
poll-tax evidence for the 1690s from Midlothian and West Lothian
demonstrates, had been so for many decades before the later eighteenth century.[14] When factual information is provided it tends to be
derived from the parish reports of the *Old Statistical Account.* But the
OSA, however invaluable as an historical source in general terms, is not
very reliable as a means of tracing tenant depletion. Local ministers
often did not make a clear enough distinction between small tenants,
subtenants and cottars to enable systematic conclusions to be drawn.
It is clear that the two latter groups were being removed in large
numbers.[15] But it cannot simply be assumed that the experience of the
rural underclass was also shared by the poorer tenantry without hard
evidence. It is a remarkable fact, however, that this is rarely forthcoming. One of the key assumptions of Scottish social history in this period
lacks any real systematic documentation. Some years ago, Dodgshon
did try to describe tenant reduction in Roxburgh and Berwick on the
basis of farm rentals and estate correspondence, the only valid sources
for tracing tenant numbers over long periods of time.[16] Yet his re-
searches were confined to the decades before the 1760s and hence say
nothing about the last quarter of the eighteenth century which is
regarded as the classic period of land consolidation. Historians have

tended to fall back for this era on what contemporary improving propagandists said should happen to small farms rather in attempting to discover what did happen.

However, in one part of the rural Lowlands, historical analysis has gone further than this and revealed a more complicated picture than that conveyed by the orthodox interpretation. Carter and Gray in their studies of the north east region of Aberdeen, Banff, Kincardine and Moray, have shown how misleading the 'Lothiancentric' approach is.[17] Throughout these counties small holdings survived, large farms, though increasing in significance, were usually moderate in extent and new small units or 'crofts' were being established even as consolidation was proceeding elsewhere. Because of the survival of comprehensive poll tax records for Aberdeen for the 1690s, it is possible to quantify changing number of holdings in that county from the seventeenth to the nineteenth centuries in a way which cannot be done for any other Lowland region. An investigation into fifteen sample parishes reveals that there had been an actual *increase* in the number of holdings of around 8 per cent between the 1790s and 1870.[18] Closer focus on the century from the 1690s to the 1790s indicates, in a five parish sample, that in one direct tenancies fell considerably, in two there was little overall change and in two a significant increase in tenants took place. In all five cases, however, the number of tenancies rose substantially between the 1790s and 1870. This important research on the north east demonstrates that the orthodox thinking of the improvers was complicated in this region by the constraints of climate, land endowment and existing tenurial patterns. The decisive regional factor was that much of the land awaited reclamation. The spread of cultivation cross the moors and into other marginal areas encouraged landlords to let tracts of territory to smallholders or crofters at low rental whose families would then provide the labour power to clear and exploit the new holdings. The social revolution in the north east was not simply or mainly the creation of a farming elite. Fragmentation in many parishes was just as likely as consolidation and the crofter and small tenant was as representative of the new age as the 'big farmer'.

In a sense, however, the research results from this region have merely strengthened the traditional interpretation of an irresistible and widespread consolidation of holdings. The north east can be seen as aberrant and exceptional, forced into a distinctive tenurial system by the exigencies of the problem of marginal land which was unique to the area. The experience of Aberdeen, Banff and Kincardine is depicted as one which contrasts with developments elsewhere in the Lowlands where the more orthodox interpretation is still relevant.[19]

It is certainly the case that no other lowland region evolved the same widespread structure of crofts as the north east. However, a number of Scottish counties displayed similar characteristics, most notably in the survival of a large small farm sector despite the ritual disapproval of many improving propagandists. It can be argued that those historians who have interpreted the period c.1750 to c.1850 as the rise of the big farm at the expense of the small holding have at the very least overstated their case and hence oversimplified a social process of great complexity and diversity. The evidence considered below provides the basis for an attempt to reinterpret the changing composition of the tenant class in the age of improvement.

II

In the early 1770s, Robert Ainslie, improving theorist and estate factor to the Duke of Douglas in his extensive lands in Lanarkshire, Renfrewshire and Angus, carried out a series of farm surveys during which he described the optimum size of mixed agricultural holdings.[20] The key factor was the relationship between unit size and the working capacity of a plough team. He estimated that 50 acres 'in a good climate and middling soil' gave enough work for one plough. However, in the improved regime about half of all land should be in grass and the remainder under cultivation. Therefore, 100 acres were actually the optimum minimum size for a sound agricultural holding. Even larger farms than this would, however, convey additional benefits in the efficient use of labour.

How far the plans of improvers such as Ainslie became a reality can be partly determined from the Board of Agriculture returns on holding size in Scotland published more than a century after he compiled his reports. The data extracted from the official figures are set out in Tables 1 to 5. Tables 1 and 2 provide evidence on the national pattern, including information on the Border counties and the Highlands as well as the Lowlands. The inclusion of the Highlands is obviously likely to increase the significance of smaller holdings while data from the Borders inflates the total of large stock farms above 500 acres. More meaningful and useful, therefore, are the detailed breakdown of figures from the specifically Lowland counties contained in Table 3.

To some extent these data confirm the conventional interpretation. According to Table 2, almost half (44 per cent) of the farm acreage in Scotland was held in units of 100 to 300 acres. These were the distinctively 'capitalist' farms: 100 acres were reckoned to be the maximum that could be managed by using family labour alone. After that a farmer was forced into becoming an employer, hiring one or two permanent servants and additional numbers of casual workers. However, despite the territorial dominance of this class, what is remarkable is the survival of the small farm sector. Table 1 suggests that no less than 80 per cent of all holdings in the 1880s were still below 100 acres and 68 per cent were at or below 50 acres.

That these results cannot simply be explained away by the inclusion of the numerous crofts of the Highlands is suggested in Tables 3 to 5. Tables 3 and 4 indicate that in sixteen out of the eighteen Lowland counties enumerated, at least half of all holdings were at or below 100 acres in extent. In nine counties, the proportion of holdings in this category reached 70 per cent or over of the total. Not surprisingly, the counties where small farms were particularly thin on the ground tended to concentrate in the south east region. Haddington, Linlithgow and Berwick had much smaller numbers than elsewhere. On the other hand, the large size of the small farm sector in the north east is clearly demonstrated. But it is important to recognise that this pattern was not simply confined to the northern counties. Holdings of below the improving minimum of 100 acres were also very numerous in Stirling, Dumbarton, Renfrew, Lanark and Ayr. Even when the percentage acreage by larger farms is calculated, as in Table 5, the resilience of the small holdings is confirmed. In the south eastern counties the big farmers were overwhelmingly dominant. Yet the Lothians social system was but one variant among several in the rural Lowlands. Elsewhere, even judged by acreage farmed, the smaller men retained an important position. They had not been swept away by the later eighteenth century mania for consolidation. Of the eighteen Lowland counties, farms at

Table 1. *Number and Percentage of Agricultural Holdings in Each Class, Scotland, 1885*

Class (in acres)	Total	Percentage
1/4 to under 1 —		
1–5	21,463	27
5–20	22,132	28
20–50	10,677	13
50–100	9,778	12
100–300	12,549	16
300–500	2,034	2
500–1000	90	0.2
Total (1 acre and above)	79,355	100

Source: PP, c.4848 (1886) Board of Agriculture Return of Allotments and of Agricultural Holdings in Great Britain.

Table 2. Acreage of Holdings in Each Class, Scotland 1885

Class	Total Acreage (pasture and arable)	Percentage
¼ to under 1	—	
1–5	68,619	1
5–20	236,995	5
20–50	361,675	7
50–100	725,499	16
100–300	2,139,133	44
300–500	768,823	16
500–1000	409,641	8
Above 1000	137,104	3
Total (1 acre and above)	4,847,489	100

Source: PP, c.4848 (1886) Board of Agriculture Return of Allotments and of Agricultural Holdings in Great Britain.

or under 100 acres in size controlled at least one third of the land in six counties. Within this pattern there was much local complexity, with hill farms ranging from around 500 to several thousand acres while in the more low lying western districts smaller holdings remained the norm.

In the arable areas of Lanarkshire and Dumbartonshire it has been claimed that most farms in the era before improvement ran to 50 or 80 acres. The late nineteenth century data suggest that many of these small tenancies survived and flourished despite the *dicta* of the improving strategists.

This evaluation of figures on holding size supports the conclusions of a recent study on agrarian and social change in eighteenth century Lowland Scotland.[21] This examined a large number of rentals from estates in Lanarkshire, Ayrshire, Fife and Angus, together with relevant court records and landlord correspondence, to construct a profile of regional patterns of tenant depletion over the period c.1620 to 1815. The analysis seemed to demonstrate that a decline in tenant numbers was occurring throughout this almost 200 year time-scale, especially as a result of the eradication of multiple tenancies in the decades before the mid eighteenth century. However, during the classic period of improvement after c.1760, while tenants continued to lose land, the process was much more gradual and limited than is often suggested. Between the years c.1760 to 1815 few of the estates investigated shed more than 20 per cent of their tenant numbers and the rate of tenant turnover was either broadly similar to or only marginally above that which had already existed earlier in the eighteenth century.[22] Examination of writs of removal in local sheriff courts seemed to confirm

Table 3. *Number of Agricultural Holdings by Acreage in each Class by Scottish Lowland County, 1885*

County	¼–1	1–5	5–20	20–50	50–100	100–300	300–500	500–1000	above 1000	Total
Aberdeen	77	1,799	8,509	2,003	2,056	1,849	124	9	1	11,510
Ayr	29	450	529	461	758	1,193	77	13	2	3,512
Banff	39	966	1,282	719	549	456	32	3	—	4,046
Berwick	33	172	113	53	74	212	115	104	23	899
Clackmannan	10	54	51	22	21	51	11	1	—	221
Dumbarton	29	165	136	95	118	189	5	3	—	740
Edinburgh	22	174	246	117	111	286	76	50	7	1,089
Moray	15	475	535	336	308	280	39	6	1	1,994
Fife	48	510	309	235	227	637	200	37	—	2,294
Forfar	43	433	625	325	394	684	171	26	2	2,701
Haddington	19	86	77	43	34	122	127	51	—	561
Kincardine	20	261	463	239	311	387	42	7	—	1,730
Kinross	1	62	50	25	27	107	22	1	—	295
Lanark	91	362	530	432	702	862	74	13	1	3,062
Linlithgow	11	86	67	51	90	199	26	7	1	538
Nairn	2	44	86	75	85	75	7	2	—	376
Renfrew	27	199	206	181	319	341	9	5	1	1,288
Stirling	15	221	231	258	363	370	28	5	1	1,492

Source PP, c.4848 (1886) Board of Agriculture Return of Allotments and of Agricultural Holdings in Great Britain.

*Table 4. Percentage of Agricultural
Holdings at or below 100 acres by Scottish
Lowland County, 1885*

County	Percentage of Holdings
Aberdeen	82–
Ayr	63–
Banff	89–
Berwick	49
Clackmannan	71–
Dumbarton	73–
Edinburgh	61–
Moray	84–
Fife	62–
Forfar	67–
Haddington	45
Kincardine	75[ms]
Kinross	56–
Lanark	69–
Linlithgow	57–
Nairn	78–
Renfrew	72–
Stirling	73–

Source: PP, c.4848 (1886) Board of
Agriculture Return of Allotments and
of Agricultural Holdings in Great
Britain.

that the depletion of the tenantry was much less extensive than is often
supposed. It was a story of piecemeal, slow and essentially undramatic
evolution, quite different from the experience of wholesale and systematic
removal characteristic of the Highland Clearances. Only in hill country,
suitable for large-scale pastoral farming, was the social impact of
consolidation at all comparable with the Highland experience. The
empirical and laborious investigation of primary sources for the eighteenth
century therefore produced results which correspond in general terms
with the discussion of late nineteenth aggregative data on holding size.[23]

III

The question why the revolutionary plans of the improving theorists
were never implemented on anything like the scale believed by many
historians cannot be answered in simple terms. One explanation is that
the improvers' attitudes were actually more sensitive to economic and
social realities than is sometimes allowed. Estate factors, were primarily
concerned with a tenant's capacity to pay an increasing rental than

Table 5. *Percentage acreage in each Lowland county occupied by holdings at or under 100 acres in size*

County	Percentage acreage occupied by holdings of 100 acres or less
Aberdeen	43
Ayr	26
Banff	49
Berwick	4
Clackmannan	18
Dumbarton	30
Edinburgh	11
Moray	40
Fife	12
Forfar	19
Haddington	5
Kincardine	20
Kinross	12
Lanark	30
Linlithgow	17
Nairn	38
Renfrew	36
Stirling	35

Source: PP, c.4848 (1886) Board of Agriculture Return of Allotments and of Agricultural Holdings in Great Britain.

with holding size *per se*. Ironically, the new systems of rotation, by allowing a remarkable improvement in yields over a short time-scale, probably helped many poorer farmers to cope with their landlord's rent exactions and hence preserve their place on the land. But some theorists were also less devoted to the idea of the large, consolidated farm than many of their peers. The idea of mass clearance was often attacked as 'a dangerous and destructive experiment'.[24] It could disturb social harmony and by threatening dispossession destroy that sense of security so vital if the tenantry were to be slowly weaned away from their old ways and encouraged towards the new and more efficient methods of improved agriculture. Comparisons were sometimes drawn with the cruder and less effective tactics of the Highland lairds.[25] These policies were not recommended because they threatened the loss of an economically valuable population. The consequences for social stability were also to be feared. In 1800 the agricultural reporter for Fife emphasised the problems of removing too many small units and concentrating too much land in the hands of a few. He drove home his argument with reference to the contemporary political turmoil in France as proof of the connection between economic discontent on the one hand and revolution and social anarchy on the other.[26]

In addition, behind the generalised faith in big farms lay the recognition that holding size was ultimately conditioned by a whole range of influences including land endowment, climate, agrarian specialisation and tenant resources. In dairying districts, such as many parishes in Renfrewshire and Lanarkshire, the small family-run enterprise was regarded as having positive advantages over larger units.[27] Consolidation of holdings is well known. Less familiar perhaps is the evidence that larger farms were sometimes divided into two or more holdings because the new structures promised a higher rental than a single farm. As the new order took shape, surveyors seem not to have been hidebound by a single orthodoxy. Fragmentation of land, maintenance of the status quo or reduction to a greater or lesser extent of tenant numbers, were all possible responses.[28] Some forces favoured consolidation, others a different approach. One development of the period was a widespread assault on subtenancy. This could either result in complete removal or in the promotion of subtenants to the rank of direct tenants and rent payers. The numbers of tenants were also increased in some districts as cultivation moved into areas of moorland which were most cheaply and quickly exploited by colonies of smallholders.[29]

The Industrial Revolution in the countryside was a further factor making for division of land. Textile and other industries stimulated the growth of existing country towns and villages and the foundation of entirely new settlements. Many estates leased land to small tenants, smallholders and pendiclers in and around these developments. In 1791, the strategy of the Morton estate in Fife was partly influenced by the growth of the small town of Aberdour:

> As the people both in Easter and Wester Aberdour are in great need for land and as this farm lyes so near the Town and a good Road, it should be reserved for acred land which will give a much higher rent and be better cultivated than in a farm.[30]

There were similar hopes of high returns during the division of farms on the Crawford estate in Lanarkshire in 1772. Here the attraction was the provision of smallholdings for the leadminers of Wanlockhead. The surveyor specifically pointed out the attractions of small tenancies:

> This small parcel consisting of 21 acres of Crawford John with a small liberty of grassing milk cows is possest by William Watson, lead-driver, which about 13 years since only paid £15 st. and now pays £25 at which to a demonstration shows how much may be made by small possessions in this form . . .'[31]

The impact of tenant numbers of this kind of policy could sometimes be spectacular. On the Earl of Strathmore's lands in Angus, tenant numbers rose from 219 in 1762 to 475 in 1784 due mainly to the creation of smallholdings in and around Glamis and Newtown. Significantly, too, the numbers of those in multiple tenant possessions fell from 188 in 1762 to 58 in 1784. It is likely that a form of resettlement and reallocation of land was undertaken on this estate which helped to maintain a farming population despite the consolidation of holdings elsewhere.[32]

Even if the dogmatic preference for holdings of 100 acres and more had been enforced in the manner commonly understood it is highly unlikely that it would have been generally successful. A basic problem was that Scottish agricultural improvement took place in a relatively poor country which did not always possess the resources required if the ideas of the theorists were to be fully put into practice. Historians do recognise the problems of explaining how the large farms which were supposed to be becoming the norm in the later eighteenth century were financed. The answer sometimes given is that these improved holdings were not leased to the impoverished and conservative farmers of the locality but were let to incomers from progressive areas such as the Lothians who had both capital and the relevant expertise.[33] There is indeed evidence that many estates would have preferred tenants from such a background and it is also the case that efforts were often made to recruit experienced farmers from elsewhere.[34] Equally, however, these attempts were rarely successful. A survey of tenant structures in the four counties of Angus, Fife, Lanarkshire and Ayrshire reveals that in the later eighteenth century most landlords had to rely on the indigenous tenantry.[35] This in turn placed a considerable constraint on their capacity to implement widespread consolidation.

In any event, that strategy was greatly hampered by the actual experience of the farming community in the later eighteenth century. The road to improvement was much rockier than is sometimes suggested. In both 1772–3 and 1782–4 a combination of poor harvests and the contemporaneous increase in rents imposed enormous strain on the tenant class in many areas of the Lowlands. The crises produced tenant insolvencies, accumulation of rent arrears and, in some districts, the emigration of many farming families to the colonies.

In Kirkcudbright and Dumfries it was reported in 1781 that ' . . . money continues very scarce and many people of landed property and tenants are failing.' The same year brought the bankruptcy of John Tait, who was the greatest cattle dealer in the region and who left debts of more than £10,000. In 1782, no less than seven estates in this area were put up for sale with three being offered at prices over £72,000.[36]

Tenants were in acute difficulty in 1772–3 and even more seriously in 1783–4. On the Douglas estate in Lanarkshire, the arrears of 1772 had not been effectively reduced before they rose sharply once gain in the crisis of 1782.[37] There was a similar pattern on the Betram of Nisbet property in the same county.[38] In 1783–4, estates in the west of Scotland had to distribute seed corn among the tenantry.[39] That crisis hit hard not simply because of the deterioration in weather conditions but because farmers were still recovering from the difficulties of the previous decade. In 1780 arrears on the Hamilton estate stood at £3230 with annual book rental valued at £2742. Of the 123 tenants, 121 were in arrears to a greater or lesser extent and this on an estate where there had been very substantial landlord investment since the early 1760s.[40] Between 1781 and 1785 investment in enclosure fell to a trickle with only 3 per cent of farms reporting any activity.[41] The difficulties were eventually overcome in the last few years of the century when the boom in agricultural prices during the Napoleonic Wars gave a renewed impetus to improvement. However, in the meantime, the pace of consolidation, which ultimately depended on a sufficiently deep pool of tenants with the resources to stock large farms, was necessarily retarded.

IV

This essay has attempted to challenge the orthodox view, too uncritically based on the writings of some improving theorists, that the central social process in Scottish agrarian change was the triumph of the large farm and the related reduction or elimination of smaller holdings. It has been argued that while bigger units did become more significant, the small farm sector survived not as an archaic hangover from an older world but because it often had a rationale in the new economic order. In addition, the financial resources of the tenant class made it imperative that farms of an acreage considerably below the approved norm would remain. It is doubtful whether Lowland rural society possessed the capital to fund the kind of tenurial revolution suggested by the more enthusiastic advocates of improvement. Therefore, as the new social order developed, it was seen to be one of great complexity. The elite of 'big' farmers with holdings of two to three hundred acres and above were certainly present and especially dominant in the south eastern counties and, to a lesser extent, in Fife and Kinross. Elsewhere, however, the small holding, family farm and croft were just as prevalent and set the social tone of their localities in the same way as the great grain farms of the Lothians.

REFERENCES

1. T.M. Devine, *The Transformation of Rural Scotland: Social Change and the Agrarian Economy 1660–1815*, (Edinburgh, 1994).
2. T.C. Smout, *A History of the Scottish People, 1560–1830* (London, 1969), 308–9.
3. *Ibid.*, 309.
4. T. Robertson, *Outline of the General Report upon the Size of Farms* (Edinburgh, 1796), 43.
5. Smout, *Scottish People*, 312.
6. Malcolm Gray, 'Scottish Emigration: the Social Impact of Agrarian Change in the Rural Lowlands, 1775–1875', *Perspectives in American History*, VII (1973), 134.
7. *Ibid.*, 134–5.
8. *Ibid.*, 135.
9. See, for example, T.M. Devine, 'Social Responses to Agrarian "Improvement": the Highland and Lowland Clearances in Scotland' in R.A. Houston and I.D. Whyte eds. *Scottish Society, 1500–1800* (Cambridge, 1989), 148–168.
10. Rosalind Mitchison, *A History of Scotland* (2nd ed., London, 1982), 349.
11. Callum Brown, *The Social History of Religion in Scotland since 1730* (London, 1987), 101.
12. Anthony Slaven, *The Development of the West of Scotland 1750–1960* (London, 1975), 77.
13. Gray, 'Scottish Emigration', 136.
14. Scottish Record Office (SRO), GD86/770, Berwick Poll Lists, 1693; E79/8/A, Midlothian Poll Lists, 1693.
15. Devine, *Transformation of Rural Scotland*, ch.8.
16. R.A. Dodgshon, 'The Removal of Runrig in Roxburghshire and Berwickshire, 1680–1766',*Scottish Studies* 16 (1972).
17. Ian Carter, *Farm Life in Northeast Scotland 1840–1914* (Edinburgh, 1979); M. Gray, 'North-east Agriculture and the Labour Force, 1790–1873' in A.A. Maclaren ed. *Social Class in Scotland: Past and Present* (Edinburgh, 19760).
18. Gray, 'Scottish Emigration', 138, ftn.69.
19. For example, Gray in describing the north east prefaces his remarks by stating, 'In contrast to the movements elsewhere . . . [in the Lowlands]'. Gray, 'Scottish Emigration', 136.
20. National Register of Archives, Scotland (hereafter NRA(S)), Sir Alexander F. Douglas-Home Papers, 859/256/1, Report of Robert Ainslie, 7 September, 1769.
21. Devine, *Transformation of Rural Scotland, passim.*
22. *Ibid.*, ch.7.
23. *Ibid.*, chs.5 and 7.
24. NRA(S), Douglas-Home Papers, 859/256/1, Ainslie's Report, 1769.
25. *Ibid.*
26. J. Thomson, *General View of the Agriculture of Fife* (Edinburgh, 1800), 86.
27. L.J. Saunders, *Scottish Democracy, 1815–1840* (Edinburgh, 1950), 70.
28. Devine, *Transformation of Rural Scotland*, ch.7.
29. See, for example, SRO, Balfour of Balbirnie Muniments, GD288/241, Remarks upon Sundry of Mr. Balfour's farms, 1769; OSA (Fife), 610; SRO, Morton Papers, GD150/2404/38X, Memorial for Lord Morton concerning his Fife estate, 2 March, 1791; SRO, Leven and Melville Muniments, GD26/5/613, Memorandum for Lord Balgonie, 1793.
30. SRO, Morton Papers, GD150/1404/36–38, Memorial for Lord Morton, 1791.
31. Hamilton Public Library, 631/1, John Burrell Journals, 12 June, 1772.
32. NRA(S), Earl of Strathmore Papers, 885/117/1; 169/1; 169/160. Strathmore Rentals, 1737–1800.

33. Smout, *Scottish People*, 311.
34. Devine, *Transformation of Rural Scotland*, ch.7.
35. *Ibid.*, ch.s 5–7.
36. SRO, Oswald of Auchincruive Papers, GD213/54, Maxwell-Oswald Correspondence, 1778–83.
37. NRA(S), Douglas Home Papers, 859/142/5 Douglas Rentals, 1775–1812.
38. SRO, Bertram of Nisbet Papers, GD5/1/498, Rentals, 1770–84.
39. Hamilton Public Library, 631/1, John Burrell's Journal, 6 December, 1784 and 8 January, 1785. Cost of Seed and Corn bought over 1783 and 1784.
40. NRA(S), Hamilton Papers, 2177/E.3/74, Abstract Rentals and below, pp.
41. Hamilton Public Library, 631/1 John Burrell's Journal, 18 August, 1772.

4

The Liberal Professions within the Scottish Class Structure 1760–1860: A Comparative Study of Aberdeen Clergymen, Doctors and Lawyers[1]

A. Allan MacLaren

The most notable characteristic of the period 1760 to 1860 was the emergence and sustained development of industrial capitalism. The main features of this process are well-known but are worthy of re-statement. Industrialisation was both a cause and a consequence of a heightened entrepreneurial spirit leading to an ever-increasing competition among capitalists. Expanding markets allied with new technologies presented opportunities for social mobility perhaps greater than has been seen before or since. A highly specialised division of labour emerged within an industrial working class which was tied into a system which entailed the unresolved contradiction of mutual dependence and conflict with their competing capitalist employers. However, if the forging of new social relationships was a consequent feature it was a process shaped by external forces. Increasingly throughout the period capitalist and worker were exposed to market forces which ultimately became the fundamental determinant of prices, profits, and level of occupational income.

The issue of the location of the professions within the emerging class structure of capitalism and the role that market forces played as a determinant of professional income has long been the subject of debate. Broadly following the tradition of Durkheim[2] and the works of Carr-Saunders[3] and Marshall[4], Harold Perkin[5] has strongly argued that the professions were to a large degree structurally autonomous and relatively free from the pressures of these market forces. They enjoyed incomes which were not directly related to market bargaining but were the consequence of the value placed on these occupations by society. Indeed Perkin regards industrialisation as a great watershed in their development. Overall however, there is not a lot of evidence to give strong support to the proposition that this process of 'emancipation' from the bonds of patronage accompanied industrialisation in

Scotland.[6] The purpose of this paper is not therefore to explore the interaction between market forces and the professions but to examine more closely the location of the professions within the capitalist social structure.

Some consideration must be given to definition of what we mean by 'profession' and 'professionalism'—terms which have been the subject of a great deal of recent popular misuse. A professional service is one which is held to require a high expertise and one whose practitioners tend to claim that its exercise involves an ethical discretion which approaches a level of disinterest in immediate monetary reward. A second notable feature is that of self-regulation and the enforcement of this ethical discipline by a body set up by the practitioners. Finally this body also seeks to ensure that recruitment into the profession is based on merit in that all candidates must have undergone specified standards of training and been examined on their proficiency. There is also the tendency for this same body to seek recognition from the State of its own authority to regulate the profession.

Historically one tends to regard these professions as being associated with the Church, Education, Law, Medicine, and the Armed Forces. Neither Education nor the Armed Forces are the subject of this paper as the former overlaps and provides a vital component in all four of the others, and the Armed Forces do not fit readily into the 'learned' professions. Both are worthy of a completely separate study. In examining the Church, Law, and Medicine a distinction made by Friedson[7] between knowledge in its pure and applied form will be followed. Thus the professions will be classified broadly into scholarly (pure knowledge), and consulting (applied knowledge)—clergymen falling into the first category and lawyers and medical practitioners into the second. The focus of the analysis will be based largely on a case study of these professions within the city of Aberdeen although some attempt will be made to place these in a national and comparative perspective.

Parallel to the general urbanisation process taking place throughout Scotland, the period from 1760–1860 saw a remarkable transformation in population and socio-economic structure of Aberdeen.[8] From a population of about 12,000 the city grew to more than 72,000. The growth was not even, however, and would appear to be related to a fluctuating demand for labour within the local economy. In the first fifty years the population more than doubled—standing at 26,000 at the beginning of the nineteenth century. This was a period marked by relative stability in economic and social structural terms. The dominant industry was the stocking trade which was conducted on a domestic basis involving production not only in the city but throughout the rural north-east where it provided a vital supplement to rural incomes. Within the city the stocking-manufacturers formed a close kinship network bound by both partnerships and marital ties.[9] Not all of those families survived the collapse of the stocking trade as a consequence of the Napoleonic Wars and those that did diversified into factory-centred production of linen, woollens, and cotton. The demand for labour in the burgeoning textile industry, and in other industries such as shipbuilding, engineering, ropemaking, and paper and comb-manufacturing, saw the population soar in the first three decades of the nineteenth century, never falling below a decennial increase of 25 per cent. In those thirty years of dynamic capitalist development an industrial working class was created as a consequence of the entrepreneurial efforts of the families that had begun the process towards the end of the previous century. These families continued to dominate all the economic, social and political institutions throughout these years. However, as an unforeseen consequence of their endeavours the local economy became more and more exposed to wider capitalist crises and dramatic fluctuations took place in the local economy. In the 1840s the city staggered from a series of economic and financial disasters which saw the permanent closure of the majority of its textile mills. The collapse dragged down many of the old ruling families which had held power in the city since the eighteenth century. There was a consequent drastic slowing in population growth and by the decade 1850–60 it was down to 5.5 per cent—marginally less than the increase in the country as a whole.

In terms of overall comparison with the population growth of other Scottish cities in these hundred years, undoubtedly the most notable feature is the remarkable homogeneity of the Aberdeen population. Unlike Dundee, or other comparable urban centres, Aberdeen drew its migrants from its immediate rural hinterland. The 1851 Census shows that out of a population of 72,000 fewer than 20,000 were derived from outside the city or the immediate county. Indeed the number of English residents slightly outnumbered the Irish-born (1,270) whose numbers may have been inflated at that time by their presence on the construction of the railway which reached the city in 1850. The newcomers contributed to the development of a dynamic capitalism, which, with its associated class structure, presented a host of opportunities, not only for large capitalist entrepreneurs, but also for what we would now term small service industries. The growing needs of an urbanised population contributed to the expansion, of a new stratum of shopkeepers such as bakers, butchers, chemists, clothiers, grocers, ironmongers, mealsellers, as well as tradesmen such as builders, blacksmiths, carpenters, painters, nurserymen, and so on. Likewise opportunities presented themselves for consultant professions such as lawyers and doctors, and indeed not least, in these times of rapid change, the spiritual support of ministers of the church. This latter group will now be considered.

Clergymen Within the Class Structure

Although interdenominational animosities occurred to a not inconsiderable scale, clergymen generally were highly regarded socially. As a consequence they did not encounter any need to seek to further advance their social standing within the community. As a scholarly profession, most of their number had undergone a professional training involving university attendance. Throughout the period, presbyterianism in its various forms dominated the city but a broad Calvinist orthodoxy was prepared to include minor non-presbyterian churches and to tolerate the existence of a low-profile Episcopalianism.[10] A fairly tolerant peer-recognition took place across denominations. However such toleration was not extended to Catholics who were seen as seeking to corrupt, and what could be described as minor charismatic type churches, seen as attempting to mislead. Catholic priests and charismatic preachers were specifically excluded from professional recognition and outwith their immediate congregations possessed little social status.[11]

Within the recognised professional clergy there existed an accepted social hierarchy loosely based on stipendiary reward. A Church of Scotland minister in the West parish of the city would enjoy a salary up to five times greater than that of a clergyman attending to the needs of a congregation of a minor denomination in a less salubrious area. The source of the stipend was also of importance. Parishes endowed by the city were seen as more attractive than those where market forces—measured in terms of falling attendances—might lead to pressure to consider a reduction in stipend. In this respect the Disruption which took place in the Church of Scotland in 1843 had long-run consequences for the ministry. Although ostensibly fought out over the issue of the rights of patrons to 'intrude' a minister on a congregation, the societal implications ran much deeper and have been the subject of extensive analysis elsewhere.[12] As far as the professional development of the clergy is concerned the Disruption might be seen as a watershed. The schism produced a Free Church claiming merit as the basis of appointment and in the longer run the Church of Scotland—albeit reluctantly—was forced to follow a similar path ultimately leading to

the ending of formal patronage. It was recognised that parishioners
had a right to receive a minister who had undergone a university
education, and had been tested and licensed by the presbytery as a suitable
candidate for the ministry. Most significantly, perhaps, the same minister
had to be seen as acceptable by a new and dominant bourgeois social
composition within the kirk session. It was somewhat ironic that the
same social forces that swept aside the old bonds of patronage, now
could act to constrain freedom of expression. There is little doubt that
popular selection brought its own petty tyrannies and one consequence
of the Disruption was to draw the clergy into a much closer economic
and social relationship with their new bourgeois sponsors.

In other respects the effects of the Disruption on the profession were
complex. The increased demand for clergy as a consequence of a
massive investment in church-building offered greater opportunities
for mobility within the profession. Competitive selection also led to
new lucrative openings for an ambitious minister. On the other hand,
the enforcement of specified minimum qualifications meant that entry
into the profession had become less open in some respects than it had
been under the old system of patronage where a promising, but less
qualified, young man might have received advancement from an interested patron.

Apart from competitive advancement within the profession there
existed a number of other avenues of mobility. For those with academic
ambitions the attractions of a university chair were obvious. Indeed in
a church without bishops, a university appointment was the only
permanent office above parish level. It was from the ministry that
divinity professors, and many of the Arts professors, were recruited. For
many a university chair was regarded as an additional and undemand-
ing source of income which, unlike the office of parish minister, was
a valuable heritable property possessing rights of sale and conveyance.[13]

A more significant avenue of mobility for most ministers, rather than
academic advance, was their apparent suitability as marriage partners
for the daughters of wealthy merchants, or indeed for the rich widow.
Unlike lawyers—who tended to marry into families within the legal
profession—ministers were regarded as safe and eminently respectable
partners for the younger daughters of rich merchant families. Such
marriages avoided conflicts of interest over business as might result
from intermarriage with a rival family. Indirectly they also confirmed
and advanced the already high status enjoyed by ministers within the
community. A familiar pattern was for a young aspiring ministerial
candidate to be employed as family tutor. Alexander Dyce Davidson
provides a good example of the process. Son of a brewery

superintendent, after graduation at Marischal College in 1825, he was engaged as tutor by James Blaikie, an advocate and a member of a powerful family which dominated all aspects of the city polity and economy. The family provided a near unbroken run of lord provosts between 1833–46 and controlled the rights of patronage regarding appointments to city parishes. Davidson married Blaikie's daughter and found himself incumbent of the prestigious and lucrative West parish.[14] However, such accelerated promotion is somewhat remarkable. The more typical pattern was that of the unmarried minister of a less well-endowed parish succumbing to the attractions of financial independence associated with marriage to a rich widow.

As a profession, ministers of the church might at first appear to be the occupation least likely to be interlocked within the capitalist class structure. The nature of the occupation with its concern for abstract or pure knowledge, might suggest a certain detachment from the type of market forces bearing on the consultant professions of law and medicine practising a knowledge of more immediate application. The evidence—such as it is—suggests otherwise. Perhaps clergymen by their supposed spiritual detachment, and lack of concern for worldly goods, along with their already high status, were seen as particularly attractive marital partners. Certainly, in social, economic, and marital terms, clergy were drawn into the capitalist class structure and were no way independent of it.

However, in at least one important respect the role of clergymen differed substantially from that of the other professions. Whilst the professional boundaries of the law, could be fairly accurately described, this was less clear with regard to the ministry. In the events leading up to the Disruption the Church found itself increasingly embroiled in legal disputes over the issue of the property rights of patrons in relation to ministerial presentment. Historians in their concern to document these events may well have been diverted from two other important cases. These had little or nothing to do with ministerial presentment but had an important consequences in terms of defining the spiritual and secular boundaries of the clerical profession. Both cases were decided by the Court of Session in Edinburgh after lengthy consideration. Both reveal how secular forces were set on limiting the powers of the clergy.

The Case of Professor J. S. Blackie

The first case concerned the appointment of John Stuart Blackie to the chair of Latin in Marischal College in 1839. Blackie, unlike most of his professorial contemporaries, was prepared to make a stand on principle regarding his appointment and, in a carefully stated case, refused to sign the Confession of Faith 'except in his public professional capacity'.[15] His statement was found to be unacceptable to the Presbytery of Aberdeen and another appointment was made in his place. Blackie would appear to have anticipated this outcome and with considerable courage proceeded to take his case to the Court of Session where, in effect, he challenged the validity of the Test Act. The secular court declared that the presbytery had no rights in the matter and the deposed Blackie was reinstated to his chair. Spiritual control over the appointment to a lay chair had been refuted, and although 14 years were to pass before the Act itself was amended, the issue was clarified by the Blackie case.[16] The outcome made little or no difference with regard to professorial appointments. Apart from Blackie those appointed had found no difficulty in going through the ritual of subscribing to the Confession of Faith. However, as far as the Church was concerned a significant alteration had taken place relating to its secular powers. The redefinition disallowed the clergy, in the form of the presbytery, the right to intervene in an area long held to be its province. A important demarcation had been drawn between the spiritual and the secular.

If the presbytery had retired with a bloodied nose over the Blaikie case, worse was to follow. The issue became one of paramount importance in defining not only the role of the minister, but also, and more importantly, what a minister could say from his pulpit under the cover of professional privilege. Interestingly enough the issue at stake indirectly confirmed a right of secular freedom of expression in a popular newspaper.

The Case of Adam v. Allan

It has been said of James Adam, editor of the *Aberdeen Herald* that 'no other Scottish newspaper allowed less honour to the seceders' at the Disruption.[17] The brilliance of Adam and his contribution to the development of the Scottish press has long been overlooked. Adam successfully combined a forthright advocacy of free trade with a bitterly satirical anti-clericalism[18] in a form unknown in any other Scottish newspaper. He had a wide readership not least among those who did not share his views on free trade but eagerly awaited his weekly observations on what he held to be the hypocrisy of the evangelical clergy. In 1838 one such minister, John Allan of the Union Church, condemned Adam from the supposed protection of his pulpit. He stated *inter alia* that the editor of the *Aberdeen Herald* was an infamous infidel, an infidel villain, a blasphemous villain, a low villain, a hired agent for attacking the clergy, an agent of the devil, a Satanic agent.[19]

He had chosen the wrong man. Adam took Allan to court and, in a jury trial, was awarded £1000 in reparation for slander. The enraged Allan, furious at what amounted to the loss of about four years stipend, appealed against the verdict at the Court of Session in Edinburgh. The case was finally heard on June 1841 and was to provide a legal demarcation as to what a minister might say concerning another from his pulpit. Allan asserted that a minister held special rights in such matters. The privileges of the pulpit were such that a minister had the right to warn his flock of the dangers of 'pernicious errors and fallacious opinions' and by denouncing the editor of the *Aberdeen Herald* he was doing just that. He had done this not out of any personal malice towards Adam but as part of his professional duty as a parish minister. In order for the slander to stand malice would have to be proved by the pursuer.

He further claimed that the

office of parish minister imposed upon him the duty of watching over the spiritual interests of his flock, and also the duty of vindicating Christianity and the form of Christian faith established by law in Scotland from insult and attack, and the chief means within the power of clergymen for the performance of these duties was their pulpit ministrations.[20]

The judges were acutely aware of the wider issues involved in their deliberations and discerned that no difference could be drawn 'between a minister of the Established Church and of any other religious communion'.[21] There was a recognition that a minister possessed certain rights and privileges within the bounds of church courts such as the presbytery and kirk session but that this did not extend to a public place. On the issue of pulpit privilege there was a measure of agreement.

It was held that

great license was at one time claimed by the Church of Scotland as topics for the pulpit . . . for words there spoken, ministers were responsible to the Church only, but not to the civil courts. But such pretensions no longer exist.[22]

However on the crucial matter of where lay exactly the boundaries of pulpit privilege, the four judges failed to agree. They divided equally over the issue as to whether malice on the part of the minister had to be proved. It was agreed that further advice be sought and no fewer than nine other session judges were consulted. After much complex wrangling Allan's appeal was rejected. If the precise boundaries of what could be said in the course of a sermon were somewhat unclear the outcome reached amounted to a recognition that there was no privilege for what was uttered in the pulpit, and it stood on the same footing as if it had been uttered at the cross of a royal burgh.[23]

What had begun as little more than an unseemly squabble between two diverse forms of media—the press and the pulpit—ended with the total triumph of the former. Somewhat characteristically Adam did not even bother to record his success in the *Herald*. There is little doubt that the clergy were subdued by the outcome. Allan, confronted by a more pressing financial reality, saw the way forward as being that of embarking on a judicious marriage of the type mentioned earlier. In a sense he never fully recovered. Retiring soon after the Disruption he explained to his congregation that a throat condition was hindering the performance of his duties.[24]

Whatever the truth of such a claim, in many ways Allan's situation and the means by which he resolved it, provide an interesting example of the overall position of the clergy in the period. Considerable improvement in terms of professional development had taken place. The qualifications attached to entry into the profession were defined and there was an increasing opportunity for advancement as a consequence of church-building. Socially ministers continued to be held in high esteem and were widely sought as suitable marital partners. Although a profession basing its claims on access to pure knowledge, ministers found themselves being drawn into a closer relationship with what for many became their financial sponsors. Perhaps partly as a consequence of this a redefinition took place between the boundaries of what might be regarded as their spiritual and secular activities. Overall this demarcation acted to constrain the powers of the clergy in terms of their secular rights and privileges. As we shall see such difficulties did not arise with regard to either lawyers or medical practitioners, although each encountered their own contrasting range of problems.

Lawyers and Doctors Within the Class Structure

Unlike clergymen, both lawyers and medical practitioners throughout this period could gain access to their respective professions by means of a system of formal apprenticeship. In neither case was there any requirement to undergo university training whereas this generally would be expected of a presbyterian minister. Increasingly however, the legal profession expected university attendance from those seeking entrance although in this respect Aberdeen may have differed from other cities.[25] Certainly it is quite clear that in these years lawyers generally progressed much further down the path of professionalism than their medical counterparts.

One of the strengths of the legal profession was its clear and undisputed domain. The difficulties encountered by clergymen regarding the demarcation between spiritual and secular powers did not arise regarding lawyers. Whilst they may not always have been popular, there was a broad agreement between the public sector and the private individual as to what were the concerns of lawyers and as to what was their specific function. Unexpectedly perhaps, this did not apply to doctors. Throughout the period orthodox medicine fell into four categories comprising physic, surgery, pharmacy, and midwifery, but considerable areas of overlap occurred between all of them. Medicine remained a craft which was ill-defined in terms of the boundary between surgical skills and medical knowledge, although attempts were made to draw fine distinctions.[26] Moreover many doctors, in the public image, were not far removed from tradesmen in that they found a lucrative supplement to their income by running pharmacies selling proprietary medicines. Apothecaries providing similar services were not slow in offering their services as doctors. The issue was further confused by a whole body of 'irregular practitioners' who, at best were indistinguishable from the others, and at worst practised no more than quackery. Consequently it is not surprising that in the popular mind the practice of medicine for many retained a certain mystical association which was not far removed from the possession of magical powers. Above all these problems were made worse by the total absence of any regulative body governing the the activities of a profession often beset by notoriety and scandal.

The legal profession, on the other hand, did have the necessary institutional means, in the form of the Society of Advocates, of tackling such problems. An institution of long-standing, and one which increased in stature throughout the century, the Society, whose membership was drawn from throughout the north-east, aimed to ensure ethical standards of behaviour. Membership was sought after but was not routinely granted and the Society endeavoured to exclude those who were considered to fall below the standards expected. Indeed in at least one case the Society openly attempted to apply a black list on the court practice of a non-member.[27] In other respects the Society also worked to improve the image of the profession by acting to limit competition among lawyers over the increasing lucrative market in property conveyancing. Recommended conveyancing rates were drawn up and members were pressed to adhere to these.[28]

To a much greater extent than clergymen, lawyers were drawn from the offspring of leading city families and intermarriage within the profession was common. The Society of Advocates recognised this marital pattern in drawing up their membership admission rates. Special terms and substantial reductions were allowed for the sons of members seeking entry, and similar privileges were extended to those who married daughters of members.[29] The Society as well as taking care to scrutinize those seeking membership, also sought to regulate entry at the initial point of entry to the profession. Those seeking to become law apprentices were examined regarding their moral and educational suitability. After 1800, added to the already high cost of indenture fees, was the requirement of attendance (not necessarily graduation) for two sessions at the university. The evidence clearly indicates the success of the Society in enforcing this requirement.[30] Initially this attendance may have been regarded in the wider sense as part of the process of becoming a lawyer and a gentlemen. However, by 1819 the Society took the process a step further and funded two lectureships at Marischal College, in Scots Law and Conveyancing. Thereafter it was insisted that all apprentices who ultimately intended seeking membership must, as a prerequisite for entry, have attended these classes.[31]

Lawyers, more than either of the other two professions under consideration, had proceeded further down the path of self-regulation. They were concerned with advancing a public image of professional competency associated with a high standard of training. Through the Society of Advocates the need was stressed for an adherence by individual members to an ethic based on high moral principles. Implicitly this involved the maintenance of a supposed professional detachment from the temptations of becoming involved in the wider and corrupting forces of the capitalist market place. In this respect the Society may well have been giving due recognition to the long-standing reputation held by Aberdeen lawyers regarding their acquisitive nature.[32] In the first half of the nineteenth century the rapid economic and social changes taking place within the city presented a host of opportunities for a shrewd lawyer to make his fortune. One such man was Alexander Anderson who in a fifty year business career, involving countless financial institutions and investment companies, gained a fearsome reputation for utter ruthlessness in the market place.[33]

On the other hand, if Anderson provides a fine example of the lawyer-entrepreneur, it would be generally true to say that, lawyers as a profession, were attempting to distance themselves from overt capitalist involvement. Such a process was possible because of the public perception of where the actual boundaries of the profession lay. It was assisted by the fact that lawyers, more than either of the other two professions under consideration, were drawn from well-established city families and as a consequence shared a clearer common purpose. Indeed the pattern of intermarriage within the profession was recognised formally by the Society of Advocates by variable entry fees. Above all it was the latter institution and its regulatory function which can be seen as foremost in advancing the profession. It is when one turns to examine the medical practitioners that the distinctive characteristics of the legal profession are most effectively brought into contrast.

Although similar to lawyers in one important respect that the cornerstone of professional training lay in a system of formally indentured apprenticeship, in almost all other considerations the experience of the two professions differed quite radically. However, even in the drawing up of the indenture significant differences are apparent. Unlike law, medical apprentices were required also to undertake the duties of house servant, and to abstain from all forms of debauchery. Most revealing perhaps was the fact that they were foresworn not to reveal any of the secrets of the business to others.[34] Indenture fees were high and yet the training offered was not always of a high standard as

> private patients were unlikely to be happy with being visited by an apprentice, and might even object to his visiting with his master. Often the apprentice was only sent to visit the poor.[35]

Whilst the Society of Advocates vetted all those entering the profession as apprentices—no such body regulated entry into the medical profession. Indeed entry into medicine was absurdly open and could be accomplished in any number of ways other than by apprenticeship, although this still remained the accepted and respectable point of entry to the profession until well into the nineteenth century.[36]

Throughout most of the period neither of the two city universities offered any formal training in medicine although both had chairs which were filled. Of the two universities Kings College was the greater offender in this respect. In one notorious case the professor gave only one lecture in his 22 years incumbency and on his death the chair passed to his son who continued the same tradition.[37] Both university senates saw it as being their function not to offer medical training but to confer degrees by recommendation. This proved a lucrative source of funds. Although it was stipulated that all candidates had to be known by the person recommending them this was clearly not always the case. If a candidate's application was accompanied by a letter from a physician or other eminent person, or if the candidate had attended or graduated from one of the Aberdeen colleges, or if an Aberdeen graduate supported the application, this generally would be seen as sufficient for the award of a degree. The senate minutes abound with examples of degrees being conferred—often to overseas candidates—where there was little real indication as to the knowledge possessed or training undergone by the candidate. Indeed the readiness of the two Aberdeen universities, as well as St Andrews, to confer degrees was recognised throughout Britain by the profession and as a consequence it was held that the high quality of the degrees conferred by Edinburgh and Glasgow were being undermined.[38]

Given such ready access to degrees scandals were far from uncommon. In one notorious case in 1791 the senate of Marischal College sought advice from the Solicitor-General on how they might take action to recover a degree that they had conferred mistakenly on a candidate who now openly was practising 'impudent quackery'. They were warned that it would be most prudent to remain silent as once a degree had been conferred it could not be taken away, and that in future they should be more circumspect and cautious in their choice. However, although attempts were made, neither senate proved capable of regulating a process which provided such a ready source of income.[39]

Unlike clergymen or lawyers, those intent on entering the profession could do so by what would now be described as gaining work experience. One such person, John Milne, who rose to become an eminent doctor, began his career when

> at seventeen he went to Greenland with a sailing whaler as surgeon, a situation often held by lads of ability, whose view of life received some breadth from foreign experience.[40]

From this position he found promotion as a surgeon's mate on an East India Company ship and later became a surgeon for the company in Bombay where he made his fortune.[41]

A more familiar pattern was to enrol in the armed forces as a regimental or naval surgeon. During the Napoleonic wars there were many opportunities for young men to gain experience and 'young men of ability' were actively recruited from both the universities' Arts classes to undertake surgeons' commissions. The fact that an Aberdonian doctor, Sir James McGregor, rose to become Director of the British Army Medical Board, had a vital significance in terms of recruitment from the north-east. Others went abroad to the West Indies and elsewhere with perhaps 'a little hospital practice and some medical books' to see them on their way.[42] Many having gained practical work experience in the field returned to take up medicine, and as part of the process, would purchase a university degree in order to demonstrate proficiency to their patients.

Those entering the profession by such means found themselves in what was an overcrowded and very competitive market and one where medicine often remained a part-time occupation.[43] Unlike Law where institutional controls over entry into indentured apprenticeships aimed at maintaining a balance in the profession, no such measures are apparent in the medical profession. In an unregulated profession, the numerous private pathways into medicine were confusing to the general public. At the top of the medical hierarchy stood those who had degrees from the universities of Edinburgh and Glasgow as a consequence of attending medical classes. Such men tended to describe themselves as physicians. Beneath them lay a confusion of 'regular' practitioners who may have attended classes at Edinburgh or Glasgow, or elsewhere, or had obtained practical experience, and had subsequently used this as the basis for purchasing a degree from Aberdeen or St Andrews. One apologist for the procedure at Kings and Marischal Colleges stressed how this system of conferring degrees overall worked to unite the profession:

> The degree was the recognition by the University of general and professional attainments, however and wherever acquired. It was free from the notion of a licence to practice, superceding all such: it kept aloof from the pretensions and feuds of the surgeons and physicians: it did much to integrate physic and surgery by recognising that the chirurgeon-apothecary, who had obtained an honourable position in his calling, might be worthy of the degree equally with his brother physician who disdained to use the knife or the pestle and mortar.[44]

On the other hand, not all practitioners bothered to seek university recognition. Among the better-trained this might include former indentured apprentices within a family practice. However many apprentices received a minimum of medical training which indeed might not approach the standards of those obtaining their experience abroad or on an unsuspecting soldier or sailor. The field was further crowded by apothecaries who often dabbled successfully in medical practice. Existing alongside, rather than below, were a host of what an ill-defined 'regular profession' described as 'ignorant quacks and empiricks'. It was claimed that these preyed on the unwary, stealing patients from the qualified practitioners, whether physician or surgeon.

The evidence suggests that the public sought medical help where they could best find it and even the poorest discriminated in an openly competitive market.[45] Neither was the distinction between 'regular' and 'irregular' practice so clear as the 'regular' practitioners might like to have maintained. Clearly the general public required and sought the services of doctors. However they also held an inherent distrust of certain aspects of the scientific medicine—the basis of the training claimed by the 'regular' practitioners which set them apart from the so-called quacks and empiricks. Nowhere was this distrust so apparent as in the field of anatomical research where the need to obtain supplies of fresh corpses brought the profession into open conflict with the general public. The distrust extended far beyond the working class, who were most likely to provide the subjects for research. It involved a response from an entire cross-section of society and, interestingly enough, it also brought doctors into conflict with both the other two professions under consideration—lawyers and ministers.

An excellent example is provided by the case of the burning and total destruction of a building used as an anatomical theatre by a Dr Andrew Moir in Aberdeen in 1831. Moir was a brilliant and well-known doctor whose income suffered seriously from the fact that he was known to teach anatomy to students. This alone prevented him 'from having any medical practice' other than that received from occasional 'chance fees'. The riot which took place was extremely serious and Moir, and indeed some of his students, were fortunate to escape with their lives. The finding by a dog of some human remains in a shallow grave sparked of a riot which led to the involvement of some 20,000 people. The destruction of Moir's property—'literally not one stone of it left on the other'—was attended (although not in their official capacity!) by the lord provost and the entire city council. 'Fire engines came, and were hustled back by the angry crowd' and the 97th Regiment called out to quell the riot watched ineffectively although their presence may have deterred the mob from further action against the medical hall. The conservative *Aberdeen Journal* gave little space to what was a major incident involving law and order in the city. Only two ringleaders were ever brought to trial. One of these was pardoned on the basis of his claim that he believed that his grandmother's body had been in the building. Thereafter neither Moir or his students were safe on the streets and even those residents who lived in close proximity to his house found themselves under constant threat.[46]

Whilst the city authorities would not go as far as condone the action of the mob and the consequent destruction of Moir's property, it is clear that they were prepared to concede that the deed, to a degree, was morally justifiable. The *Aberdeen Journal* saw it as a 'lesson' and 'a warning to Dr Moir to be more careful in future'.[47] Certainly the riot brought into the open the general distrust felt by the public concerning the medical profession. The finding of bodies in Moir's premises confirmed the popular suspicion held by many members of the general public regarding the activities of certain members of the 'regular' medical profession. The action of the mob gave notice not just to Moir but to other members of the profession who might be engaging in similar scientific research.

As far as the medical profession, itself, is concerned the period did see considerable advances in terms of the acquisition of knowledge. However such gains tended to be lost in what was an increasingly competitive market for patients who, perhaps not surprisingly, were less able to discriminate amongst the contending claims made by the vast array of rival practitioners.

Under the circumstances it is not surprising that in the eyes of the general public confusion and uncertainty reigned regarding what comprised medical qualifications. Indeed in terms of medical treatment there may have been little to choose between qualified and unqualified practice.[48] The many pathways into the medical profession meant that the worsening situation was unlikely to improve until some institutional means could be created by which entry standards could be enforced and professional qualifications monitored. Given the many conflicting interests within the medical profession, it is not surprising that no such institution emerged. It was not until the 1860s that intervention by the state brought an effective regulation of the profession.[49]

The Liberal Professions in Retrospect

It has already been noted that the three main attributes of professions comprise briefly: First, an expertise in a given defined field and in which ethical standards are held to prevail over market forces; second, self-regulation takes place through institutional intervention; third, recruitment is based on merit derived from training and educational qualifications. Each of the three professions viz. clergymen, lawyers, and doctors, will be compared in the light of these three attributes and assessed in terms of their location within the bourgeois class structure.

Throughout the hundred years the clergy—certainly in terms of what one might term the mainstream ministry—continued to enjoy a high status and of the three professions they were regarded as the most eminently respectable: a respectability enforced by the activities of presbytery and kirk session. As a moral vanguard of society they were less likely to be confronted by the need to resist the market although events such as the Disruption were to direct them down new paths leading to greater exposure. Whilst the Disruption increased the element of merit in recruitment into the profession it also drew the clergy into a much closer association with the business world than had formerly been the case. The high regard given to the clergy as marital partners further cemented the connection. Indeed increasingly the secular world impinged on their activities. Midway through the period the presbytery found itself challenged by secular law and pushed back from from areas long held to be within its sphere of influence. Likewise the law was used to redefine and constrain the the so-called ministerial privileges of the pulpit.

More than either of the other professions lawyers had proceeded further down the path towards professionalism. Although not necessarily popular, lawyers were highly respected and steadily, throughout the period through their own institution, the Society of Advocates, they strove to improve their social image and attain a greater respectability. Recommended standard fees were drawn up as a clear attempt to distance the profession from market forces. Likewise by the middle of the period ever-increasing standards of training and qualifications were enforced. Comprising a much closer social network than either of the other professions, there was a tendency for families within the profession to inter-marry. This was a pattern acknowledged and given institutional encouragement by their Society in admission fees which favoured such circumstances. Finally whilst lawyers were very much part of the the bourgeois social structure it is certainly the case that increasingly they came to regard themselves as a distinct and separate body. Associated with this attitude, advancement of the profession was seen as seeking to project an image of aloof and even altruistic independence by distancing themselves from overt involvement in market forces.

Alone among the professions, doctors found themselves both weakly established within the bourgeois structure and most exposed to market forces. At the top end of the profession highly qualified men of experience, could make a good living. However the association between qualifications, experience, and earnings was not a clear one. Indeed, in a sense, any one might be obtained without the other. The precise field of medicine remained remarkably ill-defined and it seems likely the situation worsened as a consequence of industrialisation and urbanisation. Indeed the expansion in opportunities for mealsellers must have been mirrored by the new openings for those laying claim to possess medical skills, whether physician, surgeon, apothecary, or midwife. Under the competitive circumstances which they faced, it is unlikely that a professional ethic played much part in their deliberations. The situation was worsened by the absence of an effective regulatory body with powers to intervene and control the many pathways into the profession. With experience as highly rated as training and qualifications the profession remained divided and dispersed throughout the social structure. Men of high reputation were firmly embedded in the bourgeois class but a long tail led to those who made their living on the periphery of the new working class. All were confronted by the forces of economic competition for patients at whatever level they practised. Indeed, in some respects medicine stood nearer to an occupation rather than a profession until late in the period.

REFERENCES

1. In conducting this research, the author wishes to acknowledge gratefully financial support received from The Carnegie Trust for the Universities of Scotland; advice and assistance from the staff of the University of Aberdeen Department of Special Collections; the granting of access to the records of the Aberdeen Medico-Chirurgical Society, and the records of the Society of Advocates in Aberdeen.
2. E. Durkheim, *Professional Ethics and Civic Morals* (London 1957).
3. W. Carr-Saunders, *Professions: their Organisation and Place in Society* (London 1928).
4. T.H. Marshall, *Class, Citizenship, and Social Development* (London 1964).
5. H. Perkin, *The Origins of Modern English Society 1789–1880* (London 1980), pp.254–58. See also his *Rise of Professional Society: England since 1880* (London 1989).
6. See A.A. MacLaren, 'Patronage and Professionalism: The "Forgotten Middle Class" 1760–1860' in D. McCrone et al. eds. *The Making of Scotland: Nation, Culture & Social Change* (Edinburgh, 1989), pp.123–42.
7. E. Friedson, *The Profession of Medicine: A Study of the Sociology of Applied Knowledge* (New York, 1970).
8. For an account of the economic and social changes taking place in the city, see A.A. MacLaren, *Religion and Social Class: The Disruption Years in Aberdeen* (London, 1974).
9. T. Donnelly, 'The economic activities of the members of the Aberdeen Merchant Guild, 1750–1799' *Scottish Economic and Social History*, 1, no.1 (1981) p.30.
10. Episcopalianism had a long history of support in the north-east and there were five congregations in the city in 1851 when an estimated overall attendance was 3795. This comprised just over five per cent of the population, making them the third biggest denomination, and not that far behind the Established Church (7.26%).—MacLaren, *Religion and Social Class* p.215. Over the years they were successful in retaining their existing members but avoided any attempt at expansion and thus offered no challenge to presbyterian hegemony. It was said of them that 'salvation they believe, is not to be found without the walls of their own chapel, and they take care to keep it there . . .'. James Bruce, *The Aberdeen pulpit and universities* (Aberdeen 1844), p.143. This view was confirmed by the official historian of the Episcopal Church. See George Grub, *Home mission work of the Episcopal Church in Scotland* (Edinburgh 1883), p.8.
11. There was one Roman Catholic congregation in the city. Catholic clergy followed an unwritten but well-recognised code of confining their attentions to their immediate flock and at all times seeking to avoid the critical gaze of the presbytery. On occasion a priest might inadvertently step out of line and bring down the

wrath of the presbyterian clergy. Father James Gordon who spoke the local vernacular and was regarded as being overly active in assisting the city poor, was systematically attacked in a course of sermons by six presbyterian ministers. James Riddell, *Aberdeen and its folk* (Aberdeen 1868) p.79. Thereafter he was harassed continually and even money collected at the Roman Catholic chapel 'for the benefit of suffering labourers during the severe season of distress' was less than politely refused.—Sheriff Watson's diary, 27 September 1836 in M. Angus, *Sheriff Watson of Aberdeen* (Aberdeen 1913). Similar pulpit and pamphlet attacks were made on Hugh Hart who had successfully built up a large independent working-class congregation. Hart was shunned by presbyterian ministers who regarded his qualifications as inferior and were shocked by his audacity in claiming a unity of all Christian religions. His theological position, dress, mannerisms, and sermons were the subject of a vicious and routine ridicule. W. Gammie, *The Churches of Aberdeen* (Aberdeen 1909) p.377; Bruce, *Aberdeen pulpit,* pp.125, 140–2, 147.

12. See MacLaren, *Religion and Social Class, passim.*

13. See A.A. MacLaren, 'Privilege, Patronage and the Professions: Aberdeen and its Universities' in J. Carter and D.J. Withrington, *Scottish Universities—Distinctiveness and Diversity* (Edinburgh, 1992).

14. See James A. Ross, *Record of Municipal Affairs in Aberdeen* (Aberdeen 1889). MacLaren, *Religion and Social Class,* p.221. Davidson, nevertheless, seceded in 1843 to become minister of the Free West Church.

15. It is somewhat ironic that Blackie later wrote in defence of the rights of professors who had subscribed to the Free Church and now faced dismissal although, to say the least, few of them had risen to speak on his behalf in his hour of need.—See J.S. Blackie, *On subscription to Articles of Faith: A plea for the liberties of the Scottish Universities, with special reference to the Free Church professors* (Edinburgh, 1843).

16. J.M. Bulloch, *A History of the University of Aberdeen* (London, 1895), pp.184–85.

17. R.M.W. Cowan, *The Newspaper in Scotland* (Glasgow, 1946), p.149.

18. See A.A. MacLaren, 'The Disruption of the "Establishment": James Adam and the Aberdeen Clergy' in J.S. Smith and D. Stevenson eds., *Aberdeen in the Nineteenth Century: The Making of the Modern City* (Aberdeen, 1988), pp.106–20.

19. Alexander Dunlop, J.M. Bell, John Murray, James Donaldson, *Cases decided in Court of Session from November 12 to July 20, 1841,* vol.III (Edinburgh 1841), p.1058.

20. *Ibid.* p.1059.

21. *Ibid.* p.1063.

22. *Ibid.* p.1064.

23. *Ibid.* p.1072.

24. W. Walker, *The Bards of Bonaccord, 1375–1860* (Aberdeen 1887), p.660.

25. Availability of university education within the city is likely to have been a significant factor. In this respect it appeared to differ from substantially larger English cities. See Andrew Rowley, 'Professions, Class and Society: Solicitors in Nineteenth Century Birmingham,' read at Annual conference of British Sociological Association at the University of Edinburgh, 1988.

26. See I. Loudon, *Medical Care and the General Practitioner 1750–1850* (Oxford 1986), pp.18–22.

27. See the case of Alexander Laing. The Society resolved that it would 'publicly censure any member . . . who shall countenance the said Alexander Laing as an agent before any of the Courts at Aberdeen in time coming'—*Sederunt Book of the Society of Advocates in Aberdeen (dated 1776),* 24 November 1789. The dispute with Laing went back a long way. In 1779 He had sought membership of the Society and had been refused on the basis of 'sundry objections' regarding his 'character'. After a series of unsuccessful appeals he took his case to the Court of Session in Edinburgh where his application was again rejected. Ibid. 7 December 1779; 7

January, 8 March 1780; 23 February, 26 July, 2 August 1781; 8 November 1782; 6 January, 31 January 1783; 1 February 1788.

28. *Sederunt Book of the Society of Advocates in Aberdeen*, 14 November 1800.

29. The reductions were considerable and amounted to less than half the standard fee which stood at more than £63 in 1791. Members' sons were also admitted without having served a regular apprenticeship.—*Sederunt Book of the Society of Advocates in Aberdeen*, Regulations: Item XIX; Item XXI; Item XXVI.

30. Out of a total of 246 admitted to the Society between 1800 and 1860 only five had not attended university and all were admitted before 1813. Between 1760 and 1800, prior to the regulations coming into force, 42 were admitted and of these 18 had not attended. See MacLaren 'Patronage and Professionalism' p.134. The policy received something of a setback in 1873 when the right of such legal bodies to enforce such entry requirements was abolished by Parliament. Thereafter no university training—either in Arts or Law could be set as a requirement for entry to the profession. N.J.D. Kennedy, 'The Faculty of Law in Aberdeen' in P.J. Anderson ed., *Studies in the History of the University* (Aberdeen, 1896), p.301.

31. J.A.H. Henderson, *History of the Society of Advocates in Aberdeen* (Aberdeen, 1912), p.63. The Society had long been a champion of such measures. See *Sederunt Book of the Society of Advocates in Aberdeen (dated 1776)*, 4 October 1786.

32. Henderson, *Society of Advocates*. pp.xii–xiii.

33. The city ring road—named after him—has been described as resembling the man himself: 'fast, wide, and dangerous to cross'. B.M. Balfour, 'No Mean Aberdonians—Some Aberdeen Entrepreneurs' in J.S. Smith and D. Stevenson eds. *Aberdeen in the Nineteenth Century: The Making of the Modern City* (Aberdeen University Press, 1988), p.41.

34. E.H.G. Rodger, *Aberdeen Doctors at Home and Abroad* (Edinburgh, 1893), p.57.

35. Loudon, *Medical Care*, pp.28; 39.

36. *Ibid.* p.53.

37. Rodger, *Aberdeen Doctors*, p.70. W. Kennedy, *The Annals of Aberdeen*, vol.2 (London, 1818), pp.119–20. R.S. Rait, *The Universities of Aberdeen: A History* (Edinburgh, 1885), p.225.

38. Loudon, *Medical Care*, p.144.

39. P.J. Anderson, *Officers and Graduates of the University of King's College* (Aberdeen, 1893), pp.130–75; op. cit. *Fasti Academiae Mariscallanae Aberdonensis* (Aberdeen, 1898), pp.120–81 (see entry, pp.133–4); Rait, *Universities of Aberdeen*, pp.210, 212–3.

40. Rodger, *Aberdeen Doctors*, p.138. This pathway into medicine was not all that unusual although it was regarded with scorn by the 'regular' practitioners. Yorkshire also had its 'Greenland doctors . . . These are a set of mechanics of various descriptions who, failing in their respective vocations, too often from profligacy, learn to bleed and are then qualified for the place of surgeon on board a Greenland ship. On their return . . . they go into the country and are doctors until the next Greenland season'. Loudon, *Medical Care*, p.144.

41. Rodger, *Aberdeen Doctors*, pp.137–48.

42. Aberdonians were favoured 'above all others' through a wide-ranging network of patronage. Rodger, *Aberdeen Doctors*, pp.127, 104, 138, 203, 100.

43. See D. Hamilton, *The Healers: A History of Medicine in Scotland* (Edinburgh, 1981), ch.4. Loudon, *Medical Care*, pp.208–23. I. Waddington, *The Medical Profession in the Industrial Revolution* (Dublin, 1984), pp.187–89.

44. William Stephenson, 'Four centuries of medicine in Aberdeen' in P.J. Anderson ed. *Studies in the History of the University* (Aberdeen 1896), p.308.

45. W. Henderson, *Observations on the Medical Attendance of the Poor in their own Homes* (Aberdeen, 1822), p.17.

46. Rodger, *Aberdeen Doctors*, pp.235, 242–3.

47. *Ibid.* p.243.
48. Loudon, *Medical Care,* pp.208–27. See also R. Porter, *Health for Sale: Quackery in England 1660–1850* (Manchester, 1989).
49. Waddington, *Medical Profession,* pp.135–52. Although a medical society was founded in Aberdeen in 1789, for many years it remained little more than a student debating society. Its early years were marked by internal disputes and attempts to achieve a measure of 'respectable' recognition both from the medical profession and the wider society. Ultimately the institution survived and prospered although it lagged far behind its counterpart—the Society of Advocates in Aberdeen—in terms of its control over the profession. See Aberdeen Medico—Chirurgical Society, *Minute Book, 1789–92.*

5

Politics and Power in the Scottish City: Glasgow Town Council in the Nineteenth Century.

Irene Maver

I

In comparison with analyses of radicalism and the emergence of the Labour Party, the attitudes and influence of political elites in Glasgow during the nineteenth century have—until recently—been given only superficial attention in accounts of the city's development.[1] This selective focus should not necessarily be attributed to bias or inertia on the part of historians; as the nineteenth century progressed, the ruling order in Glasgow carefully cultivated its own self-image, which for years fostered the notion that among elite circles there was more to unite than to divide in terms of allegiances, thus obviating the need to critically scrutinise political behaviour. In consequence, a conventional wisdom arose about the nature of political power in Glasgow, to the effect that after the Reform Acts of the 1830s, elements of reaction were swept from their entrenched position within the city's institutions, allowing an enlightened, liberal regime to dominate until the 1880s.[2] Even after the Irish Home Rule crisis redirected politics nationally, Glasgow's reputation as a bastion of 'municipal socialism' reflected the culmination of this liberal, reforming impulse by 1900.[3] It was a story of steady, sustained progress, where the concept of the 'common good' over-rode overt political partisanship, and the excesses of sectarianism were generally muted within the electoral process.

For their part, Glasgow's elites had long understood the advantages of an effective public relations machine, to the extent that the image was consciously boosted and the reality submerged, in an effort to maintain a position of political ascendancy. As will be elaborated in this paper, such a strategy was particularly successful in the municipal sphere, where the ruling order remained remarkably resilient throughout the nineteenth century in face of sustained challenges from below. Of course, such a view of elite activity is selective, as there were other institutions in the city where politics could (and did) influence the behaviour of elected leaders within the community; for instance, the Police Board up to 1846, the Parochial Board from 1845, and the School Board from 1872. However, municipal representation was one of the most distinctively political areas of the public service, with traditional Parliamentary interconnections, which were especially apparent during the first half of the nineteenth century. Apart from the participation of women in civic elections from the 1880s, entitlement to the municipal vote broadly mirrored that of the Parliamentary vote; accordingly, the pressure for reform in both areas tended to occur conterminously, involving the same social groups and similar sets of demands.

As the key dates for electoral reform in the urban context, the years 1832–33 and 1867–68 will be used in this paper to divide the century into three distinct periods of municipal activity in Glasgow. During the first phase, the exercise of political power in Scotland's royal burghs was concentrated exclusively in the Town Councils, under a system of Parliamentary representation which seemed immutably fixed by the provisions of the 1707 Treaty of Union. The number of electors in Glasgow totalled thirty-three; a figure which can be explained by the fact that only serving councillors could vote for the city's MP—or quarter MP, as Glasgow was only one component of the Clyde Burghs constituency, along with the other royal burghs of Dumbarton, Renfrew and Rutherglen. In the wake of the 1832–33 reform legislation, a degree of accountability was introduced into Scotland's royal burghs, with the enfranchisement of the £10 male householders boosting the number of voters in the self-contained Glasgow Parliamentary constituency to just over 7,000. Yet despite this important concession to democracy and the steady expansion of the representative base from the 1830s, the pre-reform political power structure was not wholly eroded, nor did the socio-economic profile of the ruling order alter significantly. While the prevailing political orthodoxy in Glasgow tended increasingly towards Liberalism, this did not signify the replacement of one elite group by another; rather, it represented a broad shift of allegiances within elite circles, for a variety of reasons connected with the city's changing religious orientation and demographic profile. It was not until the aftermath of the 1868 Reform Act that the ideological affinities of Glasgow's elites became gradually less cohesive, as the electoral process opened out substantially to accommodate all male householders, and inter-party rivalries intensified in an effort to woo and win over the enfranchised population.

II

The group which for all practical purposes was able to dominate the city's politics during the pre-reform era—that is, the thirty-three serving town councillors—has not, on the whole, been treated with much sympathy by historians.[4] This is understandable, given the profound irony of a situation which allowed for political power to be concentrated in the hands of a small and self-elected clique, while the city itself represented such a spectacular economic success story. Moreover, the blanket reputation of the Scottish burghs for gross inefficiency prior to 1833 meant that Glasgow was inevitably tarred with the same brush of notoriety. Henry Cockburn's retrospective assessment has served, by and large, as a model to describe all the pre-reform Town Councils. 'In general', he wrote, 'they were sinks of political and municipal iniquity, steeped in the baseness which they propagated, and types and causes of the corruption which surrounded them'.[5] Although a deliberately overblown image, there undoubtedly was substance to some of these accusations, with flaws all too glaringly apparent in the municipal accountancy practices of Aberdeen, Dundee and Edinburgh.[6] In comparison, Glasgow's civic leaders took pains to maintain the city's financial credibility; indeed, fledgling municipal enterprises can be identified even before the 1800s, as councillors explored a variety of different options for exploiting community assets—favouring Glasgow Green, in particular, as a revenue raising resource.[7] It should also be cautioned that individuals like Cockburn had a political axe to grind in their lurid evocation of Scotland's closed system of civic government. As a Whig reformer, it was in Cockburn's interests to show that the pre-1833 period symbolised the darkness before the dawn, and if that implied the denigration of relatively efficient burgh administrations like Glasgow, he was not likely to go out of his way to redress the balance.

From the political perspective, the ruling order in pre-reform Glasgow constituted those representatives of the city's burgess institutions—the Merchants' House and Trades' House—who were able to wield most authority within civic circles and, ultimately, at the Parliamentary level. The burgess institutions traditionally controlled the municipality; or, more specifically, power was concentrated in the Merchants' House, which had a fixed majority in terms of Council representation, plus exclusive right for one of its members to serve as Lord Provost. The superior status of the merchants was not a phenomenon unique to Glasgow; merchant dominance was the norm in the political hierarchy of Scotland's royal burghs, although Glasgow tended to be more favourable in terms of the numerical ratio between merchants and craftsmen, reflecting the growing importance of the trades to Glasgow's economy from the seventeenth century.[8] Nevertheless, the 1707 Act of Union—which specifically stated that the rights and privileges of the royal burghs must be protected—had the effect of institutionalising the power of the merchants.[9] Not that the craftsmen were politically impotent in Glasgow up to the 1830s; their collective sense of grievance against merchant dominance had provoked them cautiously into reforming activity from the 1780s, and thereafter Trades' House leadership was to the fore in stating the case for political reform within the municipal sphere.[10]

Yet for all the efforts of individuals and interest groups to challenge this position of ascendancy, up to the 1830s the merchants were protected because of Government determination to preserve the constitutional *status quo*. On the other hand, it should be stressed that there were no rigid demarcations between members of Glasgow's burgess institutions, and that by the 1800s some of the more successful trades representatives had penetrated the ranks of the Merchants' House.[11] Nor should it be implied that the political power of the merchants was distributed evenly among all those who were admitted to Merchants' House membership. Although the dominance of the overseas sector had begun to erode by the nineteenth century, to accommodate increasingly important domestic industries like textile manufacturing, the administrative structures of the Merchants' House remained intact, with power vested in the Dean of Guild—as the leading merchant burgess—and the exclusive circle which surrounded him. Because of this self-perpetuating power-base, the merchant-dominated civic leadership had not been anxious to change the system of municipal and Parliamentary representation during the eighteenth century. In the 1780s, despite Trades' House prompting, Glasgow Town Council remained resolutely aloof from moves being made by several of the royal burghs to introduce a greater measure of accountability into municipal affairs.[12] The refusal to endorse the aims of the early burgh reform movement can be partially attributed to the successful system of political patronage which had prevailed in the city throughout the eighteenth century, and helped to perpetuate the position of the ruling order even further.[13]

From the post-Union period, Glasgow's political elites identified with the Hanoverian ascendancy as a form of economic self-protection. However, despite their vocal declarations of loyalty to Government interests, they came to be uncomfortably caught in a conundrum by the 1800s. As the city progressed economically, so the urban fabric began to deteriorate, under the mounting pressure of population numbers. City residents totalled some 31,000 during the 1750s; a figure which more than doubled to 77,300 by 1801, and nearly doubled again to 147,000 by 1821.[14] The problem was compounded because Scottish industrialisation proceeded at a comparatively brisker pace than south of the border, with profoundly dislocating effects on the environment and on existing social structures. In terms of urban development, this was reflected in the recognition that by the 1820s, Glasgow had some of the worst living conditions in the United Kingdom, and that the mechanism for servicing the city's needs had become unmanageable.[15] However, political considerations impinged on the urgent need for administrative reform, as Parliament was reluctant to sanction any interference with the Scottish system of burgh government, because of fears that this might lead to constitutional change. Over time, therefore, the loyalties of Glasgow's town councillors became increasingly divided. While they still identified strongly with Government interests, they were also prepared to concede that a measure of political reform was desirable, not least to break the legislative stalemate which was allowing the civic administration such little room for manoeuvre. This commitment ran contrary to subsequent claims that Glasgow's pre-reform ruling order consisted of 'old Tory stagers', deeply hostile to change.[16] As early as 1819 civic leaders were endorsing the view that 'reasonable and moderate' alterations should be made to the city's system of government, '. . . as may appear, after mature deliberation, to be conducive to the public welfare'.[17]

   In this context, it is revealing that the terms 'Whig' and 'Tory' became an anachronism in the city's municipal politics during the pre-reform era, because of their previous association with the old patrician hegemony. Among the civic leadership the political labels of 'Liberal' and 'Conservative' came to be much preferred, as both represented a positive affirmation of new priorities among the city's elites.[18] On the one hand, they conveyed a sense of economic progressivism, albeit in differing degrees of support for the free trade principle; on the other hand, they more meaningfully expressed contemporary attitudes towards constitutional change. In 1830, Kirkman Finlay—former MP and a dominating figure within the Merchants' House—summed up prevailing opinions when he argued: '. . . It was absolutely absurd to say that no change should take place in representation formed on the state of things two hundred years ago, or that everything in the country was to advance while the Government stood still'.[19] Finlay was also reflecting a mounting sense of frustration among the broad membership of the city's burgess institutions that Parliamentary representation should have to be shared on equal terms with three smaller burghs, whose civic representatives were able to wield disproportionate influence when it came to the return of the Clyde Burghs MP. Dumbarton, Renfrew, Rutherglen and Glasgow did not even have very much in common after the 1800s; indeed, each burgh jealously guarded local economic interests against the predatory tendencies of its neighbours. To disentangle this increasingly disharmonious union, reform was therefore the favoured option, especially as it would allow Glaswegians (or rather, an influential body of Glaswegians) to become masters of their own political destiny.

Parliamentary reform was a cause to which Glasgow's elites gradually became committed over the first three decades of the nineteenth century, and by 1830 it was the burgess institutions and the Town Council which were making much of the running to exert pressure on Westminster to support 'a safe, moderate and reasonable amelioration of the system'.[20] Yet the cause of reform was only one very obvious manifestation of changing political priorities within Glasgow at this time. Bound up with the constitutional debate was the thorny question of the role of Church and State, and—in particular—the status of the Established Church of Scotland. This was a relatively new dilemma, which had not hitherto proved to be contentious among civic circles, even although the roots of the controversy stretched back to the early eighteenth century.[21] Prior to 1800 the Town Council had been depicted as a bastion of the Establishment, in order to visibly demonstrate its devotion to the Hanoverian ascendancy; however, by the 1830s, religion was dominating municipal politics, and largely defined allegiances according to support for the Established Church. This conflict of loyalties was a reflection of divisions within the Church itself, where Moderates and Evangelicals were locked in a bitter power struggle over the issue of patronage—that is, the right of congregations to directly elect their ministers.[22] Moreover, there was a practical dimension to civic concern over the dispute, because of the obligation of councillors to serve as patrons of the city's Established churches and appoint a representative Elder to the General Assembly. As religious tensions heightened, and spilled directly into the Parliamentary domain, the municipal authority became a crucial vehicle for furthering the cause of the respective protagonists in the patronage debate.

Although Glasgow's political elites stood solidly by the Establishment throughout the pre-reform era, the increasingly acrimonious patronage dispute began to shift their ideological focus in a qualitatively different direction. Evangelicals, who challenged the prevailing Moderate orthodoxy within the Church, turned their critical scrutiny towards what they perceived as the shortcomings of contemporary society, especially in the urban context. In their quest to restore moral equilibrium, they consciously created the blue-print for an idealised society. The intention was to reconcile the classes by assimilating them into one 'Godly Commonwealth', where faith would ultimately triumph over social and sectarian divisions.[23] Their approach was unequivocally paternalistic, and sought to achieve harmonious integration through a vigorous Christian outreach programme, with especial emphasis on home-visitation and educational improvement among the poor. It was a positive, potent message, which proved enormously popular among the urban middle-classes, particularly during the unsettled political and economic climate following the Napoleonic Wars.[24] Over time, Glasgow's Evangelicals came to manifest missionary zeal towards the regeneration of the city's decaying urban fabric, which symbolised such a blighting and corrosive influence over the community. The notion of the 'common good', which traditionally underpinned civic government in the Scottish burghs, took on a new meaning in this context.[25] If town councillors were expected to exercise a guardianship role in the community—and this was certainly their perceived status in pre-reform Glasgow—then the Evangelical impulse helped to add moral legitimacy to this responsibility.

The sense of self-mission manifested by Church of Scotland Evangelicals was not, of course, unique. There were strong affinities with various revivalist religious movements south of the border, such as Methodism, whose prime rationale was to restore a sense of moral order to a seemingly dislocated society.[26] North of the border, the dissenting Presbyterian denominations—notably the Relief and Secession Churches—shared Evangelical anxieties about community fragmentation and the need for moral regeneration.[27] However, in Glasgow the traditional connection between the Established Church and the Town Council allowed the Evangelicals a direct entry into the political arena, which was not to be opened out to the dissenters until the post-reform era. Evangelicals adopted a typically dualistic attitude towards their political commitment, which combined religious radicalism with an inherently conservative approach to the Church and State connection. Ideological roots ran deep, even in a rapidly changing city like Glasgow, so that for all their vocal criticisms of Moderate inflexibility over the patronage issue, Evangelicals still firmly believed the Church to be a crucial cornerstone of the British constitutional framework. This dogged identification with the Establishment was to characterise an influential body of Glasgow's elites up to the shattering impact of the 1843 Disruption of the Church of Scotland. In terms of practical politics, this meant that allegiances tended overwhelmingly towards Conservatism, as a philosophy which was both dynamic, yet claimed to preserve the integrity of Church and Constitution.

For many among Glasgow's political elites, the charismatic Scottish Evangelical—the Rev. Dr. Thomas Chalmers—came to embody the spiritual side of this ideological coin, while the material side was represented by the Conservative leader, Sir Robert Peel. The liberal economic policies of Peel proved attractive, given the city's commercial and manufacturing base, while his innovative ideas on preventative policing accorded with those of Glasgow's civic leaders, who were anxious to instil a far greater degree of control within the rapidly expanding community—especially in the industrial districts.[29] Control of the community was also a preoccupation of Thomas Chalmers, who had been called to his first Glasgow ministry in 1815, and whose subsequent missionary endeavours among the urban poor of the St. John's parish were to leave a controversial—if lasting—legacy.[30] In 1819 he had been greatly helped in his efforts to secure the St. John's ministry by James Ewing, a leading municipal activist and close personal friend of Kirkman Finlay, who was later to distinguish himself as Lord Provost and MP for the city.[31] As a committed Evangelical and leader of the city's self-styled group of Conservatives, Ewing built up a strong personal following within the Town Council from the 1820s. Significantly, his most enthusiastic supporters tended to be younger men, who had only recently become wealthy in growth areas like textile manufacture, shipping and finance. Ewing's own personal background was mixed; while his substantial fortune derived from Glasgow's eighteenth century West India trade, like many of his peers he was by no means averse to diversifying into new business ventures, including banking and iron manufacture.[32] Yet in more than an economic sense, Ewing straddled the pre- and post-reform eras in Glasgow. His election as MP in the 1832 reform election was indicative of the support he could command outwith the confines of the Merchants' House, and although his Parliamentary career was short-lived, the solid corps of allies which he steadily cultivated during the 1820s was to have a considerable bearing on the future direction of politics in Glasgow during the nineteenth century.[33]

Men like James Burns, James Campbell and Henry Paul belonged to the younger generation of Ewing supporters, and for all that their first forays into municipal service were made during the unreformed era, their impact lingered long after the demise of the self-elected regime.[34] It was this group which played a pivotal role during the political transition period of the early 1830s by rallying the burgess institutions solidly behind the cause of reform, albeit with the proviso that this should be in strict accordance with constitutional principles. By taking the initiative, Lord Provost Ewing and his supporters aimed to deflect attention away from the radical reform movement, and outmanoeuvre more moderate reformers among the Liberal ranks. Moreover, their Evangelical commitment made a loudly-declared virtue out of the political necessity to safeguard the integrity of the British constitution. The apparently ambiguous response of the Ewingites to the reform process prompted an understandably hostile reaction from radicals and Liberals, who made scathing reference to their 'saintly' pretensions.[35] Nevertheless, for all the opposition rhetoric, the sentiments of the well-organised Conservative-Evangelical group struck a chord among many within elite circles in Glasgow, as was clearly evident in the 1832 Parliamentary election, when Ewing easily topped the poll.[36] Similarly, although the 1833 Burgh Reform Act opened out the municipal election process, Conservative-Evangelical supporters continued to be represented within the Town Council, and indeed consolidated their position up to 1843.[37] This is not to underestimate the considerable impact of Liberals and others within the municipal sphere during the immediate post-reform period; on the other hand, the suggestion that in Scotland the 'post-1832 reaction swept the Tories from the towns' begs a number of questions about the complex nature of politics at the time, given the experience of Glasgow.[38] By 1832, the term 'Tory' had long been discredited in the city, while there was no sharp break in terms of the personnel who were able to wield political power.

III

The first open election for Glasgow Town Council took place in November 1833, some ten months after the General Election which had returned Lord Provost Ewing and the moderate Liberal, James Oswald, as the city's MPs. As has been previously indicated, the number of voters within the Parliamentary burgh increased to over 7,000, while almost 5,000 were enfranchised within the more territorially restricted municipal boundaries.[39] With outright entitlement to two MPs, Glasgow now had a direct voice at Westminster, although representation re-mained—overwhelmingly—the preserve of the city's mercantile interests up to 1868.[40] As far as municipal representation was con-cerned, the burgh was divided into electoral wards; five initially, although with the gradual expansion of the city's boundaries and steady increase in the voting population, the number of wards multiplied over time.[41] One important feature of the first election campaign, with long-term ramifications, was the establishment of loosely organised ward committees, which gave voters the opportunity to meet together and decide on suitable candidates to recommend as prospective councillors. Such meetings were held in each of the five wards in 1833; most of them fairly rowdily, as the competing parties struggled for control of the proceedings.[42] There was no party machinery in the modern sense, but the rival camps were well organised and knew precisely their ideological objectives. The result showed, too, that voters were perfectly aware of their candidates' political preferences, with twenty-seven declared Liberal councillors returned out of thirty.[43] Out of fourteen candidates standing from the unreformed Council, only four were returned, including one Liberal.

Nevertheless, despite this auspicious beginning, the overwhelming Liberal domination was a transient phenomenon, and the city's Conservatives speedily began to regain the initiative. It was as if the voters of 1833 had cautioned the old guard not to make assumptions about the loyalties of the new electorate, and that conscious efforts had to be made to win back support. The lesson was taken to heart, and although the Liberals remained electorally unassailable in the city's industrial East End, they could never really be sure of their ground elsewhere. From 1834 the westerly Fifth Ward consistently favoured the Conservatives, due partly to the district's powerful shipping interests, which were a particular source of electoral strength.[44] By 1843, the Liberals managed to fully reassert themselves on the Council, but only because Conservative organisation had broken down over the Disruption of the Church of Scotland, and candidates withdrew from standing in local elections. Until this time, the balance of municipal allegiances was often on a knife-edge, resulting in a dramatic situation after the 1837 elections when both sides were able to claim an even number of Council representatives.[45] The following year the Conservatives were placed in an absolute position to direct affairs, and adopted a far more interventionist approach to municipal government than the short-lived, post-reform Liberal regime.[46] Evangelical influence helped shape priorities as far as the moral dimension was concerned; for instance, Henry Paul moved the Council's first practical temperance initiative in 1839, with the establishment of an *ad hoc* committee to examine the extent of excessive drinking in Glasgow.[47] The Peelite influence was perpetuated, too, with moves in 1841 to co-ordinate the city's policing structure and substantially extend powers of municipal jurisdiction.[48]

The Conservative-Evangelical power-base in Glasgow was considerably bolstered by the continuing influence of the burgess institutions after 1833. Under the terms of the Burgh Reform Act, the respective heads of the Merchants' House and Trades' House—that is, the Dean of Guild and Deacon Convener—were entitled to serve in a civic capacity as *ex-officio* councillors.[49] The two representatives were invariably Conservatives, even after 1843, showing that the traditional allegiance of burgess leaders did not alter substantially in the post-reform era. Their presence on the Council also meant that they were in a pivotal position to hold the balance of power during the period 1837 to 1843, when the Conservative-Evangelical alliance narrowly retained political control. Although the grip of the burgess institutions had thus theoretically been broken by the system of open election under the Burgh Reform Act, their influence remained an important factor in civic affairs. The Act even went so far as to stipulate that a councillor had to be formally enrolled as a burgess before he could take up municipal duties.[50] Up to 1846, unless burgess-ship was hereditary, this meant the payment of appropriate entry fees and the possibility that an elected councillor could be excluded from office because he was not suitably qualified. Indeed, by the end of the nineteenth century burgess-ship was still a legal requirement to become a town councillor, albeit on the basis of token enrolment.[51] Yet although burgess-ship was a requisite to assume civic office, the right to stand as a councillor was restricted to those persons having appropriate voting qualification. Not all Glasgow burgesses fell into this category in 1833, as out of an estimated 800 belonging to the Merchants' House and 3,500 belonging to the trade incorporations, a substantial percentage did not have the vote because of the lower value of property they owned or occupied.[52]

The Burgh Reform Act thus doubly reinforced municipal exclusiveness because of the continuing burgess representation on the Town Council and because of the property requirement of those it enfranchised. Nor did it bring about a shift in the socio-economic status of those who chose to actively participate in the municipal process; indeed, an analysis of the occupational profile of town councillors both before and after 1833 reveals no major differences in the categories represented, although—ironically—the merchants had more of the edge during the immediate post-reform period.[53] The textile industry was especially well represented on the Council, although coal, iron, shipping and finance were also prominent areas of interest, and remained so throughout the nineteenth century. Similarly, Council business remained substantially the same after 1833 as under the closed regime, despite the introduction of several administrative changes by Liberals and Conservatives.[54] On the other hand, the conduct of affairs was given added drama by the politico-religious rivalries of town councillors, especially with the increased representation of dissenting Liberals. Religion was understandably a contentious issue during the 'Ten Years' Conflict' in the Church of Scotland, immediately prior to the Disruption of 1843. Evangelicals continued to exert sustained pressure at the municipal level to alter the basis of Church patronage, in an effort to undermine the system of control within the Established Church. Surprisingly, they were often aided in their efforts by dissenting councillors—not because of any mutual affection between the two groups, but because the dissenters were wholly committed to disestablishment of the Church, and were thus prepared to support moves which would weaken its authority.[55]

Within both Liberal and Conservative groupings on the Town Council there were latterly strong differences of opinion over the religious debate. Thus, the dissenters were opposed by Moderate Churchmen in the Liberal ranks, who were prepared to defend the Establishment. Although the majority of Conservatives had Evangelical sympathies, when it became apparent that some were seriously considering a break with the Establishment over the issue of patronage, there were those— like ex-Lord Provost James Campbell—who refused to go so far as to abandon the Church and State connection.[56] The denouement was finally played out in 1843, when over half the worshippers of the Established Church in Glasgow seceded to form the Free Church of Scotland, under the spiritual direction of Thomas Chalmers.[57] It was testimony to his charisma that so many Glaswegians were prepared to participate in the Disruption, and thereafter the balance of political power was never quite the same again. With a wedge effectively driven between Church and State for the majority of religious adherents, the way was clear for Liberalism to become—unequivocally—the prevailing political orthodoxy in the city. Both at the Parliamentary and municipal level, Conservatives became collectively conspicuous by their absence— certainly, up to 1868.[58] Within the Town Council, the hitherto well-organised Conservative group abruptly stopped competing in elections, although individuals did periodically come forward as candidates. This meant that until the emergence of the Labour Party towards the end of the nineteenth century, political labels were not formally used to describe civic candidates in Glasgow. Over time, councillors came to make a virtue out of their supposedly non-political stance. By appearing to raise the interests of the 'common good' as a priority above partisanship, the civic authority was seen to be acting as a corporate group—in true business-like fashion—and not according to the vagaries of doctrine or ideology.

In more ways than one, the 1840s proved crucial for reshaping political priorities among Glasgow's elites. Thus, although the religious realignment arising from the 1843 Disruption cleared the way for the mid-Victorian ascendancy of Liberalism, administrative developments also influenced the city's political reorientation. In this respect, the expansion of the municipal boundaries in 1846 was especially import-ant. The Extension Act superficially seemed to be a practical measure, with a two-fold objective: firstly, to make the civic entity of Glasgow territorially conterminous with the Parliamentary burgh; secondly, to co-ordinate police jurisdiction under the control of the city's magis-trates.[59] This latter consideration reflected long-standing Peelite concerns over law enforcement in the urban context, and—in partic-ular—the need to combine the multiplicity of Police Boards which prevailed in Glasgow and environs, in order to ensure that they acted in unison. However, although there undoubtedly was a practical ratio-nale behind the proposed amalgamation of police functions, there were also political motivations on the part of the civic leadership. Put simply, the Boards could no longer be trusted to carry out their day-to-day affairs, because the elected Commissioners were deemed insufficiently responsible to hold office.[60] This was a perception rather than the reality, as there is no evidence to suggest any significant shortcomings in Police Board administration; nevertheless, from the 1830s alarm bells had been ringing among elites in Glasgow about the penchant of the electorate to return representatives who seemed to be ideologically suspect. Thus, the Chartist proclivities of certain Glasgow Police Commissioners were one source of worry within municipal circles; so too was the representation of at least one Irish Roman Catholic, at a time when religious sectarianism—though not crudely articulated—strongly underpinned elite attitudes.[61]

This concern was reinforced in the wake of serious unrest in the textile districts surrounding the city in 1837–38, which in turn prompted the Conservative-controlled municipality to attempt Police Board restructuring in 1841.[62] However, the matter was not resolved until 1846, when an administrative solution was achieved under the Liberal regime—albeit with the active encouragement of Peel's Con-servative Government. Under the provisions of the Extension Act, the territorial jurisdiction of the municipality was increased from 2,373 acres to 5,672.[63] Notwithstanding a vocal rearguard action to safeguard their status, the Police Boards of Glasgow, Anderston, Calton and Gorbals were formally dissolved, and their powers transferred wholesale to the Town Council's Police and Statute Labour Committee.[64] Yet despite the intentions of civic leaders, the abolition of the Boards did not mean that the political *status quo* was allowed to prevail undisturbed in the new municipality. If the Police Board administrative structures disappeared, the personnel still remained. Thus, boundary expansion had the effect of shifting the balance of civic representation by bringing in radical councillors from the incorporated districts, notably the industrial East End. Several of the newcomers—such as James Moir, a Gallowgate tea-dealer and former Chartist—had gained their first experience of public service as Police Commissioners.[65] By 1851, eight out of the forty-eight elected councillors could boast previous credentials as representatives to Glasgow Police Board, and their occupational profile was generally much less elevated than that of the mercantile elites who had hitherto dominated at the municipal level, with a particular focus on professionals, shopkeepers and small traders.[66]

The small but significant radical presence on Glasgow Town Council after 1846 was not a new phenomenon. The veteran activist, James Turner of Thrushgrove, had been returned during the first reform election of 1833, as had James Moir's idiosyncratic father-in-law, Robert McGavin.[67] However, political circumstances were qualitatively different in the wake of boundary expansion, given the concentration of the radical presence in the East End. This in turn reflected a growing territorial division between east and west in Glasgow, which became a dominating factor in the city's politics up to the 1890s. Again, perceptions outweighed the reality; Glasgow's residential profile was not so sharply divided between middle-class west and proletarian east as the rhetoric of the radicals liked to imply. On the other hand, by resolving previous uncertainties over policing and jurisdiction, the 1846 Extension Act did allow greater scope for development in the West End, with districts like Kelvingrove, Park and Woodside becoming favoured addresses for Glasgow's wealthier citizens.[68] As the West End grew in social standing, so the East End was seen to decline. A potent symbol of the east's eroding status was the condition of Glasgow Green, which had been promoted as something of a showpiece by the Town Council in the early decades of the century, but which was depicted by the 1850s as the unsavoury refuge of denizens from the adjacent slum quarters.[69] While James Moir led a tireless campaign to effect improvements which would reclaim the territory as the historical focal point for all Glaswegians, East End sensibilities were jolted when moves were made in 1852 by the Town Council to lay out a prestigious West End Park, in the sylvan surroundings of Kelvingrove.[70] The two public spaces eventually came to embody more than just the spirit of the old city and the new; they summed up prevailing political attitudes in Glasgow, which—though broadly accepting the Liberal ethos—were caught increasingly between different class and cultural aspirations.

Religion continued to play an important part in shaping the political divisions which were played out by the competing groups at the municipal level. Despite the power-vacuum created by the withdrawal of the Conservatives from elections in 1843, the Evangelical presence was not muted within the Town Council. Indeed, it gained new impetus from 1845 by the establishment of the Evangelical Alliance—a forum of collaboration among the Presbyterian Churches in Scotland, particularly the Free Church, the Secession and Relief Churches (later the United Presbyterians), and non-seceding Evangelicals from the Established Church.[71] Denominational differences were submerged as the Alliance set about its prime task of rescinding the Government's subsidy to the Royal College of St. Patrick in Maynooth, Ireland, which was a training seminary for priests.[72] Although the campaign was ultimately unsuccessful, the Alliance—as the self-proclaimed protector of Protestantism in Scotland—organised with ruthless precision to win political influence. One of its prime targets was Glasgow Town Council, where a consciously 'moral' agenda was promoted, including issues like temperance reform and Sunday observance.[73] Of course, there was nothing new about the moral dimension, given the previous influence of James Ewing and his supporters; however, the Alliance's broad denominational base and organisational efficiency meant that it managed to make a municipal impact over a relatively short period of time. The extent of its success was demonstrated when two prominent activists, Alexander Hastie and James Anderson, became Lord Provost in 1846 and 1848 respectively.[74] Moreover, Hastie was elected one of Glasgow's two Liberal MPs in 1847—as a United Presbyterian, he was the first non-Established Churchman to represent the city in Parliament.

Understandably, there were those who viewed the rapid rise of the Evangelical Alliance with some alarm. Among this number were the East End radicals, who disliked the paternalistic overtones to Alliance pronouncements, believing them to smack too much of social control. In 1848 Lord Provost Hastie had incurred their particular ire over alleged shortcomings in his role as chief magistrate, when a demonstration in the vicinity of the East End against unemployment and rising food prices developed into a full-scale riot, and three men were shot dead.[75] Significantly, in the municipal elections of that year, James Moir—the erstwhile Police Commissioner—embarked on his long civic career by ignominiously ousting the Lord Provost from his East End seat.[76] Other prominent antagonists included a wealthy group of businessmen, led by Andrew Orr, a wholesale stationer and Chairman of the Glasgow and South Western Railway Company.[77] Although a staunch Liberal, Orr was a stalwart of the Established Church, whose intimate circle of associates included Archibald McLellan—founder of Glasgow's municipal art collection, and a self-confessed, true-blue Tory.[78] Elected Lord Provost in 1854, Orr was unquestionably one of the most astute political manipulators in mid-Victorian Glasgow, and he soon joined forces with the East Enders in an effort to undermine the Alliance power-base, and—more crucially—to build up his own. In this respect, the collaborators were helped considerably by the growing unpopularity of various temperance measures which had been promoted by the Alliance and other like-minded campaigners—notably the 1853 Forbes Mackenzie Act, which consolidated earlier licensing restrictions in Glasgow. Indeed, the temperance debate became a prominent feature of municipal elections in the 1850s, with candidates categorised according to their sympathies for or against more stringent measures to regulate the drinks' trade. Alliance supporters poured out propaganda in their efforts to promote the cause, making special efforts to influence ward committees in areas where the issue was likely to be most contentious.[79]

In response, Orr and his followers made skilful use of the media to challenge the Alliance, establishing a particularly warm relationship with the *Glasgow Herald*. Their efforts bore fruit, as over time there came to be a distinct shift away from the Alliance and the ardent brand of Protestantism it espoused. The trend became particularly clear during the 1857 General Election, where Alexander Hastie—the only sitting MP—faced a bitter onslaught against his Parliamentary record. He was ultimately defeated by a combination of old-fashioned Whiggery and radical Liberalism in the persons of Walter Buchanan and Robert Dalglish, junior; much to the satisfaction of the *Glasgow Herald*, which attributed Hastie's downfall to his 'gloomy and impracticable views as regards the social matters of everyday life'.[80] The populist rhetoric used by Dalglish in the course of the election campaign was also evidence that—in anticipation of further Parliamentary reform—groups like the East Enders were deemed worthy of cultivation by the city's political elites.[81] The lesson was not lost on the militant evangelicals after 1857, in their continuing crusade to instil a sense of moral order into the community, and they began to rethink their strategy to win back electoral support and build up their base among prospective working-class voters.[82] From this time onwards, the temperance issue became the prime focus of evangelical attention, and the Town Council—as the authority which determined municipal licensing policy—came to be the area where the movement felt it could make the most meaningful impact.

The era of the temperance movement's greatest success came in the decade or so following the 1868 Reform Act, although there had already been clear indications that it could wield considerable clout in the municipal sphere. In particular, the defeat of Lord Provost John Blackie, junior, in the 1866 Council elections was largely orchestrated by temperance activists, who still nurtured a sense of grievance over the events of 1857.[83] It has been pervasively asserted that Blackie's unpopularity was the result of a ratepayers' backlash against his ambitious scheme to inaugurate a municipal slum clearance programme, under the auspices of the City Improvement Trust.[84] However, this was only part of a complex story. For the more militant evangelicals, the motivations of the civic leadership had become too much open to question, with individuals like Blackie seeming to blur the line between moral and material interests. It had not passed unnoticed that Blackie had taken over the centrally-located municipal seat vacated by ex-Lord Provost Orr in 1860, or that Orr had a keen personal interest in promoting slum clearance in order to open out the inner-city for railway terminals.[85] This dark side of municipal enterprise jarred with the sense of civic pride which had been carefully fostered by the city fathers during the 1850s, when Orr had referred glowingly to Glasgow's future as 'the perfect model of a great city entirely governing itself'.[86] Orr's lofty objective was greeted with a jaundiced reaction by many within the city, who felt that such pronouncements were simply an expedient to mute criticism and bind a disparate community together. Blackie's deeply held Free Church commitment rendered his motivations even more ambiguous, because of his personal connections with men like Orr and his conscious distancing from the temperance cause.[87]

Despite the doubters, there was certainly cause for the civic leadership to congratulate itself over its achievements after 1846, when boundary expansion opened out new opportunities for developing the city. The West End Park was the initial symbol of Glasgow's municipally-inspired regeneration, notwithstanding the controversy over who precisely would benefit from its location and amenity value. The acquisition of Archibald McLellan's art collection in 1856 was another municipal venture which proved to be of enormous long-term benefit to Glasgow citizens, yet aroused hostile feelings when it was first proposed to spend £44,500 of public money.[88] (McLellan's great friend, Lord Provost Orr, was to the fore in promoting the purchase, while Evangelical Alliance supporters were against.) However, most significant to Glasgow's changing civic image during the mid-Victorian era was the inauguration of the Loch Katrine water supply, which had been approved by Parliament after protracted negotiations in 1855.[89] The prestige of the project was demonstrated four years later, when Queen Victoria formally opened the Water Works in one of the most lavish ceremonials ever staged by the municipality.[90] The subsequent success of Loch Katrine set the standards for the future, because civic enterprise and community well-being became mutually identified. Whatever the sometimes questionable reality behind municipal interventionism—as in the 1866 City Improvement Trust—the urgent need for improvement was generally recognised in Glasgow, not least to restore a sense of order to the decaying urban heartland and reconcile perceived east-west polarities. In this respect, Glasgow's civic rulers showed remarkable adroitness in making a virtue out of sheer social necessity; an ability which reflected their shrewd understanding of power politics, despite their professedly 'non-partisan' stance after 1843.

IV

The extension of the franchise to male householders in 1868 did not, immediately, mean that the balance of political power shifted at either the Parliamentary or municipal level in Glasgow.[91] Despite the re-emergence of Conservative organisation, Liberalism continued to remain the prevailing orthodoxy in the city, with the majority of MPs and councillors identified as adherents to the cause. On the other hand, the various divisions among Liberals intensified, and contributed eventually towards the Unionist split of 1886. Evidence of Liberalism's multi-faceted profile was demonstrated by the entry of candidates after 1868 who consciously designated themselves as representatives of the 'working man', although even then there was by no means a focus for mutual agreement. For instance, James Martin, the forthright 'East End Tribune', represented a brand of libertarian radicalism which was deeply distrustful of government, and—in particular—the power to impose taxation.[92] Municipal enterprise aroused Martin's worst fears, as he believed that the profits were rarely used for the common good, but went into a 'bottomless pit', guarded over by Council bureaucrats.[93] Consequently, Martin was a vocal critic of the municipalisation of Glasgow's gas supply in 1869.[94] George Jackson—a protege of James Moir—represented another strand of Liberalism, which identified closely with Glasgow's emerging trade union movement.[95] As Secretary to Glasgow Trades' Council and later a leading figure in the Glasgow Liberal Working Men's Electoral Union, Jackson cultivated a personal power base which would have projected him into Parliament, but for his untimely death. The temperance evangelicals represented one more dimension to popular Liberalism in the wake of the Reform Act, securing notable victories in the municipal polls of 1868 and 1869, with the return of leading activists like William Collins and James Torrens.[96] Significantly, Jackson and Martin strongly echoed the long-standing sentiments of the East End radicals in their shared antipathy towards the apparent moral pretensions of this group.

There were also continuities with the earlier period as far as the temperance movement was concerned. During the 1840s, it had been able to gain considerable ground in Glasgow because of fears that drink was helping to create pauperism, and was thus draining ratepayers' resources.[97] Some twenty years later the argument was revived, although this time with more positive emphasis. Temperance was depicted as the key to resolving all social problems; accordingly, if the supply of alcohol could be restricted, then there would be less need to raise taxes to pay for policing or welfare services. Prohibition was the ultimate aim of the temperance radicals; a step which many with liberal sensibilities regarded as too much of an intrusion on individual freedom, but which some were prepared to accept as a necessary evil in order to bring cohesion to a seemingly disjointed society.[98] While the moral argument was pitched in the direction of Glasgow's middle-classes, the argument linking temperance with lower taxation was used as a conscious inducement to the 'working man', who was perceived as the main beneficiary of electoral reform. Understandably, the drinks' trade was alerted to the dangers of this populist appeal. In order to stem the attraction of temperance as a panacea to Glasgow's social ills, and above all ensure that the representative 'working man' did not succumb to temperance propaganda, the 'trade'—along with a varied assortment of political allies—attempted to stamp its presence on civic affairs.[99] Thereafter, the trade *versus* temperance confrontation was to profoundly influence the direction of municipal politics in Glasgow, and remained a key issue in elections even after 1900.[100] By this time the 'trade' had constructed a base of financial support, with the help of large brewers and distillers. The funding factor had been a crucial weakness during the early period, which allowed the wealthy backers of the temperance movement to initially take the initiative.[101]

Foremost among the figures who directed the temperance cause at the municipal level was the formidable personality of William Collins— a Free Churchman, who served as the city's first avowed teetotal Lord Provost between 1877 and 1880.[102] Collins' personal background reflected even more continuities with the past, and illustrated how far the city's political elites were able to merge tradition with progressivism during the course of the nineteenth century. His father—also William Collins—had founded the famous publishing firm in 1819, the same year as his close friend, Thomas Chalmers, committed himself to the pastorate of St. John's parish.[103] Indeed, the very first Collins' publication was Chalmers' famous indictment of Scotland's growing urban crisis, *The Christian and Civic Economy of Large Towns.*[104] Collins, senior, also had a high regard for the politics of Sir Robert Peel, and thus exemplified the kind of support the Conservative-Evangelical alliance could depend on in Glasgow up to 1843.[105] However, the events of the Disruption altered the family's political orientation, and Collins, junior, came to describe himself as a progressive Liberal, with strong ideological affinities with Willam Ewart Gladstone. Collins' identification with Gladstone was scarcely surprising, given that the latter's politics have been described as 'a radical conservatism, which fused at times with an advanced liberalism'.[106] Gladstone's enormous popularity in Glasgow—at least up to the 1880s—can be partly explained by this dualistic political approach, which had been such a characteristic of the city's elites since the early decades of the nineteenth century.[107] For all their zealous prohibitionist commitment, therefore, the ascendancy of the Collins group represented no significant generational shift within municipal circles after 1868.

In the aftermath of the Second Reform Act, municipal politics were forced to alter not from the ideological perspective but through the organisation and conduct of elections. The political process was substantially opened out, with an increase in the number of Glasgow's registered voters from 18,000 to 48,000 in 1868.[108] By 1900, in the considerably enlarged municipality, the figure had risen to over 135,000, of whom some seventeen per cent were women voters, under the provisions of the 1881 Municipal Elections Amendment (Scotland) Act.[109] Until boundary reorganisation in the 1890s, the bulk of the new voters tended to be located in the predominantly working-class wards, notably in the city centre and East End. Given their high concentration of spirit shops and public houses, these were precisely the areas that Collins and his circle were anxious to cultivate, and the drinks' trade determined to defend. During the 1870s a highly personalised dimension entered into municipal elections, with the anti-Collins lobby contrasting the fussy paternalism of temperance reformers with the sturdy individualism of 'working men', who did not require to be told what was good for them.[110] This crude class element was extended to Glasgow's territorial divide; in the East End wards, especially, resentment was fuelled at the intrusion of teetotal zealots, who often had comfortable homes in the more salubrious western districts of the city.

Glasgow's Wine, Spirit and Beer Trade Association worked hard to promote its favoured candidates, to the extent that overtures were made to the Irish Catholic community, which had hitherto not been represented at the municipal level.[111] In 1872 the Irishman, James Lynch, was put forward for the central Sixth Ward in an electoral campaign which was conducted in pugnacious fashion, with forthright attacks on the insidious nature of the temperance machine in the municipality.[112] Lynch was ultimately unsuccessful, but the fact that his candidacy was actively encouraged by the Liberal James Martin and the Conservative ex-councillor, Alexander McLaren, reveals that curious alliances had come to be formed against the teetotal caucus.[113]

Collins' fifteen year municipal career marked the spectacular rise of the temperance party as a municipal force in Glasgow. The temperance philosophy accorded well with prevailing middle-class values in the city, at a time when salvation was being promoted through a positive agenda of moral regeneration.[114] The mood of revivalism was most energetically articulated in 1874, when the American evangelists—Dwight Moody and Ira Sankey—spread their gospel message to rapturous middle-class audiences, including not a few town councillors.[115] Pure water was a particularly potent symbol of the crusade to cleanse and reinvigorate urban society. In 1872, the inauguration of the Loch Katrine Memorial Fountain as a central feature of the West End Park represented more than just a celebration of past municipal achievement; it was an affirmation of the civic leadership's determination to create a more open, healthy and wholesome society.[116] Yet the revivalist momentum was not to be sustained among Glasgow's middle-classes and with it went the moral base which had given the temperance movement so much of its legitimacy during the 1870s. In this context, the 1878 City of Glasgow Bank crash had a profoundly destabilising effect on perceptions of urban progress, notwithstanding the leadership role of Lord Provost Collins during the crisis.[117] The subsequent conviction of the Bank Directors on charges of fraud and embezzlement undermined public confidence in the authority of the city's elites, especially as two of the accused were former municipal representatives.[118] The 1880s therefore marked a shift away from the overtly moral agenda in civic affairs, despite the continuing presence of the temperance evangelicals on the Town Council.[119] A new sense of realism had come to prevail about the nature and function of the city's government, especially as economic circumstances were not so buoyant as before 1878. To restore faith in the city—and bring in much-needed ratepayers' revenue—the focus of Council endeavours came to be the pursuit of the significantly enlarged municipality, incorporating a plethora of outlying residential districts. Once again, the force of changing circumstances was turned to electoral advantage by the civic leadership, as the image of 'Greater Glasgow' was steadily cultivated.

The objective of the 'Greater Glasgow' was by no means new. As far back as 1856, Lord Provost Orr had spoken of the desirability of incorporating populous areas in close proximity to Glasgow, notably the rising shipbuilding communities of Govan and Partick.[120] A determined campaign was launched at the time of discussions over the Second Reform Bill, which aimed to expand Glasgow's jurisdiction substantially.[121] The increasing preference of the middle-classes to reside outwith the municipality—in more amenable surroundings, where rates were lower—caused concern among the civic leadership, who saw this as financially draining to the inner-city and conducive to even more class polarisation. However, political considerations were a major factor in thwarting moves to extend Glasgow's boundaries during the 1860s and 1870s. According to an influential body of Liberal opinion, the balance of Parliamentary representation between the burgh and county constituencies would become too disturbed if Glasgow was allowed jurisdiction over populous surrounding districts, and the counties would thus become an easy target for revitalised Conservative organisation.[122] Despite small territorial gains, therefore, Glasgow's boundaries remained largely unaltered after 1846, with the result that the social and industrial changes overwhelming the city by the 1880s had rendered the physical structure of the municipality obsolete. The distribution of population within the sixteen wards had become particularly skewed, and there were considerable fluctuations in terms of the number of voters. Thus, in 1886 the Second Ward (located in the East End) had 9,211 electors, while the Seventh Ward (in the central business district) had 1,594 electors.[123] With an equal number of three councillors allocated to each ward, there were understandably grievances about the balance of representation, with wealthy residential and business districts being unduly favoured. The quest for the 'Greater Glasgow' was therefore set in the context of this increasingly undemocratic municipal profile, although—ironically—the proposed addition of wealthy outlying districts like Kelvinside and Pollokshields clearly muted the impact of any ward restructuring within the old city.

The 'Greater Glasgow' became the priority of the civic leadership during the 1880s, and much energy was channelled into presenting the best possible case for the city. Directing the campaign was James D. Marwick, Glasgow's Town Clerk, who had the distinction of being the highest-paid local government official in the United Kingdom, and who was certainly indispensable as far as the city's legal and administrative affairs were concerned.[124] Marwick represented a long line of shrewd and strong-minded public servants in Glasgow, including figures like James Cleland, James Reddie and John Burnet, who even during the pre-reform era had done much to build up the civic bureaucracy.[125] All were astute publicists for the city, whether in the sphere of finance, policing or public utilities, like water and gas. True to this tradition, Marwick promoted the virtues of the 'Greater Glasgow' with a missionary fervour as zealous as that of the temperance campaigners (whose views he did not endorse). When Parliament set up a Boundary Commission in 1887, Marwick vigorously presented the case for Glasgow, arguing that, firstly, the suburban residents had gained an unfair advantage from civic amenities like parks and galleries, as there was no rates' burden; secondly, the inner-city was declining at the expense of the outlying districts, which were making no contribution to its improvement; and thirdly, policing and environmental health arrangements would be better co-ordinated under the central control of Glasgow.[126] Of course, there was nothing substantially new in Marwick's approach, but it was enough to convince the Commissioners in 1888 that '. . . the City of Glasgow should be extended so as to include the whole continuous urban area'.[127] The 'Greater Glasgow' was thus achieved with much civic celebration in 1891, and the city's territorial expanse more than doubled to 11,861 acres.[128] The annexed districts had an overwhelmingly middle-class residential profile, and did not include Govan and Partick, which still jealously guarded their autonomy until they became part of an even 'Greater Glasgow' in 1912.[129]

The movement towards the city's consolidation established a formidable public relations machine within the civic administration, which was to flourish for the remainder of the nineteenth century. Much as Lord Provost Orr had predicted, Glasgow came to be depicted as the model of civic excellence, and in 1888 the opening of the new City Chambers and the successful inauguration of the first International Exhibition did much to impress the municipal presence on the public consciousness.[130] The following year, Albert Shaw—an American analyst of urban government—wrote glowingly of Glasgow in the *Political Science Quarterly*, and thereafter held up the Scottish city as a guiding light to his fellow countrymen.[131] For their part, Glasgow's civic representatives were highly flattered by the attention of outsiders like Shaw, and assiduously fuelled the notion that the city held prime position in the international league table of municipal government. Indeed, when an American magazine claimed in 1890 that Birmingham was the best-administered city in the world, Glaswegians responded with a mixture of scepticism and amusement, as if to demonstrate their own superior wisdom.[132] In an editorial, the *Glasgow Herald* put Birmingham firmly in its place by suggesting that the Midlands city was merely 'a mushroom in comparison with the venerable Corporation of the Clyde', while the description of Birmingham as 'a business city, run by business men, on business principles', elicited the curt response that, 'Glasgow is about as business-like a city as is to be found in the three kingdoms'.[133] Yet while useful for fostering a sense of unity and civic pride, the Glasgow-Birmingham connection was also significant in the political context. This was because an influential body of municipal activists in Glasgow had come to hold a particularly high regard for the ideas of Joseph Chamberlain, three times Mayor of Birmingham, erstwhile rising star of the radical Liberals, and leader of the Unionist breakaway arising from the Irish Home Rule crisis of 1886.[134]

Chamberlain firmly believed that the municipality was an organically developing entity, with roots in localism, but that larger administrative units were necessary to serve the needs of the wider community.[135] His views would have struck a chord with many Glasgow councillors even during the pre-reform era, as they attempted to overcome the constraints of the burgh constitution and open out the city's government. However, the Chamberlainite ethos had especial appeal during the 1880s, and it was not without significance that many of the leading architects of the annexationist strategy within the Town Council became adherents to the Unionist cause, including Town Clerk Marwick.[136] Of course, there was a complex variety of reasons why so many Glasgow councillors severed their connection with Gladstonian Liberalism after 1886, not least the continuing high profile of evangelicals within the party. Their emphasis on issues like temperance and Church disestablishment were particularly alienating, as they were seen to be too much out of step with the more secular climate of the times.[137] Moreover, the tendency for fragmentation among the Liberal ranks had long been apparent in Glasgow, and so 1886 represented the culmination of a gradually accumulating process. Accordingly, between 1886 and 1891 declared Unionists made up approximately a quarter of the fifty civic representatives, while committed Liberals comprised around thirty-one per cent and Conservatives almost eighteen per cent.[138] There was also a significant group of Liberal 'waverers', who could never quite bring themselves to join the Unionists, but remained unpredictable in their allegiances.[139] After the Unionist split, the balance in favour of Liberalism was tenuous, despite the party's seeming numerical domination. Until 1899, no Liberal was successfully elected as Lord Provost; a highly revealing phenomenon, as it was during this time that Glasgow's reputation for civic excellence was firmly established.[139] Not that too much should be construed from these political labels, as Glasgow—unlike Birmingham—did not operate a party machine in local government. For all their sometimes bitter differences, councillors adhered to the tradition established during the 1840s, and remained ostensibly non-partisan.

Nevertheless, the origins of Glasgow's reputation as the bastion of 'municipal socialism' must be placed firmly in the 1880s and attributed firmly to the Unionists. The first town councillor to talk consistently of the 'municipal socialist' ideal at this time was Robert Crawford, who remained an unswerving adherent to the Chamberlainite cause until his death in 1915.[140] Like his mentor, Crawford had been an outspoken radical in his pre-Unionist days, and encouraged a generation of political activists, including Robert Bontine Cunninghame Graham, co-founder of the Scottish Labour Party.[141] Crawford also came to be known as one of Glasgow's most forward looking councillors; it was his original idea in 1891 to establish the People's Palace on Glasgow Green, and he was a guiding force in the municipalisation of the tramways, also approved that year.[142] However, a highly revealing assessment was made of Crawford in his obituary, which stated, '. . . though he was essentially a democrat, he was 'on the large' (to use a phrase much used by him in a spirit of humour) conservative'.[143] The strand of conservative-progressivism which ran through Glasgow's nineteenth century civic history was thus present, in a qualitatively different way, among the Unionists. Even the use of the term 'municipal socialism' was highly ambiguous, despite its value-laden overtones. Crawford was making the 'socialist' connection at a time when the Labour presence on the Town Council was negligible, and was thus displaying a populist edge to his politics typical of the Chamberlainites. Essentially, Crawford was attempting to woo both the working-class and the middle-class by implying that municipal policy in Glasgow represented socialism, but of an eminently safe and responsible variety.

The fact that a comprehensive ward distribution did not take place until 1896, under the requirements of the 1891 Annexation Act, also meant that Crawford could speak from a position of electoral security, as the basis of representation remained grossly weighted against voters in working-class districts. This imbalance was distorted even further during the five years after 1891, with the addition of highly-rated but sparsely populated areas like Kelvinside, which under generous 'no detriment' provisions had initially been allowed three councillors with a total electorate of less than 700.[144] At the same time, nearly forty per cent of Glasgow's voters were concentrated in the six working-class wards of the city centre and East End, yet returned less than a quarter of the councillors.[145] The broad implications of all this are not difficult to determine. Up to 1896, civic control remained firmly in the hands of what Albert Shaw admiringly described as 'the best elements of business life', under whose guidance there was room for even Robert Crawford's brand of 'municipal socialism'.[146] The remarkable unanimity among councillors of all political persuasions over various municipalising decisions—notably electricity (1890) and the tramways (1891)—can be partly understood in this context.[147] In both cases, there had been no meaningful ideological debate about the respective merits of public monopoly and private enterprise; to most councillors it was simply a question of maximum efficiency under effective management at the best possible economic rates, which unquestionably made good business sense.[148]

The so-called 'General Election' of 1896, whereby all seats were contested in the twenty-five newly-delineated wards, was something of a watershed for Glasgow's civic politics. Of course, this has to be set in perspective, as many of the personalities from the old administration returned to the City Chambers and there was no immediate shift in the balance of power.[149] Yet despite a number of continuities, one feature of the 1896 election was to have a considerable impact on the direction of civic affairs in the twentieth century. Most crucially, the Trades' Council Municipal Elections Committee had been working diligently to bring together a broad alliance to contest elections under the Labour platform—a strategy which bore fruit when nine so-called 'Stalwarts' were returned as councillors.[150] The emergence of the Stalwarts and their impact on the fledgling Labour Party in Glasgow has been well-documented elsewhere; suffice it to say that in the longer term, the Stalwart victories brought an overtly political dimension to the election process, and—despite its narrow power-base—made Labour very much a disturbing influence in the municipal sphere.[151] By promoting a programme of measures with a directly populist appeal, the Stalwarts claimed 'municipal socialism' as their own; a strategy which was immediately seized upon by opponents, who—in a rapid *volte-face*—began to impute dangerously subversive overtones to the term.[152] This was a sign that Stalwart successes had placed the civic leadership uncomfortably on the defensive, particularly as the steady expansion of the electorate since 1868 had introduced a far more competitive dimension in the municipal sphere. By the 1900s, the city's elites could no longer be sure of their ground, as the rise of Labour had shown that a substantial number of working-class voters had forthrightly nailed their colours to the political mast, and were no longer prepared to compromise. Accordingly, while many individual interest groups lingered on into the twentieth century—including the temperance campaigners, drinks' trade defenders, Chamberlainites and East End radicals—the old priorities became less relevant as municipal allegiances polarised starkly along Labour and anti-Labour lines.[153]

V

This chapter has endeavoured to show that strong continuities under-pinned the political profile of Glasgow's civic elites during the nineteenth century, despite the appearance of radical changes after the implementation of reforming policies. Indeed, it can be realistically claimed that the years 1843 (marking the Disruption of the Church of Scotland) and 1886 (marking the Unionist split in the Liberal Party) were far more pivotal in terms of fundamentally altering the political preferences of Glaswegians than the legislative turning points of the First and Second Reform Acts. Not that Glasgow's governing classes constituted a wholly homogeneous entity, as they were frequently divided among themselves, even those declaring the same party allegiances. There were also those who made repeated attempts at cross-class collaboration, usually to protect or promote their own interests, and with varying degrees of success. However, as this discussion has emphasised, Glasgow's municipal representatives were able to retain much of the initiative by anticipating the mood of reform and consciously cultivating those most likely to be the beneficiaries of any opening out of the electoral process. The city's elites were—if any-thing—dynamic in their approach, and prepared to adapt to the dramatic changes which characterised the city throughout the nine-teenth century. It was only latterly that this dynamism began to slow down, and a much more defensive stance was adopted towards an assortment of political challenges, not least the rise of independent labour.

REFERENCES

1. Despite an abundance of source material, Scotland has generally not been well served for nineteenth century urban history, especially in comparison with cities south of the border, like Birmingham and Manchester. The forthcoming three

volume *History of Glasgow,* covering the period 1660 to the present and published—ironically—by Manchester University Press, should remedy some of these deficiencies.

2. See, for instance, Sir James Bell and James Paton, *Glasgow: Its Municipal Organisation and Administration,* (Glasgow, 1896), pp.52–4, for an articulation of this view.

3. Glasgow's late nineteenth century reputation for civic efficiency is discussed in W. Hamish Fraser, 'From Civic Gospel to Municipal Socialism', in Derek Fraser (ed.), *Cities, Class and Communication: Essays in Honour of Asa Briggs,* (Hemel Hempstead, 1990), pp.58–80; Bernard Aspinwall, *Portable Utopia: Glasgow and the United States, 1820–1920,* (Aberdeen, 1984), pp.151–84; and Irene Sweeney, *The Municipal Administration of Glasgow, 1833–1912 Public Service and the Scottish Civic Identity,* (unpublished Ph.D thesis, Strathclyde University, 1990), pp.426–67.

4. Peter Mackenzie, radical journalist of the reform era in Glasgow, had much to do with cultivating the notorious image of the Town Council prior to 1833. See Mackenzie, *Old Reminiscences of Glasgow and the West of Scotland,* (Glasgow, 1890; first published 1865), volume II, especially pages 182–99. His views are clearly perpetuated in George Eyre Todd, *History of Glasgow, Volume III: From the Revolution to the Reform Acts,* (Glasgow, 1934), pp.478–87, and David Daiches, *Glasgow,* (London, 1982; first published 1977), pp.133–41.

5. Henry Cockburn, *Memorials of His Time, 1779–1830,* (Edinburgh, 1910; first published 1856), pp.90–1.

6. *Report from the Select Committee into the Royal Burghs of Scotland,* pp., VI, 1819, pp.4–26.

7. James Cleland, *A Description of the Manner of Improving the Green of Glasgow, of Raising Water for the Supply of Public Buildings for the City, &c., &c.,* (Glasgow, 1813).

8. Theodora Pagan, *The Convention of the Burghs of Scotland,* (Glasgow, 1926), pp.75–6.

9. Under Article XXI. See Geoffrey W. Iredell, *The Lyon Enchained: A Study of the 1707 Act of Union,* (Glasgow, 1960), p.98.

10. Robert Renwick (ed.), *Extracts from the Records of the Burgh of Glasgow, VIII, 1781–95,* (Glasgow, 1913), pp.160–61.

11. Until 1846, exclusive trading privileges prevailed in Glasgow, whereby burgess enrolment was a requirement to conduct business within the burgh boundaries. However, given the city's rapid growth and economic success, such a prerequisite was becoming increasingly anachronistic even during the early decades of the nineteenth century. Burgess membership therefore became a mark of social rather than occupational status, and many trades' burgesses ultimately did not practise the craft they adhered to within the Trades' House.

12. Sweeney, *Municipal Administration,* pp.16–7.

13. In an effort not to undermine the city's developing status as a trading and commercial centre in the eighteenth century, close connections were forged with influential Government figures—notably Archibald Campbell, later third Duke of Argyll—who were prepared to promote Glaswegian interests at Westminster in return for control of the Clyde Burghs Parliamentary constituency.

14. J. Cunnison and J.B.S. Gilfillan (eds.), *The Third Statistical Account of Scotland: Glasgow,* (Glasgow, 1958), p.799; T.M. Devine, 'Urbanisation', in T.M. Devine and Rosalind Mitchison (eds.), *People and Society in Scotland: Volume I, 1760–1830,* (Edinburgh, 1988), p.35.

15. A.K. Chalmers, *The Health of Glasgow, 1818–1925,* (Glasgow, 1930), p.3.

16. John Strang, *Glasgow and Its Clubs; or, Glimpses of the Condition, Manners, Characters, and Oddities of the City, during the Past and Present Century,* (London, 1856), pp.533–5.

17. Robert Renwick (ed.), *Extracts from the Records of the Burgh of Glasgow, X, 1809–1822,* (Glasgow, 1915), p.489.

18. See Strang, *Glasgow and Its Clubs,* pp.523–41. As the Liberal Strang put it, (p.523),

Glasgow pre-reform ". . . may be justly said to be the very beau ideal of Conservatism".

19.   *Scots Times*, 24th August 1830.
20.   *Ibid.*, 16th October 1830. The speaker was Dean of Guild, James Ewing.
21.   Callum Brown, *The Social History of Religion in Scotland since 1730*, (London, 1987), pp.29–30.
22.   *Ibid.*, p.32.
23.   Stewart J. Brown, *Thomas Chalmers and the Godly Commonwealth in Scotland*, (Oxford, 1982), pp.81–2 and 111–2.
24.   L.J. Saunders, *Scottish Democracy, 1815–1840: The Social and Intellectual Background*, (Edinburgh, 1950), pp.210–3.
25.   The 'common good' is discussed in Mabel Atkinson, *Local Government in Scotland*, (Edinburgh and London, 1904), pp.288–91. Technically the term describes the community assets of a burgh, but it came to be a useful general term for community well-being in the municipal context.
26.   Brown, *Social History of Religion*, p.141.
27.   *Ibid.* p.142.
28.   Sweeney, *Municipal Administration*, p.49.
29.   *Ibid.*, pp.96–7.
30.   Brown, *Social History of Religion*, p.144.
31.   Brown, *Thomas Chalmers*, pp.122–4.
32.   For biographical information on Ewing, see J.M. Reid, *The History of the Merchants' House of Glasgow*, (Glasgow, not dated, but c. 1967), pp.38–40, and James Gourlay, *The Provosts of Glasgow from 1609 to 1832*, (Glasgow, 1942), pp.135–6.
33.   Ewing fell out of favour with the Glasgow Parliamentary electorate because he had supported the King's dismissal of the Whig ministry in 1834.
34.   For brief biographical information about Burns, Campbell and Paul, see Sweeney, *Municipal Administration*, pp.866–7, 869–70 and 949.
35.   *Ibid.*, p.48.
36.   Ewing received 3,214 votes, to Oswald's 2,838. J. Vincent and M. Stenton (eds.), *McCalmont's Parliamentary Poll Book: British Election Results, 1832–1918*, (Brighton, 1971), p.119.
37.   Sweeney, *Municipal Administration*, p.41.
38.   Morris, 'Urbanisation and Scotland', in W. Hamish Fraser and R.J. Morris (eds.), *People and Society in Scotland: Volume II, 1830–1914*, (Edinburgh, 1990), p.95.
39.   There is some dubiety about the precise number of voters, both at the municipal and Parliamentary level. The *Glasgow Herald* of 28th October 1833 cites 4,821 for the municipal figures, while 6,994 is the figure given for Parliamentary voters in Vincent and Stenton, *McCalmont's Parliamentary Poll Book*, p.119. However, the figures of 5,506 and 8,783 are cited in Cunison and Gilfillan, *Third Statistical Account: Glasgow*, p.423.
40.   Pre-1868 MPs like John Dennistoun, Robert Dalglish, James Ewing, Alexander Hastie and James Oswald all had close connections with the Merchants' House.
41.   After boundary expansion in 1846, sixteen wards were created. Adjustments were made to the territory of the wards after 1868, but it was not until 1891 when the number of wards increased to twenty-five.
42.   See, for instance, the *Glasgow Argus*, 31st October 1833, for an evocation of the rowdy proceedings of ward meetings.
43.   The allegiances of all the candidates are identified in the *Reformers' Gazette*, 2nd November 1833.
44.   Sweeney, *Municipal Administration*, p.41.
45.   Peter Mackenzie, *Old Reminiscences of Glasgow and the West of Scotland*, volume III, (Glasgow, 1868), pp.432–9.
46.   Sweeney, *Municipal Administration*, pp.66–9.

47. *Glasgow Herald*, 23rd March 1838.
48. *Ibid.*, 15th September 1841.
49. George Crawfurd, *A Sketch of the Rise and Progress of the Trades' House of Glasgow: Its Constitution, Funds, and Bye-Laws*, (Glasgow, 1858), pages 116–7.
50. According to section XXII of the Burgh Reform Act.
51. Bell and Paton, *Glasgow*, p.70.
52. *Glasgow Herald*, 12th April 1833.
53. Sweeney, *Municipal Administration*, pp.36–8.
54. *Ibid.*, pp.62–5.
55. Callum Brown, *Religion and the Development of an Urban Society: Glasgow, 1780–1914*, (unpublished Ph.D thesis, Glasgow University, 1981), pp.220–2.
56. James Maclehose (publisher), *Memoirs and Portraits of One Hundred Glasgow Men*, volume I, (Glasgow, 1886), p.72.
57. Brown, *Social History of Religion*, p.133.
58. I.G.C. Hutcheson, *A Political History of Scotland, 1832–1924: Parties, Elections and Issues*, (Edinburgh, 1986), pp.84–91.
59. Sweeney, *Municipal Administration*, pp.121–2.
60. *Ibid.*, pp.113–20.
61. The identified Irish Roman Catholic was John O'Neil, a pawnbroker to trade. See ibid., pp.791–4, for a discussion of his political career in Glasgow.
62. W. Hamish Fraser, *Conflict and Class: Scottish Workers, 1700–1838*, (Edinburgh, 1988), pp.153–8.
63. Bell and Paton, *Glasgow*, p.26.
64. *Ibid.*, pp.114–5. Understandably, the reasons for the Boards' abolition are made to appear much more positive in this context.
65. I.G.C. Hutcheson, 'Glasgow Working Class Politics', in R.A. Cage (ed.), *The Working Class in Glasgow, 1750–1914*, (London, 1987), p.106.
66. Sweeney, *Municipal Administration*, p.709.
67. For brief biographical information on Turner and McGavin, see ibid., pp.924 and 973.
68. M.A. Simpson, 'The West End of Glasgow, 1830–1914', in M.A. Simpson and T.H. Lloyd (eds.), *Middle Class Housing in Britain*, (Newton Abbot, 1977), pp.55–67.
69. Hugh Macdonald, *Rambles Round Glasgow: Descriptive, Historical, Traditional*, (Glasgow, 1910; first published 1854), pp.5–6.
70. Duncan McLellan, *Glasgow Public Parks*, (Glasgow, 1894), pp.41–2.
71. Hutcheson, *Political History of Scotland*, pp.62–3.
72. *Glasgow Herald*, 18th April 1845.
73. Sweeney, *Municipal Administration*, pp.597–8.
74. John Tweed (publisher), *Biographical Sketches of the Hon. the Lord Provosts of Glasgow, 1833–1883, with Appendix*, (Glasgow, 1883), pp.102–6 and 129–31.
75. For two retrospective eye-witness accounts of the riot, see Alexander Smith, *A Summer in Skye*, (Edinburgh, 1907; first published 1856), pp.522–8; and John Urie, *Reminiscences of Eighty Years*, (Paisley, 1908), pp.62–73.
76. *Glasgow Herald*, 10th November 1848.
77. For biographical information on Orr, see Tweed, *Lord Provosts*, pp.169–72, and Maclehose, *100 Glasgow Men*, volume II, pp.253–4.
78. Orr's relationship with McLellan is discussed in detail in Sweeney, *Municipal Administration*, pp.269–80.
79. Glasgow's civic politics during the 1850s are lampooned in Anonymous, *The Chronicles of Gotham: or, the Facetious History of Official Proceedings*, (Glasgow, 1856). See especially pp.93–7 for an account of efforts to rally temperance support in the working-class Cowcaddens area. The *Glasgow Herald*, 5th November 1855, puts the account into clearer perspective.

80. *Ibid.*, 1st April 1857.
81. J.S. Jeans, *Western Worthies: A Gallery of Biographical and Critical Sketches of West of Scotland Celebrities*, (Glasgow, 1872), p.38.
82. Sweeney, *Municipal Administration*, p.605.
83. *Ibid.*, pp.302–24.
84. Bell and Paton, *Glasgow*, p.222.
85. Sweeney, *Municipal Administration*, pp.291–3; John R. Kellett, *Railways and Victorian Cities*, (London, 1979), pp.222–4.
86. *Glasgow Herald*, 10th October 1856.
87. Tweed, *Lord Provosts*, pp.237–40.
88. *Glasgow Herald*, 16th May 1856.
89. Sir James D. Marwick, *Glasgow: the Water Supply of the City from the Earliest Period of Record, with Notes on Various Developments of the City till the Close of 1900*, (Glasgow, 1901), pp.133–9.
90. *Glasgow Herald*, 15th October 1859.
91. Under the terms of the Scottish version of the Second Reform Act and the Municipal Elections Amendment (Scotland) Act, both 1868.
92. See Anonymous, *The Life of the Late Bailie James Martin ('Oor Jeems')*, (not dated, but c. 1892).
93. *Ibid.*, p.24.
94. Glasgow Town Council, *Minutes*, 7th January 1869, pp.426–8, Strathclyde Regional Archives, Cl.1.69.
95. Hutcheson, *Working Class Politics*, pp.108–9.
96. For Torrens' background, see P.T. Winskill, *The Temperance Movement and its Workers*, volume III, (Glasgow & Edinburgh, 1892), pp.97–8.
97. Daniel C. Paton, *Drink and the Temperance Movement in Nineteenth Century Scotland*, (unpublished Ph.D thesis, Edinburgh University, 1976), p.163.
98. Sweeney, *Municipal Administration*, pp.608–9.
99. Norma D. Logan, *Drink and Society in Scotland, 1870–1914*, (unpublished Ph.D thesis, Glasgow University, 1983), pp.373–407.
100. Irene Sweeney, 'Local Party Politics and the Temperance Crusade: Glasgow, 1890–1902', in *Journal of the Scottish Labour History Society*, (27, 1992), pp.44–63.
101. *Ibid.*, p.46.
102. David Keir, *The House of Collins: The Story of a Scottish Family of Publishers from 1789 to the Present Day*, (London, 1952), pp.158–96.
103. *Ibid.*, pp.26–42.
104. *Ibid.*, p.41.
105. *Ibid.*, pp.116–117.
106. H.C.G. Matthew, *Gladstone, 1809–1874*, (Oxford, 1986), p.1.
107. For an impression of Gladstone's appeal in nineteenth century Glasgow, see James Nicol, *Gladstone in Glasgow; Addresses of the Rt. Hon. William Ewart Gladstone when Installed an Honorary Burgess of the City and Lord Rector of the University, together with Glasgow's Appreciation of his Statesmanship and Service*, (Glasgow, 1902).
108. Hutcheson, *Political History of Scotland*, p.132.
109. Glasgow Corporation, *Diaries*, (1900–01), Strathclyde Regional Archives, D-TC 8 1–26.
110. Sweeney, 'Local Party Politics', pp.45–6.
111. Sweeney, *Municipal Administration*, pp.787–802.
112. *Glasgow Herald*, 5th November 1872.
113. *Ibid.*, 28th November 1872.
114. Brown, *Social History of Religion*, pp.138–9.
115. Sweeney, *Municipal Administration*, pp.622–3.
116. *Glasgow Herald*, 15th August 1872.
117. Keir, *House of Collins*, pp.190–3.

118. S.G. Checkland, *Scottish Banking: A History, 1695–1973*, (Glasgow & London, 1975), pp.471–81. The two former municipal representatives were John Stewart and William Taylor.
119. Indeed, the temperance evangelicals were to survive on Glasgow Corporation until the 1920s, albeit in substantially depleted numbers.
120. *Glasgow Herald*, 10th October 1856.
121. Sweeney, *Municipal Administration*, pp.135–46.
122. *Ibid.*, p.140.
123. James Nicol, *Vital, Social and Economic Statistics of the City of Glasgow, 1885–91, with Observations Thereon*, (Glasgow, 1891), p.90.
124. See John Gray McKendrick, *Memoir of Sir James David Marwick, 1826–1908*, (Glasgow, 1909).
125. For Cleland (Superintendent of Public Works), see 'James Cleland, LL.D (1770–1840): the Distinguished Statist', in *Glasgow Chamber of Commerce Journal*, (July, 1971), pp.288–91; for Town Clerk Reddie, see George Blair, *Biographical and Descriptive Sketches of the Glasgow Necropolis*, (Glasgow, 1857), pp.143–8; for Burnet (Clerk to the Water Commissioners), see John Lindsay, *Review of Municipal Government in Glasgow: A Lecture Delivered under the Auspices of the Old Glasgow Club on 15th December 1909*, (Glasgow, 1909), pp.18–9.
126. *Glasgow Boundaries Commission, 1888: Report of the Glasgow Boundary Commissioners, Volume I, with Appendix*, (Cd. 5382), PP., XLVI.1, 1888, pp.46–8.
127. *Ibid.*, p.xlix.
128. Bell and Paton, *Glasgow*, p.27.
129. Sweeney, *Municipal Administration*, pp.191–3.
130. For the opening of the City Chambers, see the *Glasgow Herald*, 23rd August 1888; for the 1888 International Exhibition, see Perilla and Juliet Kinchin, *Glasgow's Great Exhibitions: 1888; 1901; 1911; 1938; 1988*, (Bicester, 1988), pp.17–53.
131. Albert Shaw, 'Municipal Government in Great Britain', in the *Political Science Quarterly*, (IV, 1889), pp.197–229.
132. *Glasgow Herald*, 27th May 1890.
133. *Ibid.*
134. Michael Balfour, *Britain and Joseph Chamberlain*, (London, 1985), especially pp.78–9.
135. As articulated in Chamberlain's 'Radical Scotland' speech, made in Glasgow during 1885. See the *Glasgow Herald*, 16th September 1885.
136. Sweeney, *Municipal Administration*, p.178.
137. Sweeney, 'Local Party Politics', pp.48–9.
138. Sweeney, *Municipal Administration*, p.435.
139. Glasgow's Lord Provosts from 1883 to 1899 were: Sir William McOnie, Conservative; Sir James King, Conservative; Sir John Muir, Unionist; Sir James Bell, Unionist; Sir David Richmond, Unionist.
140. Sweeney, *Municipal Administration*, p.428.
141. Both Crawford and Cunninghame Graham were in prominent attendance when Chamberlain delivered his 'Radical Scotland' speech in 1885.
142. For biographical information about Crawford, see the *Glasgow Echo*, 13th January 1894. See also, Robert Crawford, *The People's Palace of the Arts for the City of Glasgow*, (Glasgow, 1891).
143. *Glasgow News*, 8th March 1915.
144. Sweeney, *Municipal Administration*, p.438.
145. *Ibid.*
146. Albert Shaw, *Municipal Government in Great Britain*, (London, 1895), p.53.
147. The decision to municipalise the tramways was taken in 1890 and 1891 respectively, but not implemented until 1893 and 1894.
148. The business reaction against 'municipal socialism' was a feature of the late

1890s and 1900s. See Richard Roberts, 'Businessmen, Politics and Municipal Socialism', in John Turner (ed.), *Businessmen and Politics: Studies of Business Activity in British Politics, 1900–1945*, (London, 1984), pp.20–32.

149. Sweeney, *Municipal Administration*, p.438, gives a breakdown of political allegiances on the Council immediately before and after the 1896 election.

150. It should be stressed that the Stalwarts were initially a broad alliance, and that not all councillors were ILPers. For instance, the Irish Nationalist leader, John Ferguson, was prominent among this group.

151. See, for instance, W. Hamish Fraser, 'Labour and the Changing City', in George Gordon (ed.), *Perspectives of the Scottish City*, (Aberdeen, 1985), and James J. Smyth, 'The ILP in Glasgow, 1888–1906: the Struggle for Identity', in Alan McKinlay and R.J. Morris (eds.), *The ILP on Clydeside, 1983–1932: from Foundation to Disintegration*, (Manchester, 1991), pp.20–55.

152. Sweeney, *Municipal Administration*, p.444.

6

The Nobility and Politics in Scotland, c1880–1939

I. G. C. Hutchison

It has long been established that despite the first and second Reform Acts, the peerage continued to give considerable influence over the personnel of the House of Commons. The most direct method was by exercising patronage rights over certain seats; the other aspect was the presence as M.P.s of members of noble families. On both counts, there is evidence for aristocratic involvement in Scottish politics, but not to the same degree as in England and Wales. Hanham estimates that in about 1880, there were 53 English seats (out of 449) subject to patronage, and 6 Welsh (out of 33). Of the 58 seats in Scotland, only 2 were controlled in this manner.[1] These were Sutherland and Argyll, with the respective patrons being the eponymous dukes. A good instance of the complete power wielded by these patrons was Sutherlandshire, where the M.P. from 1867 was Ronald Leveson-Gower, brother of the duke. Leveson-Gower was asked by his brother to step down in 1874 on the occasion of the marquess of Stafford, the heir to the dukedom, attaining his majority and so being eligible to sit in parliament.[2]

By the other yardstick, relatives of peers sitting in the Commons, there were in 1880 six brothers or sons of the nobility holding Scottish seats, whereas in the rest of the country there were 134.[3] Weak as the position of the Scottish peerage was in comparison to England, by the eve of the First World War it had deteriorated sharply. Only three close relatives of peers sat for Scottish seats,[4] and in the two seats subject to patrons in 1880, both now returned M.P.s of the party opposed by the relevant peer. Indeed in Sutherland, the new marquess of Stafford was defeated at the poll in the December 1910 election, so underlining the loss of aristocratic political power. At a lower level of political importance, the aristocracy also found themselves in this same period being elbowed out of county government. Up until 1891, the landowning class had constituted a self-appointed unelected body administering county affairs. The introduction of county councils voted in on a democratic franchise meant that new forces came to the front. In Sutherland, the duke's candidates were defeated, while in

Aberdeenshire the marquess of Huntly lost the contest for the convenorship to a big tenant-farmer.[5] In 1895, when the new system had
settled down, in only eight county authorities did a peer or peer's
relative occupy the convenor's chair.

There were a number of factors which account for the slighter
aristocratic presence in Scottish parliamentary politics. One was that
the social relationships seen by many historians as the crucial under-
pinning of aristocratic power in rural England did not operate to the
same degree in Scotland. This was the idea of social deference, carefully
nurtured by the upper classes, and closely connected with the concept
of a common identity of interests and values among the entire rural
community.[6] The main agencies for fostering the deferential dialectic
were mostly lacking in Scotland. The great rural sports of cricket and
fox-hunting were virtually absent from Scotland. The nearest substitute
was curling, at which Lord Balfour of Burleigh and the duke of Atholl
were ardent exponents, but this sport was never socially all-embracing,
as its English counterparts were, and it did not acquire the almost
mystical veneration cricket and fox-hunting received south of the
border. Again, such typical devices for bonding rural society to the
landowner in England as building churches and founding village
schools were not available in Scotland. In the latter, the bulk of the
population was presbyterian, but most of the landed elite were episcopalian. Even for Church of Scotland adherents among the peerage,
building a state church would only heighten tension with the dissenters
in the locality. As to schools, the long Scottish tradition of providing
at least a basic education for all through some form of public funding
reduced the need for private provision. Again, the closed village, where
deference flourished in England, was relatively rare in Scotland.

Aspects of the organisation of agricultural work and the legal framework of Scottish agriculture worked against the creation of a deferential
rural society. Whereas in England agricultural labourers were totally
dependent on the landowner for employment, by contrast, the Scottish
agricultural labourer was a much more independent and mobile individual. Although there were significant regional variations in the causes
of this independence, the upshot was that Scottish farm-workers were
not at all deferential to landlord or to farmer.[7] Politically the
farmworkers were sturdy radicals in the main, so their acquisition of
the franchise in 1884 posed a grave threat to landlord influence in
county constituencies. A repeated refrain in Conservative circles was
the pernicious influence of the radical farm labourers: R.B. Haldane's
seizure of Haddingtonshire (East Lothian) in 1885 was ascribed to the
farmworkers; in 1910 A.J. Balfour blamed his party's electoral setback

in rural seats to 'the ploughmen who I presume are the difficulty in Roxburghshire as they are elsewhere in the Lowlands of Scotland'.[8]

The Scottish legal system served to alienate much of the tenant-farming element from the landowning class in the middle 1860s. Two issues were primarily at work here. Firstly, the landlords began in the 1860s to apply vigorously the game laws, which worked in their interest and to the detriment of the tenantry, or so the farmers felt. Farmers who killed hares and rabbits to try to stop their depredations on crops were prosecuted. The other legal power was that of hypothec, which placed the landlord as a preferential creditor on the estate of a tenant for rent due. This meant, it was claimed, that rents could be imposed at very high levels, as the landlord was assured that whatever else happened, he would recoup his debt if the farmer failed.[9] Farmers objected to the economic pressure these burdens placed them under. This was linked with a growing social and political self-confidence which resulted in defeats at the polls in the 1865 and 1868 general elections for many landowner candidates. The response of the governing class was to give in to a large degree to the demands of the farmers for reform of the game and hypothec laws. By 1880, the political revolt of the tenantry seemed to have passed, but there would never again be the automatic assumption of leadership by one class and an acquiescence in it by the other. As the earl of Hopetoun remarked in 1886 to another member of the aristocracy:

> I am anxious to live more at home and less in London, as I find it absolutely necessary for many reasons to be amongst my tenantry and people, as it is only by continuous personal contact with the former that I can get things to go *smoothly* in these bad times.[10]

These tense relations with farmers reflected a wider, more overtly political hazard confronting the nobility. The land question as a political issue bulked much larger in the Scottish political agenda than it did in England. In the latter, it was an occasional factor, but only really came to prominence with Lloyd George's Budget of 1909. In the former, it had a long and prominent pedigree. Firstly, there was the fact that landownership was more concentrated than in England, with a handful of individual, mostly peers, owning vast tracts of land. Bateman's survey of 1883 revealed that the duke of Sutherland owned over one million acres in Scotland, the duke of Buccleuch, 433,000 acres, the marquess of Breadalbane, 438,000, the duke of Richmond and Gordon, 280,000, the duke of Fife, 249,000. Few landowners in England could begin to match these estates in size, even although in terms of wealth the Scottish landowners were not necessarily superior.[11] The anti-landlord feelings were often fomented by access disputes, which attracted much attention and drew opprobrium on recalcitrant landowners who insisted on their right to privacy. The most famous was the Glen Tilt episode in the early 1850s, but similar struggles went on elsewhere. It is recorded that there were continual disputes over rights of way between the locals and successive earls of Loudoun over a period of 60 years from 1831.[12]

Further impetus to the saliency of the land question was provided with the crofters' revolt of the 1880s. This directly weakened the political power of the aristocracy by sweeping away their control of the Highland constituencies: the house of Argyll was dislodged from the county seat, as happened to the Sutherlands in their eponymous shire. But the crofter campaign did more. It put the land question firmly on the agenda of Scottish politics, and set up links with urban radicals, working class socialists and Irish nationalists in Scotland, all of whom could unite in denouncing the evils of landlordism.[13] For urban Liberals, in particular, there was a natural progression from disapproving of landowners in the rural context to advocating an assault on urban landlordism. It became commonplace among the more advanced Liberals in the 1890s and 1900s that one of the root causes of urban social problems was that private owners of land profited from the demand for land which an expanding city population made. The single tax remedy (which would shift the main burden of main on to land-holders, especially those enjoying an unearned increment) attracted a great deal of support in the major Lowland cities, one of the leading apologists for this being Sir Samuel Chisholm, Lord Provost of Glasgow.

Given this background, the reaction of Scottish opinion to Lloyd George's Budget of 1909 was predictable. It was warmly applauded across a wide spectrum, and its popularity was probably enhanced by the action in 1906 of the landowners, who formed the Scottish Land and Property Federation. Its leading office holders embodied all that the Scottish radicals inveighed against. Peers prominent in the associ-ation included the dukes of Atholl and Buccleuch. This heightened the political divide produced by the land issue, and the sole beneficiary was the Liberal party. In the general election of January 1910, while the Unionist share of the vote rose from its 1906 level in England by 4.6% (to 50.0%), in Scotland it rose by a mere 0.2% (to 39.7%).[14] The pre-eminence which the land question occupied in Scotland was ac-knowledged by the Labour party. Disappointed by Labour's failure to poll as well in Scotland as in England in the 1910 elections, the party in London sent a high-powered committee up to Scotland to investi-gate. The committee, which included the Scottish-born Arthur Henderson, found the Labour party in Scotland to be in difficulties, and it saw little likelihood of an early change. It pointed out the prime reason for the backwardness of Labour:

> . . . the Land Question in Scotland dominates everything else. Scotland has stood by the Liberal government so solidly because it hates the House of Lords and the landlords.[15]

Great hostility towards the landowners also arose from the Disruption in 1843, because many peers, as staunch upholders of the established church principle, refused to make land available for the erection of Free Church buildings. Some of the worst offenders were peers, with the duke of Buccleuch being regarded as a major culprit. As ever, the religious question in 19th century Scotland had a political dimension to it, and the Lowland urban Free Church adherents retained for long a disregard for the landowning class, a feeling which was reinforced by the crofters' revolt of the 1880s. This conflict had overtones of a battle between the Free Church, which enthusiastically backed the crofters, and the landlords, who were closely identified with the state church.[16] The campaign for disestablishment of the Church of Scotland, to which was put much of the political energies of the dissenting presbyterian churches from the middle 1870s, indirectly kept this animosity in the forefront. Several peers took up the cause of the Church of Scotland with vigour, Lord Balfour of Burleigh being especially conspicuous in the state church's defence.[17] It is difficult to find many noblemen championing the demands of the United Presbyterian and Free Churches, who after all constituted perhaps 60% of presbyterians.

What made the plight of the erosion of political influence difficult for the aristocracy to redress was that the economic base of the class was being weakened. This was not caused by death duties or even Lloyd George's land taxes, neither of which was particularly onerous before the outbreak of the Great War. Much of it was due to extravagance by individuals. The 5th earl of Rosslyn came into his inheritance in 1890 and in 1897 he became bankrupt, owing £125,000, mainly gambling debts. R.H. Campbell has shown how grandiose building projects laid low the finances of the earl of Galloway.[18] Matters were complicated by the onset of a downturn in agricultural prices, which meant that on some estates rents were cut by anything from one-third to one half. In certain areas the crisis was so acute that no tenants could be found, so the earl of Polwarth took some estate farms in hand himself.[19]

Although Scotland had a number of noblemen with very large estates, a good number actually enjoyed a relatively small rental income: in 1883, about 20, or just under one quarter, had estate revenue of under £10,000 per annum. A few did acquire business directorates but the demand for these seems to have peaked in the 1890s, and thereafter there was less opportunity to adorn the board of a public company. Still, in 1896, 36 Scottish peers did hold directorships, several holding more than one, and Tweeddale, with 19, had easily the most. But many of these peers did not have financial problems, for they included the dukes of Buccleuch, Richmond & Gordon and Sutherland. For many, therefore, selling up land, either the entire estate or portions of it, became the only way of keeping going. Galloway thus disposed of a good part of his property while in Perthshire Lord Kinnoull realised £127,000 by selling his estate. Others sold up for different, somewhat quirky reasons. The marquess of Queensberry quit Dumfries-shire in the late 1880s in a pique at some imagined slight. The duke of Fife sold off his north-east estate on the eve of the first world war because, as he told the marquess of Huntly, he was concerned at the socialistic tendencies of the people of Banff and Moray—proclivities which, it must be said, were not apparent to the naked eye of most observers.[20] With depleted and ever-shrinking economic resources, the wherewithal for a come-back, even if the political climate grew more favourable, was apparently lacking.

It is also possible that a minor cause of anti-aristocratic sentiment in Scotland before the first world war may have derived from moral disapproval. Several peers were prominent racehorse owners: Rosebery won the Derby twice, the earl of Minto was a champion amateur jockey. This might well have offended middle class presbyterian morality. The heavy drinking in which some sectors of the aristocracy indulged would have been censured by many, especially given the great support for temperance in Scotland. The earl of Rosslyn, for instance, when not gambling his estate away, drank it away: he recounts that at the age of twenty one his daily intake was two bottles of port. Not surprisingly he became an alcoholic and underwent a treatment cure which lasted all of one year.[21] The Scottish aristocracy also committed many breaches of the sexual moral code. One of the most notorious divorce cases of the 1880s involved the duke of Argyll's son, Lord Colin Campbell, and his wife. One son of the 12th earl of Kinnoull married a daughter of the duke of Fife and then divorced on grounds of adultery, while the marriage of another son also ended in divorce. The marquess of Queensberry's son, Lord Alfred Douglas, featured prominently in the trial of Oscar Wilde. Queensberry himself was married to a bigamist, as well as being an ardent secularist and of course a prominent boxer. The significance of these instance of sexual misconduct is that they would offend not just presbyterians but also Roman Catholics, who might perhaps have adopted a more relaxed view of the racing and drinking peers. It must be remembered that the Roman Catholic population in Lowland Scotland was proportionately larger than in England. In addition there was in Scotland no sizeable episcopalian element who might be presumed to be more tolerant of moral lapses than presbyterians or Roman Catholics. What was possible in London, or regarded simply as raffish conduct, would be assessed differently in Scotland.

The first general election held after the First World War was conducted with a broader franchise than previously, and it seemed to herald the definitive eclipse of the peerage. Only two aristocrats were successful in Scotland. They were the brothers of Lord Elibank: Gideon Murray won Glasgow St Rollox as a Unionist, Arthur Murray took West Aberdeenshire as a Liberal. The 1918 election was fought under the most favourable conditions since the first reform act for the Conservative party in Scotland, and the absence of relatives of peers is therefore very telling: the bulk of the M.P.s elected on the Coalition ticket were business or professional men. At first glance, moreover, it looked as if circumstances would become ever less propitious for a resurgence of aristocratic participation in Scottish politics.

The two decades after the end of the war seemed to usher in a precipitate decline in the economic condition of the peerage, with further substantial shedding of land. Death duties had risen quite sharply by 1918, a factor which took on a particular significance because several peers or heirs were killed in action. Of the 225 relatives of Scottish peers who were in the armed forces during the 1914–18 war, 42 were killed, including the earl of Seafield and the heirs to Lords Balfour of Burleigh, Belhaven and Kinnaird. Income tax was much higher after 1918 and local taxes and rates went up steeply as democratic local government expanded its scope beyond the confines set by the landowners in the pre-reform years. So the marquess of Aberdeen found that his annual estate bill for taxes had grown from £800 in 1870 to £19,000 in 1920.[22] The cost of maintaining houses which had suffered years of neglect or conversion to hospital or military use for four years was immense. Moreover, labour was scarce after 1918, and wage costs had soared. Many houses were closed either permanently or for long periods at a time. The duke of Hamilton vacated Hamilton Palace in 1922, Lord Linlithgow closed Hopetoun House for several years at a stretch and the earl of Airlie used Cortachy Castle only intermittently. Even the duke of Sutherland was not unscathed, as he disposed of his London house. The marquess of Aberdeen left Haddo for Cromar House, where he and his wife lived in extremely straitened circumstances in the 1930s. The rent for Cromar was actually paid by a wealthy neighbour on condition that he acquired the house on the marquess's death. Others sold off the family jewellery: the Atholls did this several times in the 1920s, while Lord Loudoun put his paintings up for sale.

For many these devices merely stalled the inevitable, which was to sell off land. Between 1918 and 1921 it was claimed that one fifth of all Scottish land (about four million acres) changed hands.[23] Lord Lovat sold 100,000 acres, along with his prize herd of shorthorn cattle in the 1920s. The marquess of Breadalbane also put 100,000 acres around Loch Tay on the market shortly after the war, and the new duke of Montrose had to dispose of his Stirlingshire estate of some 70,000 acres to meet death duties on succeeding to the title in 1925. The duke of Richmond and Gordon reduced his north-east estates around the same time, Lord Loudoun liquidated his Ayrshire holdings in 1921, the earl of Eglinton following suit in the same county in 1930. Other steep reductions were the earl of Glasgow, whose holding fell from 38,000 acres in 1883 to 2,500 in 1938, and Lord Rollo who shrank from 17,000 acres in Perth and Dumfries to 1,250 over the same time. The duke of Atholl sold half of his estate in 1926, and a few years later, so heavily in debt that he could not pay his workers, surrendered ownership of the rump of the estate to a limited company backed by Lady Cowdray. Atholl received in return an annual payment of £2,000.

Thus the most visible trappings of the economic power and social standing of the nobility, the great estate with its large house, disappeared in many cases. Moreover, many peers thereupon removed themselves completely from Scotland, so ending any say in the political process. Most went to England: Lord Napier and Ettrick settled in Surrey, Lord Dysart in Grantham, and Lord Northesk in Brockenhurst. Others went further afield: Lord Pentland moved to the United States and the earl of Erroll went to Kenya.

Not all went down without a struggle. Clearly if the estate was no longer even marginally viable, it was necessary to find alternative sources of income. Business was one possibility, and company directorships the obvious berth to look to. However, the number of Scottish peers who were directors, 36 in 1896, barely altered a quarter of a century later. In 1920 there were 45 peers sitting on company boards, but seven of these were new 'business' creations, leaving 38 'traditional' peers. The standard survey of the business elite in Scotland also reveals that the aristocratic element remained static between 1904–5 and the eve of the second world war.[24] The sorts of companies which tended to favour having a nobleman on the board were banking, insurance, railways and public utilities generally. These were all subject to a wave of mergers in the post-1918 years, so eliminating prospects for peers, who were on the whole less likely to serve in, say, an electrical engineering company.

Others entered business directly as entrepreneurs or as professional men. The 6th duke of Montrose was a practising engineer, and became president of the Institute of Naval Architects. The 19th Lord Sempill became an aeronautics engineer, publishing several books on the topic. The 15th earl of Lauderdale was an accountant. Some peers ended up in rather more dubious occupations. The 10th marquess of Queensberry managed a roadside house in Canada, and took part in the Australian goldrush before settling down, relatively speaking, as a journalist in America. But the numbers engaging in these sorts of activity remained very small indeed: most of the nobility did not seem capable or willing to do so. Even for the small group who did, inexperience and desperation could lead to disaster. The 8th duke of Atholl, whose straitened financial circumstances have been noted, aimed to put his money affairs in order by joining William Beardmore (Lord Invernairn) in a project to build metal houses. This was a complete flop, probably because the Weir company had already established itself in this sector. Losing about £20,000 on this scheme, the duke sought to restore financial stability by investing in what seemed a copper-bottomed plan to develop sugar plantations in the West Indies. Unfortunately the island chosen for this venture proved to be virtually the one spot in the region quite unsuited to cultivating sugar. Atholl lost a further £20,000 and this tipped the estate into the near-bankruptcy of the early 1930s.[25]

An alternative source of revenue was, as ever, to marry into money. Yet in practice most matches made between the wars involving a peer or the heir to the title were still confined within aristocratic circles, or extended only as far as the traditional landed and military caste. There is a slight tendency detectable for rather more marriages to North American women to occur, with the 12th earl of Haddington and the 5th earl of Minto marrying Canadian sisters. There was remarkably little intermarriage with the new peerage creations drawn from industrial and business backgrounds. One such, however, was the engagement of the heir presumptive to the dukedom of Atholl, Anthony Murray. His wife was to be the daughter of the dowager Lady Cowdray, and it was on the basis of this projected marriage that Lady Cowdray agreed to pump money into the Atholl estate coffers. Initially she was led to understand the deficiency was in the region of £50,000, then little by little the true extent of the crisis was unveiled to her. She ended up making about £380,000 available. Unfortunately Anthony

Murray died before inheriting the title, so Lady Cowdray's investment did not pay off, at least in the non-material dividend.[26] It is also significant that very few peers of the new, non-landed variety married into the older aristocracy. Only Lords Inverclyde and Glenconner broke into the magic circle.

This apparent deepening economic crisis after 1918 points toward the extinction of the peerage as significant participants in Scottish politics. It is therefore remarkable that after the 1935 general election, the last before the outbreak of the second world war, the number of M.P.s with close peerage links numbered eight. In addition there were two other M.P.s with slightly more distant ties with the nobility.[27] This was the highest figure since 1880. Moreover, it would have been nine, but for the death of the earl of Mansfield a few months before the general election. He was succeeded by his son, Lord Scone, who sat for Perth East. It is instructive that only one of the eight, MacLay, belonged to the new 'business' peerage creations; all the rest came from the traditional nobility.

Hardly any of these aristocrats can be deemed to owe their seats to a lingering trace of deference or influence. The nearest to this traditional factor was Lord William Scott, whose father, the duke of Buccleuch, had substantial property in Roxburghshire. Scott inherited the constituency in 1935 from his brother, the earl of Dalkeith, who had sat since 1923. Although the duchess of Atholl's seat contained the family estate, she did not initially intend to stand there. Sir William Younger advised her to contest an urban constituency, as it would be less physically demanding to fight. The West Perthshire seat became available quite unexpectedly on the retiral of the sitting M.P.[28] James Stuart did sit for an area in which his family still owned estates, but the circumstances of his nomination and election were not of his making. In 1923 he was waiting to go to America to resume his business career in the oil industry when a telegram from the Moray and Nairn Conservative Association inviting him to fight the seat arrived quite unsolicitedly. Stuart remarks: 'I had never for a moment entertained any thought of standing for Parliament.' Nothing was further from his thoughts than fighting the seat, but he told his father, 'merely as a matter of interest', of the invitation: 'To my utter surprise, not to say consternation, he said why didn't I "have a shot". It wouldn't do me "any harm", and it would be "an experience".' As the seat had been safely Liberal since time immemorial, Stuart stood, certain of defeat. His victory came as a total and not at first pleasant surprise: when told by his agent that he looked like winning he retorted, 'I have a job in America and I have to get back to it'.[29] Although Dunglass's father owned land in the constituency, the mining vote far outweighed any Home influence in South Lanark. But for Lord Clydesdale and Scrymgeour-Wedderburn, being selected for two suburban and semi-industrial seats removed from any family influence shows that other factors were at work. Some of the forces behind the resurgence of aristocratic political involvement may be suggested.

The impression of a financially ruined peerage in headlong flight from their estates is misleading and overstates the case. Many peers remained with considerable estates. A good number did not have to sell off all or any part of their land. A comparison of the size of estates in 1883 and in 1938 shows that, for instance, Lords Bute, Lothian, Haddington, Roxburghe, Southesk and Tweeddale still owned the same acreage.[30] In other instances even after selling up, the remaining estate area was pretty substantial: the duke of Sutherland had several hundred thousand acres left after disposing of large tracts of his estate, while Breadalbane was down to a mere 150,000 acres after selling off his Perthshire lands. Some indeed sold up in one place to move into sizeable estates elsewhere. The earl of Caithness, whose original Caithness estate had been disposed of in 1889, became a very substantial landowner and public figure in Aberdeenshire where he owned Auchmacoy. For several, slimming down their lands proved to be very beneficial. In the case of Lord Lovat, the sale of outlying areas reduced the costs of the estate, and accordingly the 1920s 'were the most prosperous in his life'.[31] Again, in some cases it did prove possible to diversify income sources, retaining the estate as the core activity but augmenting revenue by business income. The earl of Elgin by the 1920s had managed to derive half his annual income from landownership and the other half from directorates such as the Royal Bank of Scotland and several building societies. There was thus still a background of reasonable economic stability for several peers to maintain a political presence.[32]

It may be suggested that the reasons for the return of aristocrats to a political role are to be found in the changing political and social nature of inter-war Scotland. After 1918 several of the issues which had militated against the landowning peerage diminished. The land question itself slipped in importance after the First World War. In the context of the problems of Scottish industry, land seemed marginal to economic recovery. The emergence of the Labour party placed urban social matters in the forefront, and the solution to these was seen as the application of socialism, rather than the introduction of the single tax, which now seemed a 'cranky' issue. Also the influx of Highlanders to lowland cities reduced between the wars, so making the emotional charge of the Clearances less immediate.

In rural areas, the break-up of the large estates was frequently accompanied by the tenantry being offered the opportunity to buy their farms and turn into owner-occupiers. In 1914, there were around 5,900 owner-occupied farms (about 7.5% of all farms), but by the start of the next war, the figure was 17,700, representing about 25% of all farms in 1939.[33] The implications of this shift were considerable. Firstly, the tenant-farmers' sense of injustice against landlords was no longer felt to be irremediable: the prospect of acquiring their own farm or buying elsewhere was now for tenants a reality to an extent unknown before 1914. So, politically anti-landlordism had less mileage among this class. Secondly, however, the proportion of farms rented in Scotland was much higher than in England: in Scotland in 1950 43%, in England 28%.[34] This accordingly left the aristocracy with some degree of social and economic linkage with the farmers. Thirdly, the creation of a united agricultural interest became a reality in the inter-war years, neatly encapsulated in the decision by landowners to admit owner-occupier farmers into their pressure group.[35] It was remarked by a landowner in 1921 that the farmers having purchased their farms were 'beginning to realise what the burdens on heritable property really mean.'[36] In the depths of the depression landowners and farmers in many parts of Scotland held joint meetings to denounce the failure of the government to give any real assistance to Scottish agriculture.[37] An extra bonding ingredient was the rise after the first world war of an organised farmworkers movement, led by the legendary Joseph Duncan. Demands and strike action for higher wages and better conditions pulled farmer and landowner together in a joint resistance.[38] This factor had a second dimension to it. Although the flexing of the muscles of farm labourers had a unifying political effect on the other sectors in agriculture, the actual electoral threat of the labourers' vote was less serious. The number of farmworkers fell by between one fifth and one quarter over the period from 1911 to 1939, with the radical ploughboy of Tory demonology increasingly marginalised by the tractor and other advanced technological innovations in farm machinery.[39] Manifest evidence of this political shift was seen in the apparent interchangeability in many rural seats of candidates for the same party who were landowners or tenant farmers, whereas before 1914 an unbridgeable enmity between the two was seen to exist. In West Perthshire and Kinross, it was a farmer who retired in 1923 to let the duchess of Atholl stand. The retiring M.P., James Gardiner, said that he would only go if the duchess replaced him. In turn the duchess was ousted by a farmer who was enthusiastically backed by many prominent Tory landowners in the county.[40]

Religion also became of less political relevance. The disestablishment movement had essentially lost momentum by the 1900s, but after 1918 it was readily apparent to all presbyterians that there would be a re-union of the mainstream under the leadership of the Church of Scotland. Not only did the issue decline, so eliminating the basis for an anti-aristocratic dissenting vote, but the aristocracy may have gained in prestige as a result of the church union of 1929. For one thing, a key proponent of presbyterian union was Lord Balfour of Burleigh, and his genial nature did much to smooth the negotiations and to enhance the esteem of the nobility in non-established church circles. Secondly, the Church of Scotland now assumed a heightened import-ance among the national institutions of Scotland. It was no longer a sect, but the national church. In the nineteenth century, the position of Lord High Commissioner to the General Assembly had not always been very highly rated. The 4th earl of Rosslyn got the job from Disraeli in lieu of a royal household post he had been pencilled in for, because the prime minister feared the earl's prolific swearing would upset the queen. However, after the First World War, the Commissioner became a most influential figure; standing in for the monarch, the Commis-sioner embodied a sense of national identity. With only one exception the Commissioners between the wars all came from upper class families, including the dukes of Atholl and Sutherland, and Lords Elgin, Elphinstone and Stair.[41]

It is difficult to establish, but it seems probable that the loosening of strict moral codes occurring in the inter-war years even in Scotland may have helped the aristocracy. Divorce was less uncommon among all sections of society, while temperance declined as a social and political force. In addition, the flight to other places removed some of the more decadent sprigs of the nobility. The 22nd earl of Erroll, a notorious womaniser, disported himself in the 'Happy Valley' of Kenya until he was murdered, allegedly by a cuckolded baronet. For others, notoriety might be of short duration. The 14th earl of Kinnoull was declared bankrupt at 24, divorced his first wife, and married 'a noto-rious keeper of night clubs' before dying aged 36.[42]

But it was not just the removal of longstanding barriers which pushed the peers back into political activity. Another important factor was that the Conservatives faced a difficult and delicate problem in Scotland between the wars. There was above all the necessity of retaining the solid core of Liberal voters, who before 1914 had been greater than in England. The choice in 1918 of many businessmen of rather right-wing views was believed to have alienated Liberals. In the great Tory reassertion of separate political identity in 1922, the overwhelming view of Conservative M.P.s in Scotland was to retain the Coalition, in contrast to the bulk of those in England. As John Gilmour put it, the party would face 'great difficulty in holding many seats in Scotland without the help of the Liberals.'[43] As part of the strategy of creating the image of the Conservatives as the 'national' party, which Stanley Baldwin effected so brilliantly for England, it may be plausible to wonder if the aristocracy did not play a central role in the effort to do the same in Scotland.[44]

Four areas may be identified as establishing a connection between the titled classes and some of the components of the Scottish sense of nationality at this time. The importance of the Empire to Scots has increasingly attracted the attention of historians of popular culture and politics.[45] Many Scottish peers had been governors of colonies in the nineteenth century—Elgin, Minto, Dalhousie, Glasgow—so that the rising sentiment of popular imperialism stamped the role of the peerage in the consciousness of many. In the inter-war years, this was maintained by, among others, the second Marquess of Linlithgow, who was Viceroy of India in the late 1930s.

Secondly, there was the militaristic tendency. Again, the attention of historians to this important strand in Scottishness has only just begun to be developed.[46] The traditional military prowess of the Scots was matched by the leading role taken by peers in military commands. One of the most famous bands of fighting men formed in the twentieth century, the Lovat Scouts, was of course the brainchild of the 16th Lord Lovat. Several of its officer corps were drawn from other noble houses, the earl of Melville being one example.[47] The First World War served to reinforce these connections. The Scots, it must be remembered, volunteered in disproportionately large numbers from the very start of the war. Casualties among the peerage of Scotland were very high— nearly one-fifth of all aristocrats on active military service were killed. These militaristic sentiments lingered throughout the inter-war period, and were arguably as widespread in many sections of Scottish society as were the anti-war feelings held with fervour on the left. It is significant that the inspiration and the driving force behind the scheme to build the Scottish National War Memorial, which was completed in 1926, was the duke of Atholl, who himself had a distinguished war record.[48] Again, it can be no coincidence that in a book published in 1932 under the revealing title *A Scotsman's Heritage*, the very first chapter should be by Atholl. Headed 'Scottish Courage and Loyalty', this chapter argued that 'Traditions of valour, loyal service and self-sacrifice have been built up and passed on by one generation to another in an ever accumulating heritage' which culminated in the First World War.[49] These, of course, were the ancient idealised virtues of nobility, which Atholl now ascribed to the whole nation.

A third field was the growth of interest in the Scottish past, and here too the peerage played a leading role. Whereas for perhaps 150 years up until the last quarter of the nineteenth century Scottish aristocrats had seemed hell-bent on total anglicisation, they increasingly strove from the 1880s to re-position themselves within the currents of Scottish identity then emerging. The third marquess of Bute devoted much time and great amounts of money to promoting many aspects of Scottish identity, particularly those of an historical aspect. The earl of Rosebery was the first president of the Scottish History Society, and in his collected essays there is a section running to 150 pages devoted to 'Scottish History and Character'.[50] Interest in things Scottish at a less rarefied level also took place. The 11th marquess of Huntly frequently wore a kilt, a thing his forebears evidently rarely did, and in 1870 he became the first peer to attend the House of Lords wearing a kilt. The 1st marquess of Aberdeen collected couthy Scots phrases and interested himself in Lallans. He and his wife called their first volume of memoirs *'We Twa'*, and for the follow-up book, gave it the toe-curling title *More Cracks with 'We Twa'*. Lord Balfour of Burleigh became for his biographer, herself the member of a noble family, the epitome of the Scottish character—'the true Scot, Alexander Hugh Bruce, Lord Balfour of Burleigh.'[51]

The last area to be looked at in this category of re-integrating trends is freemasonry. A large number of peers seem to have been prominent freemasons, and they were evidently proud of being so, for references to their positions in the brotherhood frequently occur in works of reference like Burke's *Peerage*. For instance, 13 of the 20 Grand Master Masons of Scotland between 1880 and 1939 were peers, including the 11th earl of Haddington, the 16th earl of Eglinton, the 12th earl of Stair, the 11th Baron Belhaven and the 19th Baron Saltoun. There was apparently a measure of social mixing found in freemasonry, as Lord Rosslyn nostalgically recalled: 'These were happy days when one could hobnob with the tradesmen and miners of the village [Dysart] in a lodge of equality and good fellowship'.[52] In the inter-war years, with high unemployment and continuing sectarianism, especially in the West of Scotland, the masonic order retained its importance for men of all social walks.[53] The continuing presence of aristocrats must have done much to refurbish their image among those who might previously have been somewhat critical of the landowner-peer.[54]

Between the wars the status of the aristocracy also benefitted from the spread of quangos, as it sometimes appeared that no Scottish public body could function unless at least one peer sat on it. Lord Elgin sat on the boards of the Royal Highland Association, the National Library of Scotland, the Scottish Development Council and was a Scottish governor of the BBC. Lord Wemyss presided over the Historic Buildings Commission; Lord Linlithgow chaired the Medical Research Council; the earl of Stair's brother sat on the board of the National Gallery of Scotland; Lord Lovat was the first chairman of the Forestry Commission; while Lord Polwarth served as chairman of the Scottish Prison Board for many years. Most universities had a peer as Chancellor and sometimes another as a lay court member. Colleges of agriculture were often stuffed with aristocratic governors. Frequently, a peer as chairman of an official enquiry gave a semblance of impartiality: Lovat chaired a committee investigating how Scottish local authorities had implemented the cuts in public spending imposed during the 1931 crisis.

As well as having a central position in the bid by the Conservatives to create a sense of the 'national' party, the other attractive quality of the nobility was that on the whole they were not identified with the extreme political views of out and out capitalists. These latter, who had tended to prevail in the 1918 election, had been largely removed in the 1922 election, and thereafter in any event the cyclone sweeping through Scottish capitalism presumably kept them preoccupied with holding their business heads above water, and with no time for politics. The peers now began to take on the character of moderate, progressive individuals in whom the wavering Liberals could repose more trust that a humane stance would be adopted than could be expected from hard-faced industrialists. Indeed, compared to their English counterparts, the record of Scottish peers is reasonably liberal. There were only 12 Scottish as against 112 English members of the Lords who can be categorised as Die-hards during the constitutional crisis of 1909–14. Put another way, 48% of English, but only 18% of Scottish, peers were Die-hards.[55] During the 1930s when many English aristocrats dabbled with fascism, very few Scottish peers did so. Only the 8th earl of Glasgow and the 19th baron Sempill were openly associated with fascism. While one or two others—notably the duke of Buccleuch and the earl of Lothian—seem to have been sympathetic to the Germans, they were by no means fascistic.[56]

On a range of social questions, the aristocracy proved quite forward-looking. Thus, the Highland peers after 1918 performed a massive *volte face* by allowing land to be re-settled. The duke of Sutherland, of all people, made 12,000 acres of Borgie Farm available for smallholders and ex-service men to try to establish a livelihood. In Inverness-shire,

Lord Lovat released land in the Beauly and Morar districts for the same purpose.[57] On matters such as labour relations, peers seemed relatively advanced. Several were invited to adjudicate between capital and labour, because they were not seen as committed to one side. In 1912 the duke of Atholl took up the cause of the dockers during the London dock strike, charging Lord Devonport with lack of good faith.[58] Lord Balfour of Burleigh was part of the government committee sent in to investigate the unrest on Clydeside in the first world war. While civil servants fretted at socialistic influences and employers ranted about Bolshevik penetration, Lord Balfour was not convinced by this ultra rhetoric. Visiting some arrested shipwrights in gaol, he was deeply impressed to hear the workmen singing psalms in the metrical version: 'It was the spirit of the old Covenanters in modern fashion.' His report called for considerable modification of the harsher aspects of the Munitions Act.[59]

Peers presented a progressive face on other social issues. The duchess of Atholl began her public service work by sitting on commissions looking into health provision and the problems of travelling people. She was always concerned about women's and children's matters, and the latter question led her into her most famous episode, championing the Republican cause in the Spanish Civil War. In the early 1920s indeed she and her husband were advocating the formation of a centre party, to avoid what they saw as the extremist policies being pursued by the Conservatives.[60] In the 1935 election, aristocratic candidates espoused rather enlightened policies. Lord Dunglass expressed some support for the demands of the miners, while Scrymgeour-Wedderburn advocated speedier moves to implementing social reforms. The duke of Montrose was a spectacular convert to Scottish nationalism in the mid 1930s. He did not make this move because of his commitment to some semi-fascist high nationalist doctrines. He couched the reasons for his new affiliation in words that still have a resonance:

> For some time the industrial situation in Scotland has been causing me some concern. The division of Scotland into derelict areas, and the appointment of an Economic Committee to investigate the problem is a mere palliative; no lasting good in my opinion can result until we are granted decentralised government, with a Legislature in Scotland. I consider that Parliament at Westminster is so completely absorbed and overburdened in foreign policy and questions of National Defence that under the present centralised system Scottish life and development is stultified.[61]

Further evidence of the social concern being evinced by the peers comes from local government. As we have seen, in the initial phase of the reorganised county council system, there seemed little room for aristocrats. In the inter-war years their presence was more marked. In 1895, 8 county council convenors were aristocrats, by 1938 this had risen to 13. In addition, a good number of ad hoc authorities were chaired by members of the nobility. Both the duchess of Atholl and Lord Scone had served terms in charge of the Perthshire Education Authority. Lord Polwarth, on the East Lothian council, immersed himself in matters like rural housing reform. It is striking that only one new 'business' peer—Lord Forteviot—was sufficiently involved in local government to hold the convenorship of a county.

Yet it is important to emphasise that the recovery by the peerage of a political role in Scotland was little more than a fig-leaf. Never at any time in the post-war years did these noble individuals hold key government posts. Between 1885 and 1905 there were four peers who were Scottish secretaries (Richmond and Gordon, Lothian, Balfour of Burleigh, Linlithgow). After 1918 no 'old' aristocrat held that office. Few of them even rose to junior office: the duchess of Atholl experienced a difficult time at the Department of Education in the 1920s, and was not offered a position in the 1930s.

The relationship between aristocrats and democratic politics in Scotland can be captured in two instances. In 1926 the duke of Sutherland applied to the new Scottish Secretary to be given a ministerial position at the Scottish Office. He wrote, somewhat ambiguously: 'You will not find me lacking in keenness and enthusiasm for the cause of Scotland, which is no doubt only right and proper, as my family has had such a long association with Scotland.'[62] It is difficult to envisage any nineteenth century duke of Sutherland writing a letter along these lines. It is equally noteworthy that the duke's request, far from being acceded to, was not granted. Instead he was left in his position as Paymaster-General, a job he described as 'a humdrum one', for another two years, much to his dismay.[63] The other instance is the very well-known deposition of the duchess of Atholl by her Conservative constituency association.[64] Here the duchess's increasingly rebellious and wayward political conduct provoked the West Perthshire rank and file to splitting from her. When the duchess decided to force a by-election, the official candidate received the backing of almost all prominent local activists. The duchess lost the by-election. Clearly the message was that aristocrats did not hold these seats on their own terms, free to pursue whatever political course of action they wished. Now they were accountable to mass democracy, which would have no lingering deferential tendencies making it reluctant to assert its will.

REFERENCES

1. H.J. Hanham, *Elections and Party Management* (London, 1959) pp.19–25, 405–12.
2. R. Leveson-Gower, *My Reminiscences* (London, 1883), I, pp.276–8; II, p.84. Cf. his *Old Diaries, 1881–1901* (London, 1902), pp.47–8.
3. W.C. Lubenow, *Parliamentary Politics and the Home Rule Crisis: The British House of Commons in 1886* (Oxford, 1988), p.169, table 4.1. The M.P.s were: R.P. Bruce (brother of the earl of Elgin), for Fife; Lord Colin Campbell (son of the duke of Argyll), for Argyllshire; Lord Elcho (son of the earl of Wemyss), for Haddingtonshire; A.R.D. Elliot (son of the earl of Minto), for Roxburghshire; A.H. Gordon (brother of the marquess of Huntly), for Aberdeenshire West; the marquess of Stafford (son of the duke of Sutherland), for Sutherland.
4. These were: Viscount Dalrymple (son of the earl of Stair). M.P. for Wigtownshire; A.C. Murray (son of Baron Elibank), M.P. for Kincardineshire; and the marquess of Tullibardine (son of the duke of Atholl), M.P. for Perthshire West.
5. Marquess of Huntly, *Milestones* (London, 1925), pp.112–3.
6. J.V. Beckett, *The Aristocracy in England, 1660–1914* (London, 1986), pp.323–73 contains the most recent and fullest statement of deference.
7. I. Carter, *Farm Life in the North East of Scotland 1830–1914.* (Edinburgh, 1979); T.M. Devine (ed.), *Farm Servants and Farm Labour in Lowland Scotland, 1770–1914* (Edinburgh, 1984); R.H. Campbell, *Owners and Occupiers* (Aberdeen, 1991), especially 29–93.
8. British Library, Balfour MSS, Add. Ms 49,860, ff. pp.245–6, A.J. Balfour to earl of Dalkeith, 28 Apr. 1910 (Copy).
9. Campbell, *Owners and Occupiers*, pp.109–28; I.G.C. Hutchison, *A Political History of Scotland 1832–1924* (Edinburgh, 1986), pp.104–11.
10. Elrick House, Kincardine-shire, Earl of Kintore MSS, Bundle 192: Lord Hopetoun to K. Keith-Falconer, 22 Dec. [1886]. The stress is in the original.
11. J. Bateman, *The Great Landowners of Great Britain and Ireland* (4th edn, London, 1883).
12. J. Strawhorn and W. Boyd eds., *The Third Statistical Account of Scotland: Ayrshire* (Glasgow, 1951), pp.505–6.
13. J. Hunter, 'The Gaelic Connection: the Highlands, Ireland and Nationalism, 1873–1922', *Scottish Historical Review*, liv (1975), pp.178–204; J. Hunter, 'The Politics of Highland Land Reform, 1873–95', *ibid.*, liii (1974), pp.45–68.
14. H. Pelling, *Social Geography of British Elections 1885–1910* (London, 1967), p.415, table 52.
15. Labour Party Offices. London, Labour Party MSS, Minutes of National Executive, 1911.
16. G. Beith, *The Crofter Question and Church Endowments in the Highlands, viewed politically and socially* (Glasgow, 1884), esp. pp.9–16.
17. Lady F. Balfour, *A Memoir of Lord Balfour of Burleigh, KT* (London, c1925), pp.31–54.
18. Lord Rosslyn, *My Gamble with Life* (London, 1928), pp.113–18; Campbell, *Owners and Occupiers*, pp.160–80.
19. G.F. Barbour, *Lord Polwarth. 1864–1944* (Edinburgh, n.d.), pp.4–8.
20. Huntly, *Milestones*, pp.168.
21. Rosslyn, *My Gamble with Life*, p.161.
22. Lord and Lady Aberdeen, *'We Twa'* (London, 1925), II, pp.323–4.
23. *Scottish Farmer*, 24 Dec. 1921.
24. GEC, *The Complete Peerage* (London, 1910–40), V, App. C; J Scott and M. Hughes, *The Anatomy of Scottish Capital* (London, 1980), pp.47–8, 98–9.

25. S.J. Hetherington, *Katharine Atholl, 1874–1960. Agaainst the Tide* (Aberdeen, 1989), pp.125–6.
26. *Ibid.*, pp.127–9.
27. These were: the Duchess of Atholl, M.P. for West Perth and Kinross; A.D. Cochrane (son of Baron Cochrane of Cults), Dumbartonshire; the Marquess of Douglas and Clydesdale—customarily styled Lord Clydesdale—(son of the duke of Hamilton), Renfrew East; Lord Dunglass (son of the earl of Home), South Lanark; J.P. MacLay (son of Lord MacLay), Montrose; Lord Wiliam Scott (son of the duke of Buccleuch), Roxburgh and Selkirk; James Stuart (son of the earl of Moray), Moray and Nairn; Scrymgeour-Wedderburn (the claimant to the earldom of Dundee, which title he assumed in 1953), Renfrew West. The two M.P.s with near noble backgrounds were: Capt. A. Ramsay, related to the earl of Dalhousie, and C.I. Kerr, a kinsman of Lord Lothian.
28. Duchess of Atholl, *Working Partnership*.
29. J. Stuart, *Within the Fringe* (London, 1967), pp.69–70.
30. Based on Bateman, *Great Landowners* and evidence in *Scottish Biographies 1938* (Edinburgh, 1938). It must be noted that the 1938 figures are claimed by the peers themselves but there is no obvious reason why they should give misleading data.
31. Sir F. Lindley, *Lord Lovat* (London, n.d.), pp.241–6.
32. F.M.L. Thompson, 'English Landed Society in the Twentieth Century: I. Property Collapse and Survival', *Transactions of the Royal Historical Society*, 5th series, xl (1990), pp.1–24; and 'English Landed Society in the Twentieth Century: II. New Poor and New Rich', *Ibid.*, 6th series, i (1991), pp.1–20, give the argument for survival and resilience. D. Cannadine, *The Decline and Fall of the British Aristocracy* (New Haven, 1990), pp.88–138 is more negative.
33. Ministry of Agriculture, Fisheries and Food & Department of Agriculture and Fisheries for Scotland, *A Century of Agricultural Statistics. Great Britain 1866–1966* (London, 1968), p. 29, table 12.
34. *Ibid.*, pp. 24, 29, tables 10, 12. No figures exist for England between 1922 and 1950. In 1922, 10% of Scottish and 15% of English farms were owned by farmers.
35. Scottish Record Office [SRO], Scottish Landowners Federation MSS, GD 325/1/451, Circular letter by the duke of Hamilton and others (printed); W. Young to G.E. Jackson, 9 Dec. 1926; J.E. Johnston-Ferguosn to Jackson, 4 May 1922.
36. SRO, Scottish Landowners Federation MSS, GD 325/1/451, W.R.T. Middleton to G.E. Jackson, 22 Dec. 1921.
37. SRO, Scottish Landowners Federation MSS, GD 325/1/451, Secretary, North-East branch of the Federation to G.E. Jackson, 28 Apr. 1933; W.R.T. Middleton to Jackson, 1, 23 Mar. 1933; Sir R. Brooke to Jackson, 1 Mar. 1933.
38. Hutchison. *Political History of Scotland*, pp.320–1.
39. Department of Agriculture, *Century of Agricultural Statistics*, p. 62, table 26.
40. Atholl, *Working Partnership*, pp.134; S. Ball, 'The Politics of Appeasement: the Fall of the Duchess of Atholl and the Kinross and West Perth By-election, December 1938', *Scottish Historical Review*, lxix (1990), pp.68–9.
41. The exception was James Brown, a Labour M.P. and veteran leader of the Ayrshire miners who was a devout member of the Church of Scotland. He was appointed by Ramsay MacDonald in one of the few radical gestures of his second administration. After an initial frisson among the noble entourage at the Assembly, all passed off smoothly, thanks in part to the good sense of the dowager Lady Airlie: J. Ellis (ed.), *Thatched with Gold. The Memoirs of Mabell, Countess of Airlie* (London, 1962), p. 191.
42. GEC, *Complete Peerage*, entry for Kinnoull.
43. Birmingham University Library, Austen Chamberlain MSS, AC 33/2/4, Undated memorandum.

44. J. Ramsden, *The Age of Balfour and Baldwin* (London, 1978), pp. 207–15 is a full account of Baldwin's strategy as it applied to England.
45. E.g., M. Fry's forthcoming book on this topic.
46. I. Wood, 'Protestantism and Scottish Military Tradition', in G. Walker and T. Gallagher (eds.), *Sermons and Battle Hymns* (Edinburgh, 1990), pp.112–26.
47. Lindley, *Lord Lovat*, pp.77–80.
48. Atholl, *Working Partnership*, pp.113–17, 129–33, 151–2, 159–64.
49. His Grace the Duke of Atholl *et al.*, *A Scotsman's Heritage* (London, 1932), pp.3–30, esp. p. 25.
50. D.O.H. Blair, *John Patrick, Third Marquess of Bute, K.T., 1847–1900. A Memoir* (London, 1921), esp. pp.129–48; Lord Rosebery, *Miscellanies: Literary and Historical* (London, 1921), II, pp.39–183.
51. Balfour, *Balfour of Burleigh*, p. 203, cf. pp.1–11.
52. Rosslyn, *My Gamble with Life*, p.76.
53. C. Harvie, *No Gods and Precious Few Heroes* (London, 1981), p.126.
54. G.P.T. Flynn, 'In the Grip? A Psychological and Historical Exploration of the Social Significance of Freemasonry in Scotland', in Walker and Gallagher eds., *Sermons and Battle Hymns*, pp.160–92.
55. G.D. Phillips, *The Diehards. Aristocratic Society and Politics in Edwardian England* (Cambridge, Mass., 1979), pp.161–74, cf. p. 29. See also table 3.2.
56. R. Griffiths, *Fellow Travellers of the Right* (London, 1980), is a full discussion of the British upper-class's infatuation with fascism and nazism.
57. *Looking Back. The Autobiography of the Duke of Sutherland*, (London, 1957), pp.82–5; Lindley, *Lord Lovat*, pp.249–50. L. Leneman, *Fit for Heroes? Land Settlement in Scotland after World War I* (Aberdeen, 1989), is more critical of landowners, notably Lovat: cf. pp.78–9.
58. Atholl, *Working Partnership*, pp.61–5.
59. Balfour, *Balfour of Burleigh*, p.209; I. McLean, *The Legend of Red Clydeside* (Edinburgh, 1983), pp.42–3.
60. SRO, Waring MSS, GD 398/137, Duchess of Atholl to Lady Waring, 28 Dec. 1922.
61. Duke of Montrose, *My Ditty Box* (London, 1952), p.192.
62. SRO, Gilmour of Montrave MSS, GD 383/23/14, Duke of Sutherland to J. Gilmour, 26 Oct. [1926].
63. Sutherland, *Looking Back*, pp.147, 162.
64. Ball, 'The Politics of Appeasement', pp.49–83; Hetherington, *Katharine Atholl*, pp.186–218.

7

The Origins and Economic and Social Roles of Scottish Business Leaders, 1860–1960

Anthony Slaven with the assistance of Dong-Woon Kim

The Entrepreneur in Scotland

In the heyday of Victorian business, Scottish business leaders were the subject of much biographic writing, at least at a local level. One of the first studies was J S Jeans *Western Worthies*[1] published in 1872. In similar vein was the two volume study of *Memoirs and Portraits of One Hundred Glasgow Men*,[2] and Eddington's contemporary biographies for Edinburgh and the Lothians.[3] This curiosity about the men who created our modern economy has not continued in any systematic way into the present century, and with the exception of a few great names, the Scottish businessman has remained essentially anonymous.

It was this lack of information on our modern business leaders that lay behind the design of a research project whose primary aim was to explore the origins, characteristics, and economic and social roles of Scotland's business leaders from the middle of the nineteenth century to the 1960s, the period encompassing the ascendancy of our basic industries and their subsequent decline. This chapter presents a preliminary analysis of some of the data collected in that project.[4] The account also draws on the business biographies assembled in the resulting two volume study, the *Dictionary of Scottish Business Biography*.[5] The compilation of the statistical tables has been based upon the research on the biographies by Mr D W Kim as part of his work for a doctorate under the author's supervision.[6]

In approaching this study it was decided from the outset that the businessmen to be selected for study had to be chosen in a systematic way, and by criteria that would make it possible to regard these men as representative of their industry. The approach taken was to base the selection on leading men in leading firms, and to group them in industrial sectors, using the Standard Industrial Classification main order headings. The first stage of investigation involved creating lists of leading companies in each major industrial sector at 25 year intervals from 1860 to 1960.

Leading companies were identified on a variety of criteria, notably capital employed, employment and output data. The problems of ranking companies and selecting business leaders in these companies over time, were made manageable by adopting a target population of men to be studied. A target of 400–500 men was selected, and ranking procedures were then adjusted to provide lists of companies, and a regional representation of companies. The actual number of men allocated to each sector was based upon a weighted employment share at census intervals between 1861 and 1961. The selection of the men for biographic study finally rested on factors such as seniority of position, length of service at senior level, and supplementary information on the subjects contribution to the firm in question.[7]

The first stage of this project was a biographic one intended to provide short essays which would not only deal with the businessman as an individual, but would emphasise his role in his firm, the significance of the man and his company in the context of the industry or sector of which they were a part, and thence to outline the wider public involvement of the subject during his lifetime. At the same time, more detailed data sheets were created recording information ranging from birth, marriage and death, to education, general and business interests, religion, politics and wealth. This preliminary report focuses on four main areas for which information has been most systematically collected. The paper attempts to outline general conclusions first on the origins and means of entry to business of our business leaders. Second to review the educational and training background of the men studied in the *Dictionary*; third, to explore the nature of their non-business roles, and finally to comment on how wealthy these men became, and how they used that wealth. In the broadest sense we have been interested to sketch the roles of these entrepreneurs in their firms, and in their communities, with particular emphasis on their leadership and philanthropy.

Origins and Entry to Business

In answer to the general question—how did the leading Scottish entrepreneurs enter into business careers,—there were three main routes. The men in question made their entry either as Founders of the business; as Inheritors of the business; or as Professional Managers in the business. (*Table 1*) shows that in general terms 42 per cent of

Table 1. Origin of Scottish Entrepreneurs 1840–1960

Sector	Total Men	Founders of Business		Inheritors		Managers	
		No.	%	No.	%	No.	%
Extractive	34	12	35	13	38	9	26
Metals	26	16	61	7	27	8	31
Engineering	27	12	44	8	30	7	27
Shipbuilding	18	11	61	5	28	2	11
Vehicles	10	6	60	2	20	2	20
Chemicals	10	2	20	6	60	2	20
Textiles	44	16	36	21	48	7	16
Clothing	11	6	54	3	27	2	18
Leather	12	3	25	8	67	1	8
Food & Drink	37	12	32	20	54	5	13
Bricks, pottery, cement & glass	14	10	71	2	14	2	14
Timber/ furniture	8	3	37	5	63	—	—
Construction	21	12	57	7	33	2	10
Paper, printing publishing	15	2	13	11	73	2	13
Other manufactures	10	4	40	4	40	2	20
Gas, water & electricity	4	—	—	—	—	4	100
Transport and communication	33	10	30	12	36	11	33
Distributive	33	21	64	7	21	5	15
Banking, insurance & finance	14	6	43	1	7	7	50
TOTAL	381	159	42	142	37	80	21

Compiled from data collected for the *Dictionary of Scottish Business Biography*, A. Slaven & S.G. Checkland eds 2 vols, 1986 & 1990. (*Aberdeen University Press*)

our sample were founders of their businesses, while 37 per cent were classed as inheritors, and 21 per cent as managers. The dominance of 'Founders' as the main means of entry in some sectors clearly has some connection with the trajectory of the industry. Rapidly expanding trades offering opportunities to able men would attract a high rate of new business formation. Consequently it is not surprising to find Shipbuilding, Metals, Vehicles, and the construction supply industries of Bricks, Pottery Cement and Glass, recording more than 60 per cent of all men entering as founders. Longer established and strongly family based sectors show, in contrast, a heavy representation of Inheritors, this entry route being notably prominent for Paper, Printing and Publishing, Leather and Footwear, Timber and Furniture, and Chemicals and allied trades.

These two categories account for four out of every five of our Scottish business leaders: the remaining, and least common origin of our entrepreneurs was as professional managers. Managerial talent only proved to be an effective passport to business leadership in a small number of trades. The public utilities and Banking, Insurance and Finance provided most opportunities for the deployment of professional skills in law, accountancy, and finance, while the Transport and Communication sector also proved to be an important area for managerial expertise. Among the productive industries, Metals, Engineering, and the Extractive Industries also absorbed significant numbers of expert managers to cope with the technologies of these rapidly growing trades. Conversely, dominant patterns of family ownership and control effectively froze out professional managers from senior positions in a large number of sectors; professional managers in senior positions barely existed in Timber and Furniture, Leather and Footwear, Construction, Shipbuilding, Food, Drink and Tobacco, Paper, Printing and Publishing, and many more.

The fact that nearly 80 per cent of our sample of Scottish entrepreneurs either founded or inherited their firms highlights the significance of the family as a potent influence in entrepreneurial origins. At one level, the ownership of the business by the family, and the pool of skill and experience provided by the father of the businessman, helps explain the pattern of entry to business in Scotland. Some 56 per cent of all our entrepreneurs made their way in occupations previously undertaken by their fathers (*Table 2*). The line of experience from father to son was particularly strong in the Leather and Footwear trades, Timber and Furniture, Food, Drink and Tobacco, Textiles, Paper, Printing and Publishing, and still influential in Chemicals and the Extractive industries.

The family was clearly influential in opening access to skill, information and knowledge of particular businesses, and we may assume, was also important in providing capital. A general indication of the ability of families to support the business aspirations of offsprings may be gleaned from a consideration of the social status of the fathers of our entrepreneurs. (*Table 3*). Six out of every ten fathers of our businessmen were drawn from social class I and another one from social class 2. Nearly 80 per cent were drawn from families with backgrounds in manufacturing, banking, finance, the professions, landed proprietors, teachers, book keepers, construction and so on. Our men of business emerged from a dominantly middle class background. The skilled working class provided only 17 per cent of our business leaders, and the semi-skilled and unskilled only 4 per cent. Family continuity and

Table 2. Occupations of Fathers of Scottish Businessmen: Known Cases, 1860–1960

Sector	Total Cases 381	Known Cases 293	Father in Same Occupation No	%	Father in Different Occupation No	%
Extractive	34	31	20	64	11	35
Metals	26	23	9	39	14	61
Engineering	27	23	6	26	17	74
Shipbuilding	18	15	8	53	7	47
Vehicles	10	7	2	29	5	71
Chemicals	10	9	6	67	3	33
Textiles	44	33	23	70	10	30
Clothing	11	9	4	44	5	56
Leather/ footwear	12	12	12	100	—	—
Food/drink/ tobacco	37	27	21	79	6	22
Bricks/pottery	14	10	5	50	5	50
Timber/ furniture	8	6	5	83	1	17
Construction	21	11	6	54	5	46
Paper/printing	15	12	10	83	2	17
Other manufactures	10	9	2	22	7	78
Gas/water/ electricity	4	1	1	25	—	—
Transport/ communication	33	22	12	54	10	46
Distributive	33	22	10	46	12	54
Banking/ insurance/ Finance	14	11	2	18	9	82
	381	293	164	56	129	44

Source: As Table 1, compiled by Mr D-W Kim

upward mobility as a consequence of business success is also apparent (*Table 4*). While only 37 per cent of the fathers of the founders of business were drawn from social class I, no less than 77 per cent of the Inheritors fathers had moved to that top category. The family was clearly a dominant influence in origins and in the entry of entrepreneurs to business in Scotland. It also was the starting point for the education and training of these men.

The Education and Training of Scottish Entrepreneurs

Schooling

It is very difficult to be precise on the absolute level of schooling undertaken by our group of businessmen. Scotland has long prided

Table 3. Social Status of Fathers of Scottish Businessmen 1860–1960

Sector	Social Class Status					
	Total Cases	% Class 1	% Class 2	% Class 3	% Class 4	Un-known
1 Extractive	34	56	23	9	0	12
2 Metals	26	42	11	27	8	11
3 Engineering	27	48	15	26	7	4
4 Shipbuilding	18	55	27	6	6	6
5 Vehicles	10	60	0	30	0	10
6 Chemicals	10	60	20	0	0	20
7 Textiles	44	64	7	18	2	9
8 Clothing	11	36	27	18	0	18
9 Leather & Footwear	12	83	8	0	0	8
10 Food/drink/tobacco	37	65	11	11	0	13
11 Bricks/pottery cement/glass	14	50	14	29	0	7
12 Timber/furniture	8	62	13	25	0	0
13 Construction	21	33	24	24	10	10
14 Paper/printing publishing	15	60	33	0	0	7
15 Other manufactures	10	70	10	0	10	10
16 Gas/water/electricity	4	75	0	0	0	25
17 Transport/communications	33	54	24	9	6	6
18 Distributive trades	33	39	24	24	3	9
19 Banking/insurance/finance	14	79	7	7	0	7
Totals	381	55	17	15	3	9
Total known cases	345	61	18	17	4	

Source: As for Table 1: compiled by Mr D-W Kim on the basis of a classification devised by Dr R.H. Trainor

Key

Class 1   Manufacturers, Coalmasters, Merchants, Bankers, Financiers, Fundholders, Professionals, Managers, Gentlemen, Landed Proprietors

Class 2   Agents, stewards, factors, salesmen, brokers, clerks, teachers, bookkeepers, minor public figures, contractors, builders, journalists, retailers, service trade operatives, house proprietors, lodging keepers etc.

Class 3   Foreman, Supervisors, Shop Assistants, Warehousemen, Watchmen, Messengers, Janitors, Craftsmen, Skilled Manual Workers

Class 4   Semi-skilled manual, Unskilled manual, Apprentices, domestic servants, unemployed paupers, inmates of public institutions, others

Table 4. Social Status of Fathers of the Founders, Inheritors and Managers of Scottish Business at birth of son. 1860–1960

Social Class	Inheritors		Founders		Managers		Total	
	No.	(%)	No.	(%)	No.	(%)	No.	(%)
Class 1	109	(77)	59	(37)	43	(54)	211	(55)
Class 2	14	(10)	37	(23)	13	(16)	64	(17)
Class 3	6	(4)	40	(25)	12	(15)	58	(15)
Class 4	0	—	7	(4)	5	(6)	12	(3)
Unknown	13	(9)	16	(10)	7	(9)	36	(9)
TOTAL	142	(100)	159	(100)	80	(100)	381	(100)

Source: As Table 1.

itself on being in the forefront of schooling, and it is undoubtedly true that a systematic sequence or hierarchy of schools was set out as early as 1560 by John Knox and his fellow Reformers. In the *First Book of Discipline* they sketched out a basic system. *Elementary Schools* were to be established in every Parish in which children between the ages of five and eight would be taught reading and scripture, usually by the local minister. Beyond that, *Grammar Schools* were to be set up in towns of any size to cater to children of eight to twelve years; in addition to Reading, the pupils in the Grammar Schools would receive instruction in Latin Grammar. At a third level, in the larger towns, it was proposed to develop *High Schools* for selected pupils who would have the opportunity to study Latin, Greek, Rhetoric and Logic. Finally, in the Universities, generally taking students from the age of fourteen, there would be three year courses for students taking Arts subjects, while instruction in Medicine, Law and Divinity stretched over five years.

This 'ideal' framework was never fully introduced, but the terminology and nature of the different types of schools entered into common currency, and most of our businessmen were given their schooling in one or other of these types of schools or institutions. The picture which emerges (*Table 5*) is one in which elementary education to the age of twelve was the only formal schooling undertaken by just over half our sample of entrepreneurs: another 20 per cent had another two years of secondary schooling at the High School and Grammar School level. Most of our men consequently began their business careers with only very basic formal education in reading, writing, arithmetic and scripture. Some sectors were indeed dominated by men with this background; Clothing, Bricks, Pottery, Cement and Glass making had four out of five men with only elementary education, while the Distributive Trades were not far behind.

Outside the school system, however, it is clear that many of our men

Table 5. *The Education and Training of Business Leaders in Scotland 1860–1960. Percentage Distribution by type of Education*

Sector	Elementary Only	Secondary School	Technical College	University Courses	University Degree	Professional Qualifications
Extractive	47	26	6	18	3	
Metals	44	36	12		8	4
Engineering	26	20	15	14	26	
Shipbuilding	44	15	22		28	
Vehicles	50		20		30	
Chemicals	20	60			20	
Textiles	59	18	2	7	14	
Clothing	82	9	9			
Leather/footwear	58	25	8		8	
Food, Drink, Tobacco	59	21	5		8	5
Bricks, Pottery, etc	80	7	7		7	
Timber, Furniture	62	25			13	
Construction	67	19				14
Paper, Printing	42	17		8	33	
Gas, Water, Electricity		33	33		33	
Transport, Commercial	53	31		3	12	
Distributive	74	6	3		6	10
Banking, Insurance	21	14			43	21
Other Manufacturers	60	30				10
Sample (381)	53	21	7	2	15	3

Source. As for Table 1

sought formal instruction in technical courses both in colleges and the universities. The Public Utilities, Shipbuilding, Vehicles and Engineering had significant numbers of men trained in this way. At the university level, degrees were sought in appropriate areas especially in Shipbuilding, Engineering and in the Chemical trades. In Banking and Insurance the high level of university qualification reflects degrees in the Law. In other sectors, however, the training taken at the universities was frequently part of the broadening of the mind, and deepening of culture associated with general studies in arts and humanities.

On this evidence it is difficult to avoid the conclusion that in many sectors of the economy, formal education had little to contribute to the success of our entrepreneurs, since more than half only completed elementary schooling. However, it is clear that much more stress was placed on training in the firm where experiential training was a widespread feature, and was greatly stressed and systematically cultivated.

Table 6. Type of Training Background of Scottish Business Leaders, 1860–1960
Per cent of business leaders within each training category

Sector	Apprentice	Technical/ Professional	Related	Unrelated Trade
Extractive	62	21	0	17
Metals	48	16	24	12
Engineering	44	48	8	
Shipbuilding	56	44		
Vehicles	50	50		
Chemicals/Allied	60	0		40
Textiles	98	2		
Clothing	64	0	36	
Leather/Footwear	92	8		
Food, Drink, Tobacco	81			19
Bricks, Pottery etc	50			50
Timber/Furniture	75		12	13
Construction	76		24	
Paper, Printing, Publishing	100			
Gas, Water, Electricity	0			100
Transport/ Communication	81	9		
Distributive Trades	84	10		
Banking, Insurance, Finance	0	64	36	
Other Manufacturers	20	20	20	40
Scottish Average	67	16	7	10

Source: As Table 1

Business Training

The requirement to undertake a trade training as an apprentice was
very strong among our entrepreneurs (*Table 6*). Two out of three of
our men undertook an apprenticeship specifically in the industry in
which they became business leaders. Indeed, only 10 per cent came to
prominence from a training background which was technically unre-
lated to their final line of business. In some sectors, however, such lack
of specific training was not a serious barrier. Half of the entrepreneurs
in the Bricks, Pottery Cement and Glass sector had no specific apprenticeship in these trades, but came instead from backgrounds as law
clerks, ironmongers, insurance agents, commercial travellers and salesmen. These men essentially came into the marketing, sales, and
administrative areas of the industry and brought in much needed
general skills. Men with similarly broad backgrounds in law and in
general clerical and commercial training also found the Chemicals and
Allied industries a ready outlet for their talents.

Table 7. Age at Entry to Partnership or Equivalent

Sector	(Total)	10–19	20–29	30–39	40–49	50–59	60–69	70–79	Unknown
Extractive	34	1	8	9	11	4	1	—	—
Metals	26	1	6	10	3	4	—	1	1
Engineering	27	1	11	9	4	2	—	—	—
Shipbuilding	18	—	9	5	4	—	—	—	—
Vehicles	10	—	5	2	3	—	—	—	—
Chemicals	10	1	3	1	2	1	—	—	1
Textiles	44	—	16	19	5	2	1	—	1
Clothing	11	—	6	3	1	—	—	—	1
Leather	12	2	6	3	1	—	—	—	—
Food	37	4	15	12	3	1	—	—	2
Bricks	14	1	2	8	—	3	—	—	—
Timber/Furniture	8	—	4	2	—	—	—	—	2
Construction	21	2	8	3	3	—	—	—	5
Paper, Printing	15	2	5	4	2	—	—	—	2
Other Mfr	10	1	2	5	1	—	—	—	1
Gas, Water, Elec	4	—	1	—	—	2	1	—	—
Transport/Comm	33	—	12	12	8	1	—	—	—
Distributive	33	—	15	10	5	—	—	—	3
Banking, Ins etc	14	—	7	3	3	1	—	—	—
Totals	381	16	141	120	59	21	4	1	19
% of Total known	362	4%	39%	33%	16%	6%	1%	—	

Source: As for Table 1. Compiled by Mr D-W Kim

The striking feature is the apparently very high level of apprentice training. This, however, also includes 'in-house training' in many sectors where specific craft apprenticeships did not exist. Such 'in-house' familiarisation under the eye of an experienced departmental head, or family member, was very common in Distribution, Transport and Communication, Clothing, Food, Drink and Tobacco, and Textiles. If this 'in-house' element is excluded the level of formal apprenticeship training is reduced to about 47–50 per cent of the total, still a very high level. Apprenticeships, both formal and informal were also commonly required of even the more formally educated and technically qualified men, usually after, or sometimes in parallel with their college or university training. This was easily accomplished in family dominated businesses.

This type of 'experiential' and 'apprenticeship' training was also a key to very early entry into positions of responsibility in the business. As *Table 7* makes plain, over 40 per cent of all our business leaders had become partners, or directors, or had attained some equivalent leading position in their firms before the age of thirty. More than three quarters of our men had assumed leadership roles before the age of forty. Such an early start in senior positions again reflects the family based structure of much of Scottish business. An interesting corollary of the early age of entry was a very long business life for most of our men. Sixty per cent of these men continued actively in their senior roles after the age of seventy, and only fifteen per cent ended their active careers before the age of sixty (*Table 8*). The fact that so many of Scotland's leading businessmen continued in control, or in leading positions, in their firms long after their most active physical years had passed, must raise questions about the consequences of such structural inertia in management for the health of the firms. Yet while there may be doubts about the wisdom of such long business careers for the conduct of the business, it is clear that these lengthy business associations allowed men to cultivate many non-business roles.

Non-Business Roles of Scottish Entrepreneurs

Another characteristic of these men of business was their close identification with their local communities, their civic and philanthropic roles, and less commonly their contribution to national affairs, either in politics or in the affairs of their industries. As a general rule few of these men were much involved in national affairs prior to the First World War, but thereafter a growing number slipped into national roles.

Table 8. Age at Withdrawal from Business

Known Cases Type/No	Percent in each age group					
	50 %	50–59 %	60–69 %	70–79 %	80–89 %	90+ %
Founders (126)	4	9	25	45	12	2
Inheritors (139)	2	14	23	42	17	3
Mangers (63)	3	14	32	32	21	3
Total (315)	3	12	26	39	16	3
Unknown (66)						

Source. As Table 1. Compiled by Mr D-W Kim

Prior to the First World War most of these men played prominent roles in their local communities. One in three was a Justice of the Peace, sitting in judgment of the misdemeanours of their workmen (*Table 9*). The office of Provost, and councillor attracted many of our men, and in due course many rose to the heights of Deputy Lieutenant of their counties. Local hospitals benefited from their service in life, and their bequests in death, and local education boards almost invariably attracted the support of the local leading men of business. In every local community, libraries, reading rooms, parks, bandstands, halls, hospitals and schools bore the name of local leading men of business

Table 9. Non-Business Interests and Activities of Scottish Businessmen 1860–1960

National Politics	Totals
MP	21
Other Offices	78
Local Government	
JP	121
DL	56
Lord Lieutenant	3
Provost	26
Councillor	54
Other	55
Community Service	
Hospitals/Medical	42
Education Boards	95
Welfare Organisations	29
Volunteer Military	16
Other	14
Honours Received	
Peerages/Knighthoods	62
Other Honours	49
Honorary Degrees	43

Source. As for Table 1.

as a mark of their service and their financial contribution. The local churches were particularly well endowed by our men since many were active in church affairs as elders over many years.

The evidence of these biographies suggests that these men saw themselves, and were seen by others, as a social elite which had distinct obligations to their own communities, and in return for their leadership and support they received in return a distinctive position in the social hierarchy. Their obligations were broadly philanthropic and their local social position might broadly be likened, in English terms, to an urban squirearchy. The return to these men was not only in local influence and local regard, for no fewer than 62 were rewarded with baronetcies or knighthoods, while many others received the freedom of their towns and cities, and no fewer than 43 received Honorary Degrees, mainly from the Universities of Glasgow, Edinburgh and St Andrews. Each in turn received generous bequests and endowments.

Wealthholding

Since the function of firms is to create wealth, and since our society depends so greatly on our businessmen to create that wealth and employment, it is appropriate to ask if involvement in business made these business leaders wealthy. The answer in general is yes, but it is by no means easy to delineate their wealth holding with accuracy. We know for almost all our sample the gross value of their personal estates at death, but it would be imprudent to regard these valuations as a complete assessment of the wealth of these men. The fixed capital in their businesses is unlikely to have been fully reflected in any share valuation included in their estates. Moreover, after the turn of the century and the increasing weight of death duties, it is evident that most of our men took care to transfer much of their wealth to trusts and to family members long before the tax man could get his hands on the family wealth. Nevertheless the data available provides an interesting pattern of wealth creation among our businessmen (*Table 10*). The range of estates at death extends from less than £100 to over £7 million, with an average estate of over quarter of a million pounds. No fewer than 20 of the men died as millionaires; six of them in the Textile sector, three each in Food Drink and Tobacco, and two in each of Shipbuilding and Chemicals. The Extractive Trades, Metal, Engineering, Other Manufacturing, Transport, and Banking Insurance and Finance each recorded one millionaire. The largest fortunes were made in Food Drink and Tobacco (£7 million); Engineering (£3.3 million) Chemicals (£3.1 million); Transport and Communications, and in

Table 10. Wealth at Death in £000 as recorded in gross value of personal estates

Sector	Smallest £000	Largest £000	Mean £000
Extractive	3.7	1180.8	337.1
Metals	3.8	1276.1	215.7
Engineering	0.3	3304.4	220.3
Shipbuilding	23.6	1069.7	241.9
Vehicles	2.6	246.9	83.8
Chemicals	79.3	3151.8	756.7
Textiles	14.8	1496.6	387.6
Clothing	10.2	160.0	54.7
Leather	35.4	600.8	114.3
Food/Drink	5.6	7150.0	534.2
Bricks/Pottery	2.1	99.7	35.2
Timber/Furniture	2.0	179.6	60.3
Construction	21.6	348.2	77.1
Paper Printing	35.3	630.8	139.4
Other Manufactures	3.8	1077.0	180.4
Gas Water Electricity	13.7	542.9	164.2
Transp/Communication	1.3	2183.8	296.0
Distributive	0.08	566.1	88.0
Banking Ins Finance	22.1	2174.8	233.6
Overall	0.08	7150.0	256.3

Source: As for Table 1. Compiled by D-W Kim

Banking and Finance, each with estates of £2.2 million. At the other end of the scale the least wealthy men were found in Construction, Clothing, Bricks Pottery Glass and Cement, and Timber and Furniture.

The wealthiest businessmen were concentrated in the period after 1900, reflecting the maturity of business fortunes and the long lifespan of many of Scotland's leading businessmen. The retention of wealth in the families is also shown in the fact that on average the estates of the inheritors were larger than those of the founders of the businesses, £316 thousand as against £254 thousand. Professional managers, in contrast were much less wealthy with an average estate value of £153 thousand (*Table 11*). In broad terms the accumulation of wealth reflected the pattern of expansion of the economy and the dominance of manufacturing in Scotland; 13 of the 20 millionaires were concentrated in the staple industries, and only two were properly in the service trades.

Conclusions

The origins of the leading businessmen in Scotland are clearly dictated by family influence. Roughly 80 per cent of all our entrepreneurs

Table 11. Wealth at Death by Type of Businessman

	Smallest £	Largest (£000)	Mean £(000)
Founder	84	7150.0	253.6
Inheritor	2183	4405.9	316.2
Manager	1005	1179.9	155.3

Source: As for Table 1. Compiled by D-W Kim

gained entry to business either as founders (over half of whose fathers had experience in that occupation) or as inheritors of going concerns. The chance of making the grade as a successful man of business in Scotland was also heavily influence by the social class of one's father. The upper middle class provided more than one third of all the founders, and nearly 80 per cent of the inheritors of Scottish business in our sample of men.

Family background and family influence was much more significant than formal education in cultivating our business leaders. It seems clear that formal education beyond basic elementary schooling was not a prerequisite for success in Scottish business. Rather it was experience in the job that played a more significant role than paper qualifications. It is evident, however, that the inheritors of businesses enjoyed a much more extensive formal education than did the founders, but in many cases the more extensive education was not routinely related to the needs of the business. Nonetheless the formal educational level of Scottish businessmen did improve over time. Prior to 1870 only one man in three had any post-school education; this proportion increased to one in two among the group who became business leaders after 1900. Yet, in spite of increasing levels of formal education, specific technical training, as distinct from apprenticeships, remained the exception among Scottish entrepreneurs. Founders were frequently more vocationally trained than the inheritors of the business, while the professional managers were normally more specifically trained in technical terms than the family owners. The upshot of this set of characteristic features was that access to senior and controlling positions in the boardrooms of Scottish businesses was strongly linked to family preferment, this accelerating the entry, promotion, and involvement of sons, nephews, and relations by marriage. In almost all sectors blood prevailed over professional talent in access to controlling positions in the firms. This is not to say that family structure excluded the entry of professional managers, they did not. Professional managers did enter many firms and rise to senior and influential positions, but it was rare for such men to acquire any significant interest in the capital of the firm.

The strong commitment of our businessmen to their firms and their families was paralleled by a strong identification with their local community. In this role they exercised great patronage and extensive philanthropy, notably pouring funds into schools, bursaries, libraries, hospitals, parks, churches, galleries and museums and every conceivable good cause. These involvements were particularly notable before the First World War when much of the provision of health and education lay in voluntary contribution rather than in state funding. Local government also was largely in the hands of these men. However, these roles diminished after the First World War as public expectations on the responsibilities of local government widened, and the political influence of the businessman began to be challenged by the rise of the Labour party.

A not uncommon reward for the leadership undertaken in business by these men, was the accumulation of significant personal wealth. It is most evident that the greatest wealth was accumulated before the First World War, that the earliest of Scotland's great staples, textiles, generated the greatest wealth, and that after the First World War Scottish businessmen apparently became less wealthy as steps were taken to make provision for families before death duties could deplete inheritances. It is also clear that, in analysing the estates of Scottish entrepreneurs, specific investment in the business quickly came to be only one element in family investment. Portfolios were quickly diversified, most significantly in railway stocks. However, although family investments were diversified there was little extension of business investment outside the trade of the family firm; transfers of capital into new areas to develop new business ventures were rare. Perhaps the biggest investment outside the business was in the purchase of landed estates, or simply, country houses. There was an almost universal gentrification of the pioneering families in most sectors in making such purchases. On the whole, however, these acquisitions were mainly adjuncts to business rather than alternatives to continued involvement in the firm. They were for relaxation, not for permanent escape from business.

While our investigation of Scottish businessmen has focused on individual entrepreneurs, it is evident that families have been more influential in the promotion of Scottish business than individuals. Family ownership and family control has been the major influence in almost all the main sectors of the economy. In this sense, family networks have been more important than individual attainment. This is not only true of the firms themselves, but family groups have dominated and led in the main industrial sectors. Behind the individual businessman in each sector there stands the group as a system of support, interaction, and influence. The nature of the Scottish economy at the end of the nineteenth century propelled the businessman into a kind of mutually supportive, yet competitive, community. The regional economy was small in scale, concentrated in location and characterized by a complex interdependence of supply and demand linking the great staple industries. Their entrepreneurs were likewise enshrined in contact networks, within which emerged a number of leading coterie who essentially formed Scotland's business aristocracy. In the extractive industries there were the Bairds; in metals the Colvilles and their successors; in chemicals the Tennants, in shipbuilding the Lithgows. Similar coteries with their constellations of influence were found in every sector, and each was increasingly inter-meshed through contact networks on the boards of the banks, the insurance companies and the railways.

Such patterns of interaction were frequently reinforced by marriage, and as the possibility of adopting limited liability opened up, these earlier interlocks were extended in a multiplicity of interconnected directorships. The consequences of this development are not clear, yet there is a coincidence in timing with a slackening of the momentum of the Scottish economy, and the beginning of the eclipse of domestic enterprise and local ownership and control. There may or may not have been an entrepreneurial failing post 1920, but a perceived general weakness in business activity in the economy, was perhaps due in some measure to the growing concentration of family interlocks in ownership and control. It is possible that the concentration made Scottish business less flexible and less responsive than it had been in days of more robust independence.

That, however, is speculation. Nevertheless it is clear that answers to such questions and an understanding of the economic rise and fall of Scotland, may emerge more clearly from a study of our leading businessmen and their families. Business biography is an important and powerful tool of analysis that is only beginning to open up the detail of business success and failure.

REFERENCES

1. J.S. Jeans, *Western Worthies: A Gallery of biographical and critical sketches of West of Scotland celebrities* (Glasgow, 1872)
2. Anon., *Memoirs and Portraits of One Hundred Glasgow Men* 2 vols (Glasgow, 1886)

3. A. Eddington ed. *Edinburgh and the Lothians at the Opening of the Twentieth Century* (Edinburgh, 1904)
4. ESRC, End of Grant Report No. F00230042, *The Businessman in Scotland: A Biography of Enterprise 1860–1960.*
5. A. Slaven & S.G. Checkland eds. *The Dictionary of Scottish Business Biography*
   Vol I, *The Staple Industries* (Aberdeen, 1986)
   Vol II, *Processing, Distribution, Services* (Aberdeen, 1990)
6. Mr Kim's thesis title is 'The origins and characteristics of Scottish Entrepreneurs with special reference to the Textile Industries'. It will be presented for examination in 1993.
7. Detailed information on the methodology adopted is set out in the Introduction to Vol 1, *Dictionary of Scottish Business Biography*

8

Lords & Heritages: The Transformation of the Great Lairds of Scotland

David McCrone & Angela Morris

The power and influence of the great landowners of Scotland has long been identified as one of the key distinctive characteristics of its class structure. The conventional wisdom, however, is that the considerable economic and political power of what Sidney and Olive Checkland[1] called 'the mighty magnates' went into terminal decline in the late 19th and early 20th centuries, especially as their economic power was challenged by a new industrial bourgeoisie, and as their political influence was eroded by the arrival of mass democracy.

This chapter will argue that the power of the lairds has been transformed, not ended; that new forms of economic activity have been taken up; that their influence over politics has become less direct and more informal; and that, above all, their hold over the growing 'heritage industry' at both local and national levels has allowed them new forms of cultural legitimation in the late 20th century.

The argument is in three parts:

—an outline of how lairds are portrayed in the literature—their power and influence;

—an examination of the thesis of decline and the collapse of landowning power, with particular reference to David Cannadine's study *The Decline & Fall of the British Aristocracy*[2];

—an elaboration of the thesis that the power of lairds has been transformed, not ended, and that we need to operate with a more subtle theory of power than that provided by Cannadine. Treating lairds as a status group rather than an economic class, and focusing on the role of 'heritage' provides an alternative way of understanding their social position.

Who is a Laird?

At the outset, there is an issue of nomenclature. Who exactly are we talking about? Are we referring to the great landowners—the aristocracy, or to that mass of land holders who in Scotland fall under the omnibus term 'lairds'? The term 'laird' is nicely ambiguous, as we can see from the Scots Dictionary[3]. Deriving from the old Scots word 'laverd', a lord, it can refer to (1) a prince or chief (late 14th century); (2) the landlord of landed property or an estate (15th century); (3) applied with the patronymic to the chief of a Highland clan as in the 'laird of McGregor'; (4) 'chiefly of lesser landowners, a landowner holding directly to the Crown, and so entitled to come to parliament (till the 18th century), but not a lord of parliament'; (5) or merely, an owner of property in general, but especially a house owner.

This ambiguity may present us with analytical problems, but it does convey an important ideological resource for landowners, and helps us understand just how they have sought to legitimate themselves in a society which has frequently been very hostile towards them. It seems to us more important to allow this ambiguity because it tells us much about the language used to legitimate power. In much the same way at the British level, the term 'aristocracy' emerged as a status description from the early 19th century, glossing over legal distinctions between the peerage and the wider class of landowners. As John Scott has pointed out:

> The language of class came to use 'aristocracy' to describe the social category rooted in the power bloc of the old society. The word 'gentleman' remained in use to describe its individual members.[4]

Without implying that lairds and aristocrats are the same social category, or that Timperley's analytical distinction between 'great landlords', 'lairds' and 'bonnet lairds' is not relevant[5], we will argue that the umbrella term 'lairds' serves important ideological purposes, binding the small landowner to the mighty lord. For example, it allowed James Fergusson in his apologia *Lowland Lairds* written in 1949 to say:

> They should be remembered not as picturesque antiquities, but for what they did. They cared for the land and for their dependents with as much thought as does the modern State and often with more discrimination. To them too, Scotland owes all its finest woodlands, a quantity of noble architecture, and collections great and small, of pictures, books and furniture which have made the Scottish country house a living and harmonious example of our culture at its best.[6]

These are interesting grounds on which to pitch a defence, because they convey a very modern sense of legitimacy—that the lairds are keepers of Scotland's heritage—which we will make a central part of our argument in this chapter.

Fergusson's account was written in 1949 under the continuing shadow of the powerful attack by Tom Johnston—*Our Scots Noble*

Families—published in 1911[7], which captured the hostility to the landed elite in Scotland which had been such a central feature of both Liberal politics in the 19th century and Labour's in the early 20th century. (The use of the word 'laird' as a term of abuse would also have political resonances among the urban working class, for as Christopher Smout has pointed out, such a term was also used in the towns and cities as a synonym for 'landlord'[8]).

Fergusson's use of 'laird' allowed him to present 'landowners' in much more attractive—and above all, Scottish—light. Thus he could elide social divisions between the great landowners, and 'bonnet lairds' (his family came from Kilcheran of lowland landed stock). He implies that social mobility was more obvious:

> Class distinctions were never strong in Scotland. Earls' families intermarried with knights', the small laird wedded the daughter of the great, and the great laird might choose his bride from the daughter of the prosperous burgess—while that burgess himself might be the son or grandson of some cadet of a noble house.[9]

Of course, this claim is not easily validated, but that is not its purpose. It is to ground the laird firmly in the Scottish tradition, not as some alien, anglicised imposition (post 1603 and 1707 always an accusation), but part of the fabric of Scotland's social structure. The laird almost becomes the lad o' pairts, but not quite. The contrast is with English squires (who else?), and with French seigneurs. Three factors, Fergusson argues, made for a 'kinship of feeling' which in 1949 at any rate was far from dead. This 'kinship' arose 'partly from the feudal relationship which bound the laird's Jock to the laird as it bound Harden to Buccleuch and Buccleuch to the king'. It also derived, in Fergusson's view, 'partly from a common simplicity of life and manners', and thirdly, 'perhaps partly from a community of race, since the Norman strain was assimilated in the Scottish nobility instead of overlaying society with an alien aristocracy, as happened in England.'[10]

By raising the Norman question Fergusson was alluding to an older and prevalent myth about the Scottish heritage, what Marinell Ash called the Bruce-Wallace controversy[11]. The preference for the 'proletarian' Wallace over the 'aristocratic' Bruce had long figured in arguments about the true Scotland, and had been given additional mileage by Tom Johnston in 1911. Johnston denounced the Scottish aristocracy on the grounds that 75% of them are 'descendants of foreign freebooters who forcibly took possession of our land after the Norman Conquest of 1066'[12]. Again

> Bruce, a Norman, convinced our forefathers that his fight against the English was for Scottish freedom, and lo, when the invading hosts were driven back, the Bruce handed our common fields to his fellow Normans.'[13]

Whether or not any of this carries historical accuracy is subordinated to the ideological purpose of such claims. Wallace and Bruce seem to have been recreated as political persona operating in a modern agenda. There is, then, some irony in the attempts by latter-day politicians to proclaim their roots. Shortly before the 1992 general election, for example, Conservative Central Office described the Secretary of State for Scotland's Scottish credentials thus:

> Ian Lang, a Scot whose Bruce grandmother claimed to have traced family ties back to Scotland's greatest patriot King Robert the Bruce, finds accusations by separatist opponents that he is 'unpatriotic' ironic, to say the least. Ian (whose middle name is Bruce)....

Legitimating the present by mobilising the past is a trickier business than politicians know.

Nevertheless, capturing 'heritage' for ideological purposes is a powerful means of legitimacy. What, for example, both Johnston and Fergusson were engaged in was a war of legitimacy against and for the lairds. Johnston sought to portray them as a cynical bunch of foreign freebooters, and Fergusson as indigenous creators of Scotland. He describes how the lowland lairds were important in setting up the Kirk, in transforming agriculture (as 'Improvers'), and in encouraging learning and developing politics, both local and national. Fergusson's aim in writing the 1949 book was not simply to give them a further stay of execution in a post-war world but to prolong their active life. He argued that

> the spirit that once vitalised that responsibility must not perish; it must be directed into other channels, into conscientious service of the land itself, and into the innumerable committees, from those of a county council downwards, through which local government is carried on. It is in this sphere that the traditions of the old lairds must be kept alive and renewed.[14]

Fergusson's predictions were fulfilled. From this period until the reorganisation of local government in 1974, the energies of the lairds were funnelled into county councils and committees. For example, in Roxburgh County Council, the Dukes of Buccleuch and Roxburghe between them held the convenership of the council for 43 years between 1900 and 1975. The Border lairds were to exercise their influence directly in this way, but also indirectly through the offices of Sheriff depute, and Commissioners of Supply. They were Lord-Lieutenants of the counties, and Commissioners of Peace. In 1918, the Duke of Roxburghe was convener of Roxburgh County Council; his vice-convener was the Duke of Buccleuch. In 1975, just before the county council was abolished the convener was the Duke of Roxburghe, and the Duke of Buccleuch was on the council. Not much, it seemed, had changed.

The reorganisation of local government in 1974 and the removal of the border lairds from positions of direct political power meant that new channels of influence had to be found. Fergusson, however, would not have been surprised to learn that by the 1990s the end of the lairds has not happened, and their 'spirit' had found new avenues of wealth creation and cultural legitimacy. Ironically, this involved converting the history with which Tom Johnston had tried to convict them into a commodity whereby they could save themselves.

The Power of the Laird

To focus initially on this ideological struggle concerning the lairds in Scotland does not imply that 'reality' does not matter. Indeed, historians seem well agreed that landowners have been unusually powerful in Scotland. In Timperley's words: 'Power and landownership have been synonymous in Scotland from time immemorial'[15]. Her own pioneering work on landownership in 1771 ('great landowners' were defined as owning more than £2000 Scots) shows that 'the overall control of Scotland's land by the great landlords was most complete in the Borders at around 65%, and up the east coast, 40–50%.'[16] The exceptions, she argues, were in the west and central regions where the great landlords never owned more than 35% of land. Most of the wealthiest estates were owned by titled families, and of the 123 wealthiest estates, 81 were owned by people with titles.

The 1872 survey of land was a symptom of mounting political pressure, designed some argue to show that land was far more equitably distributed than it actually was. However, as Callander comments:

> The 1500 largest landowners in Scotland had held over 90% of the country in 1872, and this had only dropped a percentage point or two thirty years later.[17]

The 20th century saw some reduction in the area held by larger estates, and an increase in the number of small owners, especially owner-occupied farms, and the expansion of land owned by the state and public agencies. The evidence for landownership in the 1970s rests on the work by Roger Millman, augmented by John McEwan[18]. Despite some reduction in the number of very large estates over 20,000 acres, 'the traditional estate survived with a fair degree of constancy during the period 1872 to 1970'[19], and the average proportion of Scotland's counties in estates of more than 1000 acres fell from 92.8% in 1872 to 62.8% in 1970. However, by the third quarter of the 20th century in

the arable South-East of Scotland, the proportion of non-owner occupied farm holdings, according to the agricultural census, stood at 45%
(in Berwickshire) and 49% in East Lothian. Some attrition had occurred. Lord Lauderdale through the Lauder Estates had owned 24,700
acres in Berwickshire in 1874, and 8100 acres in the same county in
1970. Similarly, the Earl of Haddington's landholding had dwindled
from 14,300 acres to 9,200 acres over the same period. Nevertheless,
it is the stability in landownership rather than the change which is
evident. As Callander comments

> In 1970, three-quarters of all privately owned land in Scotland was still held in
> estates of 1000 acres or more, half in estates of 5000 acres or more, and one-third
> in estates of 20,000 or more.[20]

Callander's view is that the apparently higher rate of estate turnover
in recent decades is simply the result of a small number, mostly owned
by absentee landowners, changing hands more frequently, and he
concludes that 'the present pattern of landownership in Scotland still
matches closely the earlier patterns stretching back through the last
nine centuries'[21]. He quotes the comment by Sir John Sinclair that 'In
no country in Europe are the rights of proprietors so well defined and
so carefully protected.'[22]

By and large, historians have viewed lairds (and especially the great
landowners) as a class 'in an even more powerful position than those
in England'[23]. At the top of the social scale, for example, at the turn
of this century stood the mighty magnates, men (rarely women) head-
ing the great houses of Buccleuch, Argyll, Bute, Atholl, Sutherland and
Roxburghe who owned vast tracts of the Scottish countryside and not
a little urban land forby. The historical consensus seems to be that this
was a rentier class which made its money from its substantial stake in
land, and through it control of key social institutions. In his review of
late 19th century social welfare, Ian Levitt quotes this telling comment
from the *Scots Pictorial* for 1897:

> The administration of nineteenth century welfare in Scotland was dominated not
> by new forces, the new wealth, the industrial capitalist that ruthlessly exploited the
> natural and labour resources around them, but by an older set, one that looked
> back to an earlier, seemingly golden period. Scottish government meant the laird,
> who as was said by Skelton, sought the quietness of the country life but instead
> 'lamented the encroachment of Morningside suburbia.'[24]

The gentry were also marked off from the bourgeoisie by their commitment to the country rather than the town, and in cultural terms,
they diluted their Scottishness by sending their sons to English (or
English-style) Public Schools. Roy Campbell has pointed to the

propensity of large proprietors to educate their sons in this way, for it was based on

> the belief that intellectually and culturally Scotland could not offer the wider horizon for the life of an educated and cultured gentleman. It led as a direct consequence to the need to speak and write in a language most easily understood by cultured society, and that was not to be found in Scotland for many.'[25]

In religious terms too it was a divided class, with some retaining an allegiance to Episcopalianism and even, like the Lothians and Bute, to Catholicism. Whereas in England the established Church played an important role in defining the status of 'the gentleman' and in legitimating their social and cultural ascendancy[26], in Scotland the lairds could not count on the unequivocal support of the Kirk.

Those who had access to the trappings of an older Highland culture could play the clan chief. Here we find echoes of the kind of claim to social legitimacy which James Fergusson had recourse to in 1949. Here, for example, is the Duchess of Erroll, as Hereditary Lord High Constable of Scotland, writing a preface in 1968 to a book of clan tartans:

> In too many countries the great historic families are separated from the mass of the people, but in Scotland we have been fortunate in that pride of Name has never depended on wealth and rank, and in that the clan tradition has always prevented class barriers from arising to divide our proud nation . . . We are all one family of Scots, the branches of that family being the clans and Names, and the Chief of Chiefs our Queen.[27]

The possession of country estates allowed the Scottish lairds and their families and friends to forge a distinctive lifestyle with its pastoral and sporting pursuits.

In political terms, too, the lairds were marked out as different. They had provided the leadership of the Conservative Party and had helped to give it its somewhat reactionary image right down until the 1890s[28]. Even after the issue of Irish Home Rule had split the Liberal Party there were important social differences between the Conservatives and the new dissident Liberal Unionists. In the 1895 intake of Scottish MPs, for example, 9 of those labelled Conservatives were landowners, 7 were businessmen and 1 came from the professions. In contrast, 9 Liberal Unionists were businessmen, 2 were professionals, and only 3 described themselves as landowners. In contrast to the aggressive market orientation of Liberal-Unionism, Toryism was, in Hutchison's phrase, the creed of 'lairds and law agents'[29].

For most of the 19th century, however, the lairds in Scotland were disproportionately powerful and influential, and, in the assessment of historians and contemporaries alike, overwhelmingly reactionary.

Johnston's attack on Scotland's 'Noble Families' in 1911 would not, in all probability, have been seen as other than fair comment, and Robert Burns' assault on 'yon birkie ca'd a lord' would have resonated long after it was written in the 1790s. The lairds seemed set for an inevitable fall.

The Cannadine Thesis: The Decline and Fall of the Aristocracy

Cannadine's is by no means the only account of the collapsing power of the landowner in these islands, but undoubtedly the latest and most comprehensive. His thesis is straightforward, and reflected in the title of his book. In the 1870s,

> These patricians were still the most wealthy, the most powerful and the most glamorous people in the country, corporately—and understandably—conscious of themselves as God's elect. But during the 100 years that followed, their wealth withered, their power faded, their glamour tarnished, and their collective sense of identity and purpose gradually but inexorably weakened.[30]

Cannadine is at pains to emphasise that his is a work of British rather than simply English history. Hence, he traces the interlocking elites of Scotland, England, Ireland and Wales. Landowners, he points out, were particularly dominant in late 19th century Scotland and Ireland, where 93% and 78% respectively of land was held in estates of more than 1000 acres (in contrast to 56% in England and 61% in Wales). In 1880, four out of the top ten great British landowners were Scottish (Buccleuch, Bute, Sutherland and Hamilton), and 9 out of the top 29 had Scottish estates. Land agitation against the landed classes was a feature of the late 19th century Celtic countries whereas 'the social fabric of rural England was never subjected to the same degree of stress'[31]. Cannadine argues that the charges made in these countries were exaggerated and owed more to thin soil, poor climate and what he terms 'the peasant mentality'[32].

In Ireland and Wales, as a result of religious and political agitation, the landowners virtually disappeared, whereas in England and Scotland they did not. The implication of this, of course, is that the landowners had a particular grip on Scotland, given that they started out from a much higher ownership base than in England. This economic domination was reflected in political control at the local level. Whereas in 1892, two-thirds of conveners of Scottish county councils were local landowners, 7 were peers and 5 were also lord-lieutenants. Even by 1940, one-half of conveners were local landowners, 7 were peers and 10 were also lord-lieutenants[33].

What, according to Cannadine, was to bring about the decline of this powerful class? His explanation is fairly straightforward. Their loss of material and economic power, most notably relating to the long fall in land prices since the 1880s, meant that at the local level their prestige and status deteriorated, and at the national level their political power both in the House of Lords and in the Commons suffered. By the 1980s, 'the old landed order had effectively ceased to be an economically definable class at all'[34]. Just as the old aristocracy ceased to dominate the land as the new 'plutocracy' translated their new wealth into old forms of prestige, so the landed classes took up new forms of money-making. The Buccleuchs, the largest landowners in Scotland, were no exception:

> Even a ducal family as broad-acred and illustrious as the Buccleuchs had become unprecedently involved in the City and big business by the inter-war years. In a family as rich as the Buccleuchs, it was the younger sons who took to business: the Duke himself and the heir to the title remained essentially full-time landowners.[35]

In Cannadine's view, the last hundred years have seen the decline of the landed aristocracy as a class:

> The fact remains that the traditional landed class has ceased to exist as the unchallenged and supreme elite in which wealth, status and power are highly correlated, and are underpinned by territorial pre-eminence.[36]

It is important at this stage to underline the concepts Cannadine uses. As we can see from the above, he considers the aristocracy as a 'class', and explicitly employs the analytical model of Max Weber to account for their decline. Hence, his first task is to consider the patricians' financial resources; secondly, how that wealth was translated into social prestige and status; and finally, how powerful this class was as a ruling or governing elite. His view is that as their economic base was challenged as a 'class', so they were progressively unable to translate wealth into social prestige and political power. Almost inevitably, their social position declined.

The Transformation of Power

It would be perverse to dispute the broad sweep of Cannadine's argument that the aristocracy in particular and the landed elite in general have lost power. However, we wish to argue that his model of power predisposes him to expect their demise, to predict the end rather than the transformation of their power. Our argument, on the other hand, is that there is considerable mileage in treating this group as, in Weber's terms, more of a status group rather than a class[37]. In this way we can highlight how they sought to define and adapt the boundaries of the group, to allow entry to those with new forms of power and to exclude others. Above all, such a perspective allows us to focus on aspects of life style, on social rather than economic means of control and boundary maintenance. In this way, we can see aspects of social consumption, beliefs and life style not as the inevitable outcomes of economic determinants but as relatively autonomous from class position. If we approach the lairds from this perspective we are better able to explain why, for example, 'aristocratic values' (as in so-called Public Schools) survive. To do this, we must first set out more precisely what we mean by 'status'.

In describing the three dimensions of power as economic, social and political (and their corresponding social types, class, status groups and parties/organisations) Weber wished to show that theoretically societies could be stratified in different and quite complex ways. Hence, depending on which dimension(s) was dominant and how it related to the others we would not expect societies to be identical with regard to the final configuration of power. While, for example, in capitalist societies the economic dimension of power (and hence classes) will predominate, the particular mix will reflect in large part the historical legacy of different societies. The distribution and culture of power in Britain, for example, differ noticeably from the United States despite the fact that both are capitalist societies.

In strictly ideal-typical terms, status groups for Weber are distinct from classes.

> In contrast to the purely economically determined 'class situation', we wish to designate as 'status situation' every typical component of the life of men that is determined by a specific, positive or negative, social estimation of honour. This honour may be connected with any quality shared by a plurality, and of course it can be knit to a class situation: class distinctions are linked in the most varied ways with status distinctions. Property as such is not always recognized as a status qualification, but in the long run it is, and with extraordinary regularity.[38]

The point Weber is making here is that while status groups frequently have economic dimensions, it is possible for the propertied and the propertyless to belong to the same status group. The 'clan' would be a very obvious example of such a group. However, such disparity of wealth may make a status group quite unstable in the long-run, and hence there tends to be a correlation between economic and social power. A specific style of life is normally expected from members of a status group, and because members are peculiarly dependent on social acceptance by other members, social order can be maintained. What might seem the trivia of social life—matters of dress, decorum, diet, religion and ritual—are central to it because these become the means of social control. In Barnes' words:

> A distinct life style is not an accidental consequence of how members are able to live, given their position in a hierarchy of consumption privileges. It is nearer the mark to think of the need for exclusivity and distinctiveness having to be met through consumption.[39]

In this way, matters of economic activity are derived from social interaction through the group, and not vice versa. The emphasis placed upon defining social intercourse by means of inter-marriage, shared leisure pursuits and educational experiences have to be understood in this context. That is why Weber pays particular attention to castes as examples of status groups from which economic opportunities follow (or not, as the case may be). Similarly, Weber was interested in the Junkers of late 19th and early 20th century Prussia, a group of landed aristocrats whose inability to control social and economic access to power was their undoing.

In strictly theoretical terms (although not necessarily in practice), classes and status groups are antithetical. In Weber's words

> We have seen . . . that the market and its processes knows no personal distinctions: 'functional' interests dominate it. It knows nothing of honour. The status order means precisely the reverse: stratification in terms of honour and styles of life peculiar to status groups as such.[40]

This excursus into the realms of Weberian sociology provides a valuable antidote to a sort of crude class theory in which economic interests preordain social and political privileges. It is interesting that Cannadine rests his study on Weberian ideas, but his interpretation of these is less convincing. The point to be made here is that status groups (and social honour which derives from it as means of social control) have the theoretical capacity to be independent of class interests. To reinforce this important point, consider this comment by the Weberian scholar, Randall Collins:

> Weber tends to speak of classes and status groups as antithetical phenomena. For example, he speaks of status group-based monopolies as characteristic of traditional societies, where they act as irrational constraints on the market. Thus in many feudal and patrimonial societies, the hereditary appropriation or exclusion of groups from military, landowning, mercantile or other occupations is a phenomenon antithetical to rationalised capitalism.[41]

The point Collins is making is not that status groups do not care about money. Far from it. They seek to control access to money-making very precisely, but not in ways which are determined by the 'market'. How successful they are in doing this will determine whether or not they succeed as a status group. The problem in market or capitalist societies is that such principles and procedures do not sit at all well with the new economic order. As Frank Parkin has pointed out:

> The political driving force of individualist doctrines arose in part from the opposition of the emergent middle classes to aristocratic pretensions and exclusiveness centred around the notion of descent.[42]

Parkin identifies in Weber's writings the concept of 'social closure', a process whereby social collectivities seek to maximise their rewards by restricting access to resources and opportunities to a narrow circle of eligible people. Hence, ruling groups succeed where they gain monopolistic control over valued resources such as land, esoteric knowledge or arms, most obviously in the case of aristocratic domination and reproduction via the lineage system. This capacity to capture for one's peers and descendants exclusive social privilege marks out the essence of status group domination. Where status groups cannot maintain such dominance or make adjustments to share power with new sources of power, they go to the wall, as in the case of the Prussian Junkers.

In other situations, notably the landed elites in Britain, there was a more or less successful adjustment to the new order, although a gradual loss of power and distinctiveness nonetheless. It is this process of adjustment which was referred to by Marx as the 'historic compromise' between the old and new orders. Some historians have even judged the capacity of the old society to adjust to change to be so successful that Britain never actually became a thoroughly capitalist society in terms of its dominant values at all[43]. Others, like Scott, are content to acknowledge that economic change was refracted through an older social order, recognised by the description, 'patrician capitalism'[44].

Understanding Scottish Lairds

If we consider lairds in general as a status group rather than as a class, then we can begin to see that theirs has been a continuous struggle to hold the line on social privilege. Without denying in any way that they have used their property assets as productive resources, it seems that their social behaviour can better be understood in this way. For example, the concern with the lifestyle of the 'gentleman', with the proper ways of behaving, with 'noblesse oblige', and correctness of rituals and beliefs does reveal the principles of status honour rather than class advantage.

This is not to imply, however, that there is no or little concern with forms of money-making. Cannadine's book shows that the landed elite have been quite successful in retaining economic privilege. While it is true that the old patrician class no longer forms the wealth elite, the landed elite are still well represented among the wealthy. In 1988, for example, 20% of the richest 100 in Britain were members of the nobility[45]. Of these no less than 8 had Scottish titles—in descending order of wealth, Buccleuch (£309m), Atholl (£143m), Seafield (£120m), Argyll (£87m), Sutherland (£83m), Roxburghe (£72m), Cawdor (£57m), and Stair (£54m).

The standard practice in the modern period has been for new money and old wealth to conjoin, as for example, in the fusion of the Tennant family, whose wealth had come from manufacture, and the Ogilvies[46]. This pattern of astute intermarriage has been a remarked upon feature over the last couple of centuries. In some cases it has not been needed. The wealth of the Buccleuchs is focused around the 277,000 acres and three estates they own at Bowhill & Drumlanrig in the Scottish Borders, and their English estate at Boughton. The Border estates are managed by a company of the same name, which employs over 300 people and had a turnover in 1990 of nearly £5m, on which the company makes a profit of around 12%. The fixed assets on the estates are valued at just over £7m, backed up by further investments of over £6.5m. The company is entirely in family hands, with the exception of the estates factor who has modest shareholding. The running of the estates is largely carried out by the Earl of Dalkeith, the Duke's eldest son and heir. While the estates are a central economic activity, it is clear that the Buccleuch's wealth is not dependent upon them, for they represent a mere 5% of the family's assets.

The Buccleuchs are, of course, unusual insofar as they belong to the top stratum of aristocratic grandees, rather than to that of run-of-the-mill lairds. However, they do indicate the new ways in which the economic winds were blowing. They were, too, among the first in the 1970s to embark on the stately homes business, and all three of their 'homes' are part of their heritage portfolio. The Buccleuchs had been active in local and national politics, both as local grandees and as MPs (although the Earl was to fail twice to win the Conservative nomination for a Borders constituency in the new-model Thatcherite party). The Duke's interests reflect those of the traditional laird: he is or has been chairman of the Royal Highland and Agricultural Society, the Galloway Cattle Society, Animal Diseases Research Association, as well as patron of various disabled and welfare associations.

Other lairds have a wider portfolio. Atholl, for example, is president of the Scottish Landowners Federation (not inappropriate for a great laird), is director of a couple of publishing companies Westminster

Press, and Pearson Longman, and has been chairman of the Red Deer Commission and RNLI. Perhaps the key to new forms of legitimacy and influence lies in the capture of heritage. Atholl himself is vice-president of the National Trust for Scotland, and the council lists of that body ring with aristocratic titles. NTS was founded by a handful of lairds in 1931 including Atholl, Colquhoun, Crawford & Balcarres, and Stirling-Maxwell. By 1991, Wemyss & March is president, Atholl and Bute are vice-presidents, and the council itself is seeded with lairds and titles.

The conventional wisdom about the stately home industry is that it is largely a financial device to maintain the great houses by state and voluntary means. There is clearly truth in this, but not the whole of it. The inclusion of the word 'home' helps to evoke the private as well as the public domains, just as 'house' describes the family and its name as well as its relationship to its property—titles, residences, heirlooms and land. It is these relationships which are captured by 'heritage'. As Wright remarks, the symbolism of 'home' has 'been used to romanticise the patriarchal family, to idolise domestic drudgery, and to vaunt a national heritage of "stately homes" '[47].

In essence, what we might broadly call heritage has cultural as well as economic significance. Heritage is a word which by its own self-definition cannot be defined. It is however ideologically loaded. The state itself by means of land and heritage acts in 1946, 1980 and 1983 has been responsible for giving 'heritage' its elevated status in national consciousness and mythology. This clearly operates at both the British and at the Scottish levels, and at the latter level is particularly important given the historic attacks on lairds in Scotland. 'Heritage' at both the local and national levels has provided them with means of 'capturing' national culture. In Patrick Wright's words: 'The National Trust [he is talking about the English one, but the same applies to NTS] has become an ethereal kind of holding company for the dead spirit of the nation'[48]. In Scotland, the 'nation' is itself ambiguous, referring to Scotland or to Britain.

Cannadine acknowledges that 'heritage' has become strongly associated with landowners, but his explanation for this is that it reflected their declining influence elsewhere. With the end of Empire, jobs for patrician consuls dried up, and hence becoming cultural trustees filled a gap. But there is more to it than that. Cannadine tends to see heritage as a fall-back position:

> In the mid 1970s great families who had hitherto refused to soil their hands in the stately homes business capitulated; the Roxburghes at Floors, and the Buccleuchs at Boughton, Bowhill & Drumlanrig.[49]

But this promotion of stately homes is not simply a 'capitulation' to economic pressures. What the heritage business allows the laird to do is to insinuate their own history into that of the nation. Scotland (or Britain) through the biographies of its great families (with the Royal one at the head) is what heritage allows. History becomes a means of justifying the social order rather than simply a rather colourful legacy of one's ancestors. Further, heritage fuses the national and the local— the history of the nation and that of the family through its stately 'home'. The other trick is to present the contents of these houses— their bric-a-brac—as the treasures of the nation, with the lairds as the custodians of the nation's heritage. Macro- and micro-heritage become fused in the family dynasty. In a democratic age in which the implicit authority of nobility is questioned, capturing the 'nation' in this way is quite a feat. In Cannadine's words: 'During the last 20 years or so, they have invented a new role for themselves, as the self-appointed guardians of the so-called "national" heritage'[50].

Central to this quest are bodies like the National Trust for Scotland whose ruling councils have been dominated by lairds from the outset. As a quintessential 'voluntary' body it calls into play all the old sets of duties and expectations, and manages the inclusion and exclusion of interests quite carefully. NTS has developed its own vision of 'national heritage'—'little houses', for example, which helps to avoid accusations of elitism. Its vision of society is a paternalistic one, in which there is an invisible cord binding the big house to the little house, the rich to the poor. It evokes an older set of values in which social position is a taken-for-granted duty not an opportunity to enhance one's wealth.

'National heritage' is a conservative idea, but one not easily captured by any single political party, still less a neo-liberal Conservative one. It fuses with ideas of multiple micro- or local heritages. If the nation's history can be told through the family's biography, its genealogy, then one cannot destroy one without the other. The family and the country are one. Hence, heritage techniques allow the retelling of myth, like the myth of the buck which justifies the massive landholdings of the Buccleuchs. The saving of King Kenneth by Scott of Buck-Cleugh would seem a better justification than a purely etymological one describing a local geological feature, and infinitely less embarrassing than the more likely account that lands were given as a reward for military services rendered to the family as a foreign mercenaries in the 17th century.

In this heritage account, the public and the private domains are elided. The Duke of Buccleuch 'owns' the land around Ettrick Forest because they were bestowed upon his ancestors in return for services to Robert the Bruce (him again) in the 14th century. At the same time, the Duke is, in the words of the Bowhill guidebook, only 'a life trustee dedicated to the constant improvement of a vital asset to the benefit of everyone concerned, as well as further generations of his own family, on whom the responsibility for future progress rests.' The guidebook is acting not simply as a spatial account of the family property, but as a chronological narrative of how the dynasty came to occupy the position it holds. The guidebook goes on:

> Once the links in the chain of continuity are broken, through the irreversible process of the break-up of estates, the merits of multiple land-use are lost forever. The advantage of continuity spanning many generations apply just as much to the families of those who occupy let farms and estate employees. On Buccleuch estates some family partnerships between landlord and tenant go back possibly as far as the 12th century.

Thus, the ideology of land and landownership is intricately connected and interwoven with a theory of history in a vernacular and informal sense and with a theory of everyday life. The Buccleuchs are able to exploit the ambiguity in the word 'nation'. While their works of art are part of the British 'national' heritage, their connections with Bruce and with Douglas (the family name associated with Drumlanrig in the western borders) make their Scottish credentials abundantly clear. The Buccleuchs and their fellow lairds see themselves as champions of 'history' rather than as captains of a heritage 'industry'. It is not a coincidence that Walter Scott played such an important part in the 'heritagisation' of Scotland as well as of the Buccleuchs whom he considered his (highly anomalous) 'clan chief'. Scott's own house on the banks of the Tweed is both a monument to Scottish History as well as a profitable part of the Scottish heritage industry itself. As Scotland's own place in the British state is questioned as never before, so Scotland's lairds appear to have succeeded in converting their own and the nation's history into commodities whereby they can save themselves.

REFERENCES

1. S. and O. Checkland, *Industry and Ethos: Scotland, 1832–1914*, (London, 1984).
2. D. Cannadine, *The Decline and Fall of the British Aristocracy*, (London, 1990).
3. M. Robinson, ed., *The Concise Scots Dictionary*, (Aberdeen, 1985), p.354.
4. J. Scott, *Who Rules Britain?*, (Cambridge, 1991), p.59.
5. L. Timperley, 'The Pattern of Landholding in 18th Century Scotland', in M.L. Parry and T.R. Slater, eds., *The Making of the Scottish Countryside*, (London, 1980).
6. J. Fergusson, *Lowland Lairds*, (London, 1949), p.23.

7. T. Johnston, *Our Scots Noble Families,* (Glasgow, 1911).
8. T.C. Smout, *A Century of the Scottish People, 1830–1950,* (London, 1986).
9. J. Fergusson, *Lowland Lairds,* p.14.
10. *Ibid.,* p.24.
11. M. Ash 'William Wallace and Robert the Bruce: The Life and Death of a National Myth', in R. Samuel and P. Thompson, eds., *The Myths We Live By,* (London, 1990).
12. Johnston, *Scots Noble Families,* p.ix.
13. *Ibid.,* p.viii.
14. Fegusson, *Lowland Lairds,* pp.26–7.
15. Timperley, 'Pattern of Landholding in 18th Century Scotland', p.137.
16. R. Callander, *A Pattern of Landownership in Scotland: With Particular Reference to Aberdeenshire,* (Aberdeen, 1987), p.48.
17. *Ibid.,* pp.78–9.
18. J. MacEwan, *Who Owns Scotland? A Study in Landownership,* (Edinburgh, 1977).
19. Callander, *A Pattern of Landownership in Scotland,* p.81.
20. *Ibid.,* p.92.
21. *Ibid.,* p.131.
22. *Ibid.,* p.136.
23. S. and O. Checkland, *Industry and Ethos,* p.56.
24. I. Levitt, 'Welfare, Government and the Working Class: Scotland, 1845–1894', in D. McCrone, S. Kendrick and P. Straw, eds., *The Making of Scotland: Nation, Culture and Social Change,* (Edinburgh, 1989).
25. R.H. Campbell, *The Rise and Fall of Scottish Industry,* (Edinburgh, 1988), p.103.
26. Scott *Who Rules Britain?.*
27. R. Bain, *The Clans and Tartans of Scotland,* (Glasgow, 1968), p.7.
28. M. Fry, *Patronage and Principle: A Political History of Scotland, 1832–1914,* (Aberdeen, 1987).
29. I.G.C. Hutchison, *A Political History of Scotland, 1832–1924,* (Edinburgh, 1986), p.200.
30. Cannadine, *Decline and Fall of the British Aristocracy,* p.2.
31. *Ibid.,* p.60.
32. *Ibid.,* p.62.
33. *Ibid.,* p.161.
34. *Ibid.,* p.638.
35. *Ibid.,* p.417.
36. *Ibid.,* p.693.
37. M. Weber, *Economy and Society,* (London, 1978), part IV.
38. *Ibid.,* p.32.
39. B. Barnes, 'Status Groups and Collective Action', *Sociology,* (26, 1992), p.265.
40. Weber, *Economy and Society,* p.936.
41. R. Collins, *Weberian Sociological Theory,* (Cambridge, 1986), p.128.
42. F. Parkin, *Marxism and Class Theory: a Bourgeois Critique,* (Oxford, 1979), p.64.
43. M. Wiener, *English Culture and the Decline of the Industrial Spirit, 1850–1980,* (London, 1981).
44. Scott, *Who Rules Britain?.*
45. 'Britain's Richest 200', *Money Magazine,* March 1988, p.20.
46. J. Scott and M. Hughes, *The Anatomy of Scottish Capital,* (London, 1980), pp.220–1.
47. P. Wright, *On Living in an Old Country: The National Past in Contemporary Britain,* (London, 1985), p.11.
48. *Ibid.,* p.56.
49. Cannadine, Decline and Fall of the British Aristocracy, p.656.
50. *Ibid.,* p.707.

Index

Aberdeen Herald 83–85.
Aberdeen Journal, 91.
Aberdeen Universities, 89–90.
Aberdeen, 57, 65, 78–79, 85, 87, 100.
Aberdeen, Marquess of, 137, 145.
Aberdeen, Presbytery of, 83.
Aberdeenshire, 132.
Aberdour, 72.
Absenteeism, 20.
Achnaba, 22.
Adam, James, 83–85.
Adam, William, 49, 57.
Admiralty, Court of, 43.
Advocates, Faculty of, 45.
Advocates, Society of, 86–88, 93.
Agricultural Revolution, 62.
Agriculture, Board of, 66.
Ainshe, Robert, 66.
Airlie. Earl of, 137.
Allan, John, 83–85.
American South, 23.
Anderson, Alexander, 87.
Anderson James, 112.
Angus, 66, 68, 72–73.
Annexation Act 1891, 122.
Apothecaries, 86.
Appin, 23.
Ardchattan, 22.
Ardnamurchan, 14, 18.
Ardrishaig, 18.
Argyll Colony, 24.
Argyll Company of Farmers, 15.
Argyll, Dukes of, 20, 182.
Argyll, house of, 9–12, 14, 24, 134, 175.
Argyllshire, 2–15, 17–22, 24–25, 28–29, 131.
Arichonan, Knapdale, 29.
Ash Marinell, 172.
Assembly, General of Church of Scotland, 43.
Atholl, Duchess of, 140, 142, 147–148.

Atholl, Dukes of, 132, 134, 138–139, 143–144, 147, 175, 182–183.
Auchnacoy, 141.
Awe, Loch, 18.
Ayr Bank, 21.
Ayrshire, 67, 68, 73.

Baldwin, Stanley, 144.
Balfour, A.J., 132.
Balfour, Lord of Burleigh, 132, 135, 137, 143, 145, 147–148.
Ballachulish, 23.
Ballimore, 19.
Baltic Sea, 18.
Banff, 65.
Barnes, B., 179.
Batavia, 25.
Bateman, J., 133.
BBC, 146.
Beardmore, William, 139.
Beauly, 147.
Belhaven, 11th Baron, 145.
Belhaven, Lord, 137.
Bertram of Nisbet Estate, 74.
Berwick, 64, 67.
Berwickshire, 175.
Billingsley Case, 46–47.
Birmingham, 121.
Blackie, John Stuart, 82–83.
Blackie, John, Jnr., 14.
Blackie, James, 82.
Bonawe, 17.
Borgie Farm, 146.
Boughton, 182.
Boundary Commission 1887, 120.
Bowhill, 182.
Bowmore, 18.
Breadalbane, Marquess of, 133, 138, 141.
Brecon, Wales, 48.
British Fisheries Society, 8, 14.
British Linen Company, 15.

Brown, Callum, 63.
Bruce-Wallace controversy, 172.
Brydges, James, first Duke of Chandos, 48.
Buccleuch, Dukes of, 133–136, 146, 173, 175, 178, 182, 184–185.
Buchan, George, 49.
Buchanan, Walter, 113.
Burroughs, William, 50–51, 53.
Burgh Reform Act 1833, 106, 108.
Burnett, John, 120.
Burns, James, 105.
Burns, Robert, 176.
Business Training, 160.
Bute, Marquesses of, 141, 145, 175, 183.

Caddell family, 57.
Caithness, 2, 23.
Caithness, Earl of, 141.
Caledonian Canal, Commissioners of, 19.
Callander, R., 174–175.
Campbell, Archibald, Ninth Earl of Argyll, 9.
Campbell, Archibald, Tenth Earl of Argyll, 10.
Campbell, Archibald, Third Duke of Argyll, 15.
Campbell, Daniel of Shawfield, 22.
Campbell, James, 105, 109.
Campbell, John (Inveraray Lawyer), 29.
Campbell, John George, Ninth Duke of Argyll, 15.
Campbell, John, of Cawdor, 22.
Campbell, John, Fifth Duke of Argyll, 14–15, 18.
Campbell, John, First Earl of Breadalbane, 10.
Campbell, John, First Marquis of Bredalbane, 17.
Campbell, John, Fourth Duke of Argyll, 11.
Campbell, John, Second Duke of Argyll, 14.
Campbell, John, Second Earl of Breadalbane, 23.
Campbell, John, Sixth Duke of Argyll, 15.
Campbell, Lord Colin, 136.
Campbell, Lord Neil of Ardmaddy, 10.
Campbell, Mrs Elizabeth, of Glendaruel, 17.
Campbell, Mungo Nutter, 19.
Campbell, R.H., 135, 175.

Campbell, Sir Alexander of Inverneil, 20–21, 26–27.
Campbell, Sir Duncan of Lochnell, 5.
Campbell, Sir James of Auchinbreck, 21.
Campbell, Walter of Shawfield, 20, 28.
Campbells of Ardchattan, 22.
Campbells of Kilduskland, 24.
Campbells of Orangebay, 25.
Campbells, 9, 11–12.
Campbeltown, 17, 21.
Canadian Maritimes, 24.
Cannadine, David, 179, 177–178, 180–184.
Cape Fear River, 24.
Cardigan, Wales, 48.
Caribbean, 25.
Carolinas, 24.
Carr-Saunders, W., 77.
Carter, I., 65.
Cawdor, Earl of, 182.
Chalmers, Dr Thomas, 105, 109, 117.
Chamberlain, Joseph, 121.
Chandos, Duke of, see Brydges, James, 48, 49.
Charitable Corporation for the Relief of the Industrious Poor, 44, 47, 51–58.
Checkland, Olive, 170.
Checkland, Sidney, 170.
Chisholm, Sir Samuel, 134.
Church, 78.
City Improvement Trust, 114–115.
Clarks of Braleckan, 24.
Clearances, 1, 8–9, 19, 28, 63, 70
Cleland, James, 120.
Clergymen, 80.
Climony, 15.
Clyde burghs, 99, 103.
Clyde ports, 21.
Clyde, River, 18.
Clydesdale, Lord, 141.
Clydeside, 147.
Cockburn, Henry, 100.
Cockburn, Sir John, of Ormiston, 47.
Cockenzie, 49.
Collins, Randall, 180.
Collins, William, 116–118.
Collins, William, Snr., 117.
Colonsay, 18.
Colquhoun, 183.
Commissary, Court of, 43.
Convention of Royal Burghs, 43.
Conveyancing, 87.
Corpach, 22.

Cortachy Castle, 137.
Cowal, 6–7, 9, 15, 22.
Cowdray, Lady, 138, 140.
Crawford and Balcarres, Earl of, 183.
Crawford Estate, 72.
Crawford, Robert, 122–123.
Crinan Canal, 18, 27.
Crinan Trading Company, 21.
Cromar House, 137.
Cullen, Lord, see Grant, Francis, 44, 45, 50, 52.
Customs, Scottish Board of, 43.

Dale, David, 22.
Dalglish, Robert, Jnr., 113.
Dalhousie, Earls of, see Ramsay, George, 14, 144.
Dalkeith, Earl of, 140, 182.
Dalling, Little, 17.
Dana, Mid Argyll, 26.
Darien project, 44.
Davidson, Alexander Dyce, 81–82.
Deacon Convener, 108.
Denmark, King of, 48.
Devonport, Lord, 147.
Die-hards, 146.
Disruption, Church of Scotland, 80–82, 92, 104, 107, 109–110, 135.
Dochart, Glen, 18.
Dodgshon, R.A., 64.
Douglas Estate, 73.
Douglas, Duke of, 66.
Douglas, Lord Alfred, 136.
Droving Company, 23.
Drumlanrig, 182.
Dumbartonshire, 67–68.
Dunbarton, 99, 103.
Dumfries, 73.
Duncan, Joseph, 142.
Dundee, 79, 100.
Dunglass, Lord, 140, 147.
Dunoon, 17–18.
Duntroon Castle, 19.
Durkheim, E., 77.
Dysart, Lord, 138.

Earle, Peter, 43.
Easdale Slate Company, 23.
East India Company, 53.
Eddington, A., 152.
Edinburgh, 43, 57, 100.
Edinburgh University, 89–90.
Education of Scottish Entrepreneurs, 156, 158.

Edward Island, Prince, 28.
Eglinton, Earl of, 138, 145
Egmont, Lord, 54.
Eil, Loch, 18.
Elgin, Earl of, 141, 143–144, 146.
Elibank, Lord, 137.
Elphinstone, Lord, 143.
England, Bank of, 51.
Enlightenment, Scottish, 1.
Entail or Montgomery Act, 1770, 7.
Erroll, Countess of, 176.
Erroll, Earl of, 138, 143
Etive, Loch, Meal Company, 23.
Etive, Loch, Trading Company, 22.
Etive, Loch, 22, 24.
Ettrick Forest, 184.
Evangelical Alliance, 112–114.
Evangelicals, 103–104, 109.
Ewing, James, 105–106, 112.
Exchequer, Court of, 43.
Extension Act, 110–111.

Faith, Confession of, 83.
Famine, Great Highland, 1.
Fergusson James, 171–174, 176.
Fife, 68, 73–74.
Fife, Duke of, 133, 136.
Finlay, Kirkman, 19, 22, 102, 105.
Fletcher, Andrew of Saltoun, 43.
Forbes Mackenzie Act 1853, 113.
Forbes, Sir William, 44.
Fordyce, Thomas, 49–50.
Forestry Commission, 146.
Forteviot, Lord, 148.
Founders of businesses, 154.
Foxall, Zachariah, 48.
Free Church, 80, 109, 112, 114, 135.
Friedson, E., 78.
Fyne, Loch, 18.

Gaeldom, 1, 3.
Gaelic Club of Gentlemen, 22.
Galloway, Earl of, 135, 136.
Gamrie, Banffshire, 44.
Garden, Alexander of Troup, 49–50.
Garden, Sir William, 52.
Gardiner, James, 142.
George I, 15.
Gigha, 18.
Gilmour, John, 144.
Gladstone, William Ewart, 117.
Glamis, 73.
Glasgow and South Western Railway Company, 112.

Glasgow Green, 100.
Glasgow Herald, 113, 121.
Glasgow Liberal Working Men's
    Electoral Union, 115.
Glasgow Trades' Council, 115.
Glasgow University, 89–90.
Glasgow Wine, Spirit and Beer Trade
    Association, 118.
Glasgow, 22, 98–107, 110–124.
Glasgow, City of, Bank, 118.
Glasgow, Earl of, 138, 144, 146.
Glassary, 25.
Glenaladale, 28.
Glenconner, Lord, 140.
Glenforsa, in Torosay Parish, 26.
Glenorchy, 28.
Govan, 119, 120.
Graham, Robert Bontine
    Cunninghame, 122.
Grant, Francis, (Lord Cullen), 44, 48,
    56.
Grant, Sir Archibald, of Monymusk,
    44–53, 56–58.
Grant, Sir James, of Grant, 52.
Grant, William, (Lord Prestongrange),
    44, 48, 55.
Gray, Malcolm, 63–65.
Guild, Dean of, 101, 108.
Haddington, 67.
Haddington, Earls of, 141, 145, 175.
Haddingtonshire (East Lothian), 132.
Haddo House, 137.
Haldane, R.B., 132.
Hamilton Estate, 74.
Hamilton Palace, 137.
Hamilton, Ann, 46.
Hamilton, Duke of, 137.
Hamilton, Henry, 45.
Hamilton, James, of Pencaitland, 46.
Hanham, H.J., 131.
Harburgh Lottery, 47.
Hardwicke, Lord Chancellor, 55.
Hastie, Alexander, 112–113.
Hay, George, Marquis of Tweeddale, 14.
Hebrides, 18.
Henderson, Arthur, 134.
Highland and Agricultural Society, 14.
Highland Association, Royal, 146.
Highland Society, 22.
Highlands, 1, 2, 66–67.
Historic Buildings Commission, 146.
Hopetoun House, 137.
Hopetoun, Earls of, 52, 133.
Hornings, Keeper of the, 55.

Horsey, Col. Samuel, 52.
Huntly, Marquess of, 132, 145.
Hutchison, I., 176.

India, East, Company, 26.
Indies, West, 18, 21, 23–25, 28, 89.
Industrial Revolution, 72.
Inheritors of business, 155.
International Exhibition, 120.
Inveraray, 15, 18.
Inverclyde, Lord, 140.
Inveresregan Trading Company, 22.
Inveresregan, 22.
Inverness, 2.
Ireland, 21.
Irish Home Rule crisis, 98, 121, 176.
Islay, 6, 8, 15, 17, 20, 22.
Islay, Lord, 44.

Jackson, George, 115.
Jamaica, 24–25.
James VI, 43.
James VII, 10.
Jeans, J.S., 152.
Johnson, Dr, 43.
Johnstone, Tom, 171–174, 176.
Junkers, Prussian, 180–181.
Jura, 18.
Justiciary, Court of, 43.

Katrine, Loch Memorial Fountain, 118.
Katrine, Loch, 114–115.
Kilfinichen, 14.
Kilmartin House, 19.
Kilmartin, 19.
Kincardine, 65.
King's College, 88.
Kinnaird, Lord, 137.
Kinnoull, Earls of, 136, 143.
Kinross, 74.
Kintyre, 6–9, 14–15, 18, 24–25.
Kirkcudbright, 73.
Knapdale, 21.
Knox, John, 158.

Laird, description of, 170–172.
Lanarkshire, 66–68, 72–74.
Landownership, 3–7, 13.
Lang, Ian, 173.
Lauderdale, Earls of, 139, 175.
Law apprentices, 87.
Law, 78.
Law, Scots, 87.
Legal Profession, 85–86.

Leith, 57.
Lenman, Bruce P., 44.
Letterewe Wood Company, 23.
Levison-Gower, Ronald, 131.
Levitt, Ian, 175.
Lincoln's Inn, 45.
Linen, 15.
Linlithgow, 67.
Linlithgow, Marquess of, 137, 144, 146, 148.
Lismore, 23.
Livingstone, William, 28.
Lloyd George's Budget of 1909, 133, 134.
Lochaline, 24.
Lochgilphead, 18.
Lord High Commissioner to the General Assembly, 143.
Lorne Meal Company, 23.
Lorne, 6–8, 14–15, 17, 23.
Lothian, Lord, 141, 146, 148.
Lothians, 63, 64.
Loudoun, Earls of, 134, 138.
Lovat Scouts, 144.
Lovat, Lord, 138, 141, 146–147.
Lowlands, Scottish, 1–2, 7, 9.
Lucca, Hanover Parish, 25.
Lynch, James, 118.

MacAllister, Archibald of Tarbert, 11.
MacAllisters of Balinakill, 24.
MacCorquidale, Hew, 11.
Macintyre, Duncan Ban, 28.
Mackworth, Sir Thomas, 48.
Maclaine of Lochbuy, 25.
Maclaine, Donald, 26.
Maclaines of Lochbuie, 25.
Maclean, Colonel Alexander of Ardgour, 14, 20, 26.
Macleans of Ardgour, 26, 48.
Macleans of Duart, 10.
MacNeill, John of Oakfield, 18.
MacNeill, Malcolm of Carskey, 21.
MacNeills of Lossit and Ardelay, 24.
MacNeills of Taynish, 25.
MacQuarrie, Lt. Col. Charles, 26.
MacQuarry, Lachlan, of Ulva, 26.
MacTavishes of Dunardry, 24.
Malcolm, Neill of Poltalloch, 14, 19, 21.
Malcolm, Neill, 29.
Malcolms of Poltalloch, 19, 25–28.
Malt Tax, 22.
Mansfield, Earl of, 140.
Manufacturers, Board of Trustees for, 57.

Marischal College, 82, 87, 89.
Marischal Estate, Aberdeen, 50.
Marshall, T.H., 77.
Martin, James, 115, 118.
Marwick, James, 119–121.
Masons of Scotland, Grand Master, 145.
McEwan, John, 174.
McGavin, Robert, 111.
McGregor, Sir James, 89.
McLaren, Alexander, 118.
McLellan, Archibald, 113–114.
Medicine, 78, 86, 88, 90.
Melville, Earl of, 144.
Merchants' House, 100–101, 105, 108.
Meres, Sir John, 51.
Methodism, 104.
Midlothian, 64.
Millman, Roger, 174.
Milne, John, 89.
Milton, Lord, 43.
Mineral and Battery Works, 46.
Mines Royal, 46–47.
Minto, Earl of, 136, 144.
Mitchison, R., 63.
Moidart, Loch, 18.
Moir, Dr Andrew, 91.
Moir, James, 11, 112.
Montgomery or Entail Act, 7.
Montgomery, James, 14.
Montrose, Duke of, 138–139, 147.
Monymusk, Estate of, 44–46, 57.
Monymusk, Kirkton of, 57.
Morar, 147.
Moray, 65.
Morton Estate, 72.
Morvern, 24, 48, 53.
Muckairn, 22.
Mull, 6–7, 14–15, 25–26, 28, 48.
Municipal Elections Amendment (Scotland) Act, 117.
Munitions Act, 147.
Murray, Arthur, 137.
Murray, Gideon, 137.
Murray, Sir Alexander of Stanhope, 14, 48.

Napier and Ettrick, Lord, 138.
National Trust for Scotland, 183–184.
Newtown, 73.
Norfolk, Duke of, 48.
Norris, Edward, 47.
Northesk, Lord, 138.

Oban Company, 23.

Oban, 17, 18, 22.
Ogilvie family, 182.
Oib, 29.
Orchard Park, 17.
Orchy, Glen, 18.
Orr, Andrew, 112–114, 119–120.

Panmure, Angus, 50.
Parkin, Frank, 180.
Parochial Board, Glasgow, 99.
Partick, 119–120.
Paul, Henry, 105, 107.
Peel, Sir Robert, 105, 110.
Pentland, Lord, 138.
Perkin, H., 77.
Perth, 18.
Perthshire Education Authority, 148.
Perthshire West and Kinross, 142.
Phantilans, 11.
Pitcairn, (N.E. Scotland), 50.
Police and Statute Labour Committee, Glasgow, 110.
Police Board, Glasgow, 99, 110–111.
Police Commissioners, Glasgow, 110.
Political Science Quarterly, 120.
Polwarth, Earl of, 135, 146, 148.
Port Seton, 49.
Potts, Ann, 47.
Prestongrange, Lord (see Grant, William), 44.

Queensberry, Marquess of, 136, 139.

Ramsay, George, Ninth Earl of Dalhousie, 14.
Reddie, James, 120.
Reform Acts, 98–99, 114, 116, 124, 131.
Relief Church, 104, 112.
Renfrewshire, 66–67, 72.
Richmond and Gordon, Duke of, 133, 136, 138, 148.
Riddell, James, 14.
Riddell, Sir James of Ardnamurchan, 28.
Robertson, Thomas, 63.
Robinson, Col. Samuel, 54.
Robinson, George, 50–54.
Roles (non-business) of Scottish entrepreneurs, 162.
Rollo, Lord, 138.
Rosebery, Earl of, 136, 145.
Ross and Cromarty, 2.
Rosslyn, Earls of, 135–136, 143, 145.
Roxburghshire, 133.
Roxburgh County Council, 173.

Roxburgh, 64.
Roxburghe, Duke of, 173, 175, 182.
Roxburghe, Lord, 141.

Salt laws, 17.
Saltoun, Baron, 145.
Samarang, Java, 25.
Sandys, Samuel, 54.
School Board, Glasgow, 99.
Scone, Lord, 140, 148.
Scotch Mines Company, 48, 58.
Scotland, Church of, 80, 103, 109, 112, 132, 135, 143.
Scotland, Royal Bank of, 141.
Scott, John, 171, 181.
Scott, Lord William, 140.
Scott, Walter, 185.
Scottish Labour Party, 122, 123.
Scottish Land and Property Federation, 134.
Scottish National War Memorial, 144.
Scrymgeour-Wedderburn, 141, 147.
Seafield, Earls of, 137, 182.
Secession Church, 104, 112.
Sedgewick, Romney, 50.
Sempill, Lord, 139, 146.
Session, Court of 43.
Shaw, Albert, 120, 123.
Shaw, John, 44.
Shiel, Loch, 18.
Sinclair, John, 24.
Sinclair, Sir John, 175.
Skipness, 22.
Slate quarrying, 23.
Slaven, A., 64.
Smout, T.C., 63, 172.
South Sea Bubble, 46.
Southesk, Kincardine, 50.
Southesk, Lord, 141.
Spinning, 15.
Squire, William, 47–48, 50–52.
St Andrews University, 89–90.
St Croix, Island of, 25.
St Patrick, Royal College of, Maynooth, 112.
Stafford, Marquess of, 131.
Stair, Earls of, 143, 145, 182.
Stewart, John of Ballachulish, 17.
Stewart, Larry, 49.
Stewarts of Ballachulish, 23.
Stirling, 67.
Stirling-Maxwell, 183.
Strathmore, Earl of, 72.
Strontian, 48, 52, 56.

Stuart, James, 140.
Sun Fire Office, 48.
Sunart, 14.
Sutherland, 2, 131.
Sutherland, Dukes of, 133–134, 136–137, 141, 143, 146, 148, 175, 182.
Sutton, Sir Robert, 54–55.

Tack, 3.
Tait, John, 73.
Temperance, 116–118.
Tench, William, 53.
Tennant family, 182.
Test Act, 83.
Thompson, John, 50–55.
Tilt, Glen, 134.
Timperley, L., 171, 174.
Tobermory, 8, 17–18, 24.
Tomintoul, 52.
Tomkyns, Thomas, 48.
Torrens, James, 116.
Toward Castle Estate, 19, 22.
Trades House, 100–101, 108.
Trades' Council Municipal Elections Committee, 123.
Tranent, 49, 56.
Turner, James of Thrushgrove, 111.

Tweeddale, 136.
Tweeddale, Marquesses of, 14, 141.
Tyneside, 49.

Ulva, 26.
Union, Treaty of, 21, 99, 101
United Presbyterian Church, 135.
United Presbyterians, 112.

Victoria, Queen, 115.

Wadset, 3, 4.
Walpole, Sir Robert, 54.
Wanlockhead, 72.
Watts, Thomas, 48.
Wealthholding, 164.
Weber, Max, 178–180.
Weir, Company, 139.
Wemyss and March, Earls of, 146, 183.
Whyte, I., 46.
William of Orange, 10.
Winton, Earl of, 49.
Wright, P., 183.

York Buildings Company, 47–50, 52–54, 56–58.
Younger, Sir William, 140.